The
COAST OF MAINE
Book
A Complete Guide

Windjammers rule the waters between the island of North Haven and Rockport during the annual Great Schooner Race.

THE
COAST OF MAINE
BOOK
A Complete Guide

Third Edition

Rick Ackermann and Kathryn Buxton

Berkshire House Publishers
Lee, Massachusetts

On the Cover and Frontispiece:
Photographs by Herb Swanson
Front Cover: *Harbor and village at Jonesport*
Frontispiece: *Annual Schooner Race from North Haven Island to Rockland.*
Back Cover: *Painting the scenery in Kennebunkport; Whale watchers heading out to sea via the Kennebunk River; Harbor Fish in Portland, selling lobsters right at the dock.*

Excerpt on p. 19 from
E.B.White, *Writings from* The New Yorker, *1925–1976*
HarperCollins, New York © The New Yorker

Excerpt on p. 137 from
Calvin Trillin, *Alice, Let's Eat*
Ticknor & Fields, New York © 1989 Calvin Trillin

Excerpt on p. 152 from
Sarah Orne Jewett, *The Country of the Pointed Firs*
Houghton Mifflin, Boston

Excerpt on p. 81 from
Marguerite Yourcenar, "Reflections on the Composition of Memoirs of Hadrian," from *Memoirs of Hadrian*
Farrar, Straus & Giroux, Inc. © 1954 Marguerite Yourcenar

The Coast of Maine Book: A Complete Guide
Copyright © 1992, 1996, 1997 by Berkshire House Publishers
Cover and interior photographs ©1992, 1996, 1997 by credited photographers

Library of Congress Cataloging-in-Publication Data
Ackermann, Rick, 1948–
The coast of Maine book : a complete guide / Rick Ackermann & Kathryn Buxton — 3rd ed.
    p.   cm. — (The great destinations series, ISSN 1056-7968)
Includes bibliographical references and index.
ISBN: 0-936399-91-0
1. Maine—Guidebooks. 2. Atlantic Coast (Me.)—Guidebooks. I. Buxton, Kathryn, 1958– .
II. Title. III. Series
F17.3.A25   1997
917.4104'43—dc21   97-25191
                                                                                          CIP

ISBN: 0-936399-91-0
ISSN: 1056-7968 (series)

Editor: Susan Minnich. Managing Editor: Philip Rich. Design and composition: Dianne Pinkowitz. Original design for Great Destinations™ series: Janice Lindstrom. Cover design: Jane McWhorter.

Berkshire House books are available at substantial discounts for bulk purchases by corporations and other organizations for promotions and premiums. Special personalized editions can also be produced in large quantities. For more information, contact:

Berkshire House Publishers
480 Pleasant St., Lee, MA 01238
800-321-8526
E-mail: info@berkshirehouse.com
Website: www.berkshirehouse.com

Manufactured in the United States of America
First printing 1997
10 9 8 7 6 5 4 3 2 1

No complimentary meals or lodgings were accepted by the authors and reviewers in gathering information for this work.

The **GREAT DESTINATIONS**™ Series

The Great Destinations™ series features regions in the United States rich in natural beauty and culture. Each Great Destinations™ guidebook reviews an extensive selection of lodgings, restaurants, cultural events, historic sites, shops, and recreational opportunities, and outlines the region's natural and social history. Written by resident authors, the guides are a resource for visitor and resident alike. All volumes include maps, photographs, directions to and around the region, lists of helpful phone numbers and addresses, and indexes.

Acknowledgments

We'd like to thank Kate Woodsome for her invaluable contributions to this, the third edition of *The Coast of Maine Book*. We also want to thank Herb Swanson, who is not only a good friend, but an exceptional photographer and connoisseur of coastal fast food joints. Also Wendy Keeler and Cynthia Hacinli for getting us off to a good start; Jeff Isaac, Jonathan Nolan and Paul and Robin Fagan, former Outward Bound instructors, for telling us how to dress for the Maine weather and for making us feel perpetually guilty for spending any time indoors.

We'd like to thank Heather Smith, our "advance man" in Bar Harbor; Kathryn and Ken Buxton for their recommedations in Belfast and Camden; Elizabeth Edwardsen and Tim Beidel for their reporters' critical eye and appreciation of the Gosnold Arms; and Mike White for his surfer's tips; Peter Rich and Bob Bowker for their bikers' tips. Thanks to Romaine Simenson, our island expert; Susan Stern for telling us about the bugs at Old Orchard Beach. Thanks also to Gary Lehy for a superb piece of pie and an invaluable shortcut; Barbara Ackermann for her birding advice; Edie Armstrong for great jewelry; Jackie Carlton, Lisa Blinn, and Troy for their thoughts on the Yorks, the Berwicks, Ogunquit, and Wells; Bill Sweet for his historical expertise; Deb Dalfonso, Bill Connor, Arthur Kirklian, Joan Ackermann and Greg Clement for their help finding some of the best places to eat and to stay on the coast. Julie Michaels for her kind recommendations and encouraging words. Most of all, we'd like to thank Philip Rich and Susan Minnich, our exceptionally patient and good humored editors — and the staff at Berkshire House for their support. We also are indebted to our dog Argos for her good inn manners and for taking us on a few side trips we might otherwise have overlooked.

Contents

CHAPTER ONE
From the Ice Age to Lobster Rolls
HISTORY
1

CHAPTER TWO
How to Get Here and Get Around
TRANSPORTATION
32

CHAPTER THREE
Where Sea Captains Slept
LODGING
44

CHAPTER FOUR
What to See, What to Do
CULTURE
81

CHAPTER FIVE
Shore Food
RESTAURANTS & FOOD PURVEYORS
131

CHAPTER SIX
By the Sea, By the Sea
RECREATION
177

CHAPTER SEVEN
Something Old, Something New
SHOPPING
230

CHAPTER EIGHT
INFORMATION
252

Introduction

Half of all Mainers vacation in the state. When they're not vacationing, they're getting away, in Maine, for the weekend. That's why so many cars in our Portland neighborhood have bike or ski racks on the back, an Old Town canoe or a sea kayak on top, and fishing gear, sail bags, extra battens, camping, or beach equipment (including lobster bib) in the trunk. We suspect many have several of the above ready and waiting to go at a moment's notice. Car-wise, it's hard to tell a Mainer from an out-of-stater.

Of course, vacationing is not a way of life suited to everybody. Some cars that pass through the state look as if the only thing that's ever been in them is people. Every year more than four times as many people as live in Maine visit Acadia National Park. Most of them, after a brief detour to L. L. Bean, go home again. And every year a small group of visitors decides to give up whatever it was they were doing and move here. Many open new restaurants, which is fine, since in addition to vacationing, Mainers love to eat. More than just a few of them are busy cooking up things as exciting as the best of what's served in much larger cities. Others among the newly relocated open bed & breakfasts or inns. Traveling the coast we have met an investment banker, a pilot, a state department official, a social worker, and a psychologist, all enjoying their new occupations. One woman, from Houston, had looked out her snow-covered window at sunset a few days earlier and cried. She said she cried not out of frustration with Maine's winter, which can be long, but because she was "so happy to be here."

She came for the same reason people as far back as the Abenaki Indians and European settlers came — for a better life. They came for the rocky coast, ocean storms, fog thick enough to stuff a pillow, wildflowers in spring, and vast sandy beaches at low tide. Visitors and new residents on Maine's coast come so that every day they can look out on the pen-and-ink lines of fish weirs in Johnson Bay off Lubec. They like watching the colors change during fall in the Camden Hills. They want to be able to cross-country ski the carriage paths in Acadia — one of the great off-season joys of the coast.

People are not only taken with the coastal Maine landscape and all it has to offer, but with the way of life. The state tourism office bottled this phenomenon with the slogan "Maine: The Way Life Should Be." — a phrase ridiculed among residents and recent transplants for its obviousness. Maine is a place people come to change — to slow down and try something new — and Mainers encourage this kind of behavior. People here are highly independent and extremely resourceful, and it is not rare to know someone who has done what may seem impossible — taken up mountain climbing at 80, started an opera company in a tiny seaside village, written a novel, or captured the coastal light on canvas.

Life here — and vacations — represent an ethic different from most other parts of the country. Small, family-run operations are the rule. Big shopping malls and chain restaurants are the exception (in fact, they are virtually non-existent east of Portland, the state's largest city). Shops, inns, and restaurants are run by individuals who are unremitting in their quest to offer good value. That comes from a particularly Yankee characteristic, which is to get the most out of something.

That's why almost everybody in Maine, rich or poor, knows two things: how to conduct a yard sale and how to shop at a yard sale. Someone's discarded sofa easily becomes someone else's treasured antique. Likewise, old wooden lobster boats or vintage friendship sloops, once popular coastal working boats, now are prized by weekend sailors, and sea captains' homes are made over into inns. Recycling and rejuvenation take on new meanings here.

Rick Ackermann and Kathryn Buxton
Portland, Maine

THE WAY THIS BOOK WORKS

ORGANIZATION

This book is divided into eight chapters, each with its own introduction. If you are interested in one chapter or another, you can turn to it directly and begin reading without losing a sense of continuity. You also can take the book with you on your travels and skip around, reading about the places you visit as you go. Or you can read the entire book through from start to finish. If you're interested in finding a place to eat or sleep, we suggest you first look over the restaurant and lodging charts in the Index (organized by area and price); then turn to the pages listed in the general index and read the specific entries for the places that most interest you.

Entries within most of the chapters are arranged alphabetically under five regional headings: "South Coast," "Casco Bay," "Midcoast," "Down East/Acadia" and "East of Schoodic." A map showing the entire coast divided into these five regions appears at the end of the Introduction and at the end of the book.

LIST OF MAPS

Some entries, most notably those in the lodging and restaurant chapters, include specific information (telephone, address, hours, etc.) organized for easy reference in blocks in the left-hand column. The information here, as well as the phone numbers and addresses in the descriptions, were checked as close to publication as possible. Even so, details change with frustrating frequency. It's best to call ahead.

PRICES

For the same reason, we have avoided listing specific prices, preferring instead to indicate a range of prices. Lodging price codes are based on a per-room rate, double occupancy, in the high season. Low season rates are likely to be 20–40 percent less. Again, it's best to call.

Restaurant prices indicate the cost of an individual meal including appetizer, entree, and dessert, but not including cocktails, wine, tax, or tip. Restaurants with a prix-fixe menu are noted accordingly.

Lodging rates generally increase close to Memorial Day when the summer season begins, and they are highest from July 4 weekend through the fall foliage season in mid- to late October. Special packages are often available for two or more nights' stay, and frequently there are even better values during the off-season. If breakfast and/or dinner is included with the price of a room, we do not alter the rate category, we just note that the room rate includes one or more meals. These lodging rates exclude required room taxes or service charges.

Price Codes:

	Lodging	*Dining*
Inexpensive	Up to $65	Up to $10
Moderate	$65 to $125	$10 to $20
Expensive	$125 to $180	$20 to $30
Very Expensive	$180 or more	$30 or more

Credit Cards are abbreviated as follows:

AE — American Express	DC — Diner's Club
CB — Carte Blanche	MC — Master Card
D — Discover Card	V — Visa

AREA CODE

There is one telephone area code for Maine: 207.

TOURIST INFORMATION

The best sources for year-round tourist information are: the Maine Publicity Bureau (P.O. Box 2300, Hallowell, ME 04347; 207-582-9300 in state and 800-533-9595 out-of-state) and the various chambers of commerce listed in Chapter Eight, *Information.*

WELCOME CANADIANS / BIENVENUE AUX CANADIENS

We hope this book will give Canadians an idea of all the good things there are to do on the Maine coast. We have kept our northern neighbors in mind and have tried to provide pertinent information.

Nous voulons que ce livre donne aux Canadiens une idée de tous les endroits où on peut s'amuser sur la côte du Maine. Nous apprécions la visite de nos voisins du nord, et nous essayons de leur fournir des renseignements pertinents sur cette partie du Maine. Il y a beaucoup d'aubergistes et de restaurateurs sur la côte qui parlent français. Si vous êtes en train de planifer un séjour sur la côte du Maine et vous aimeriez consulter quelqu'un qui peut vous renseigner en français, communiquez avec le Maine Publicity au 207-582-9300 (P. O. Box 2300, Hallowell, ME 04347). Ce service publie plusieurs brochures en français.

The
COAST OF MAINE
Book

A Complete Guide

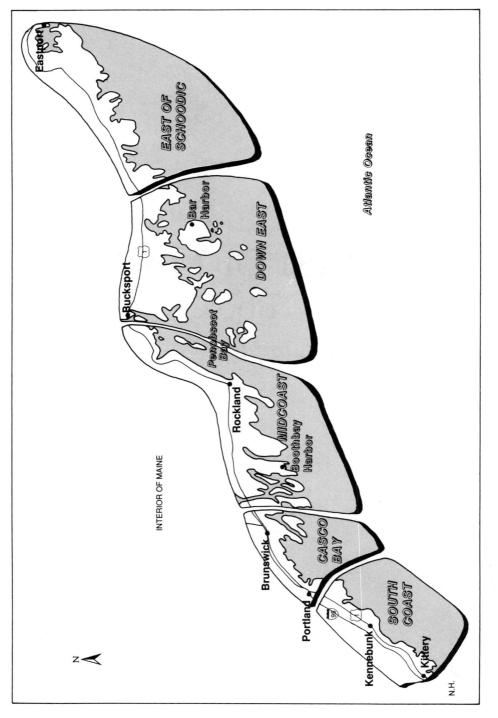

THE COAST OF MAINE — FIVE REGIONS

CHAPTER ONE
From the Ice Age to Lobster Rolls
HISTORY

Long before Europeans discovered the New World, tribes of the Algonquin nation came every summer to the coast of Maine where the sun was tempered by cool ocean breezes. "Down East," as 19th-century sailors termed the land governed by the prevailing west winds, is a place to come back to. Mainers built and sailed the wooden ships that traded with the world and rode those westerly winds "Down East" to their homes on the Maine coast.

Herb Swanson

The village of Lubec near the border with Canada.

People still come to cool off and to trade. Today, the major trading route connecting the Maine coast to the rest of the world has shifted inland to coastal Rte. 1. Tourism is second only to the paper industry in total revenues for the state. Visitors shop Maine's outlets and relax by its inlets. Many of the old working harbors have been transformed into pleasure harbors. Visitors from all over the world come to sail windjammers on Penobscot Bay, peep at the autumn leaves on Rte. 182 north of Ellsworth, cross-country ski on the carriage trails in Acadia National Park, and bed and breakfast in old sea captains' homes. For many Canadians, the south coast of Maine is the closest beach.

What visitors find is a coast that has much in common with the Maine coast of the 19th century. Artists are still intent on capturing the region's fugitive colors. Mainers today have to work just as hard to make a living.

All Yankees, and especially those who live along Maine's coast, have a reputation for keeping to themselves. Mainers are a people of few well-chosen words — all delivered with an accent flat as a clam bed at low tide. Underneath this crusty exterior, they are adventurous, inquisitive, and have a great

---

We'd like to welcome you to the third edition of *The Coast of Maine Book*. We have reserved this space at the beginning of this and most other chapters to update travelers on interesting developments, advances, changes, and "news" about life on the coast since we last wrote. We hope you find this information interesting, and while not all of it will be useful in planning your trip, it will give you an idea of what to expect once you get here.

Case in point: Maine is still the only state to have an independent governor, Angus King, a fact that demonstrates a certain amount of independence of spirit found here. In 1997, the state legislature elected its first female speaker of the house, Elizabeth Mitchell. Maine is also the only state to have a bill on the books calling for campaign finance reform — something everyone else in the country likes to talk about. Finally, we'd like to report that the Green Party is alive and well, making Maine one of the few places where the three-party political system is a work in progress. We'll keep you posted.

For your information, the state has set up shop on the information superhighway where you can pick up more germane facts about Maine, including business opportunities and information from the state tourism office. Maine's internet address is:

www.state.me.us

In closing, we would like to say that Maine remains a wonderful place to visit and live, a fact confirmed by two recent surveys. One proclaimed Maine the safest state in the union — the crime rate here is virtually nonexistent compared to more populous places to the south. Another survey found that this is one of the top ten healthiest places to live in the country. No wonder we like it here.

---

sense of humor, as Benedict Thielen discovered 30 years ago writing for *Holiday* magazine: "They never seem to look at you," he mentioned to an acquaintance. "Oh, they do, sideways, or when your back is turned," the man replied. "That fellow, he's probably off around the corner right now, looking at the license plate of your car."

The writer E. B. White once wrote to his wife, Katharine, about the apparent indifference he found frustrating but infinitely attractive. "Dear K, Santayana, whom I read on the train last night, holds out little hope for our achieving any satisfactory relationship with the Maine people." The Whites ended up spending the second half of their lives on the Blue Hill peninsula among these laconic people. Like the Whites, people "from away" find the coast a place they want to come back to year after year. Maine is not a fashionable place, but it is one where you find delicious traditions such as the four-decades-old lobster festival in Rockland. It's also a place to enjoy some of nature's most enduring pleasures, such as Ogunquit's broad sandy beach, Acadia National Park's rocky headlands, and the dramatic 18-foot tides at Cobscook Bay.

NATURAL HISTORY

Visitors are astounded by the topography of the Maine coast. Enormous tides expose rocky headlands that rise abruptly from the ocean. Two thousand to three thousand islands dot its length; inlets and fingers of land provide infinite variety. To understand what forces created the "rocky coast of Maine," you have to look at its geologic past.

ROCKS OF THE ROCKY COAST

According to the plate tectonics theory of continental drift, the European and North American tectonic plates began to collide about 450 million years ago. The impact caused the edges of both plates to buckle and crack as the ocean floor separating the two plates began to slide under the North American plate. Tons of rock were forced upward into huge mountains. Rivers of magma forced their way through cracks and formed volcanoes. In some places, magma pushed its way through cracks in the hardened granite crust to form what geologists call "black dikes." Today you can see black dikes cutting through the pink granite at Schoodic Point at the far eastern reach of Acadia National Park.

Sand and shingle beach at Roque Bluffs State Park.

Herb Swanson

The geologic past is also evident in the makeup of Maine's islands. Look at the mostly long, skinny southern coastal islands, and you'll see the remnants of the mountains that were formed when the two tectonic plates pushed together and forced the coastline to crumple. Further up the coast, islands such as Monhegan and Mount Desert are distinctly rounded mounds. These were created when molten magma forced its way up through the plate and formed volcanoes.

The two plates continued to slide together, and, about 390 million years ago, the coastal lands' layers of sedimentary materials were transformed into metamorphic rock by the immense pressure and heat of the collision. The collision created a diverse collection of rock formations and minerals along the Maine coast — sandstone, shale, and limestone in the south; shale, slate, and impure limestone in the north. The European and North American plates eventually began to drift apart, and 70 million years ago the Atlantic Ocean was formed. Today the continental plates continue to shift and the ocean to expand at the hardly perceptible rate of one inch every year.

THE DROWNED COAST

The most prominent feature of Maine's coast is a consequence of the Ice Age. Twenty thousand years ago great glaciers covered much of the northern hemisphere, including Maine. Weighed down by thousands of tons of ice, the coastal plains and many of the bordering mountains were forced downward. Water from the melting glaciers rushed into the ocean and the rising waters poured into the depressed valleys and lowlands of Maine, forming what is now called the drowned coast.

The glaciers have disappeared, and coastal lands have bounced back, at least partially, to their pre-glacial elevation. Still, much of Maine's coastal lowlands, marshes, and wide sandy beaches, part of a giant alluvial plain that once stretched the entire length of New England, now lie hidden by Gulf of Maine waters. The result of the lingering glacial depression is a meandering line where land meets water. The state's coastline stretches for 2500 miles from Kit-

Roy Zalesky

Cadillac Mountain in Acadia National Park. At 1,530 feet, it is the tallest coastal mountain in the eastern United States and affords splendid views of the bay.

tery to Eastport — a distance that is only 225 direct miles or 290 miles by car. Several major rivers empty into the ocean in Maine: the Piscataqua at the Maine–New Hampshire border; the Saco River between Biddeford and Saco in the south; the Androscoggin between Brunswick and Topsham; the Kennebec at Bath; the Penobscot near Bucksport, and the St. Croix at the border between the U.S. and Canada.

The coast has hundreds of deepwater approaches and safe ports protected by thousands of islands. Some are small piles of rocks that appear at low tide. Others are larger, like Mount Desert Island, which is the second-largest island in New England. It has 17 mountains, several towns and villages and the eastern United States' only fjord.

Major Bays of Maine

Casco	Dyer
Merrymeeting	Narraguagus
Sheepscot	Pleasant
Muscongus	Western
Penobscot (by far the largest)	Chandler
Isle au Haut	Englishman
Blue Hill	Machias
Union River	Cobscook
Frenchman	Passamaquoddy

THE ICY LABRADOR CURRENT

The Atlantic Ocean gives the coast much of its character. The waters off Maine's shore are kept cold by the icy Labrador Current that runs from the northeast over the Grand Banks off Newfoundland southwest past Nova Scotia and through the Gulf of Maine before veering east off Cape Cod.

The ocean is also responsible for two other Maine coast phenomena: fog and tide. Fog, which frequently enshrouds the coast and islands between May and September, occurs when warm moist air traveling overland from the southwest encounters cooler ocean temperatures. The air is cooled and moisture in the air condenses to form low-lying clouds — or fog. Maine's tidal range increases dramatically as you head east: the tide at Kittery is about nine feet; at Eastport it reaches nearly twenty feet as the sea rushes in and out of the Bay of Fundy's narrow confines.

VERY BIG PINES

The coast of Maine and its islands are home to more than 300 types of birds, which make the coast a birder's paradise. It's not unusual to see an eagle

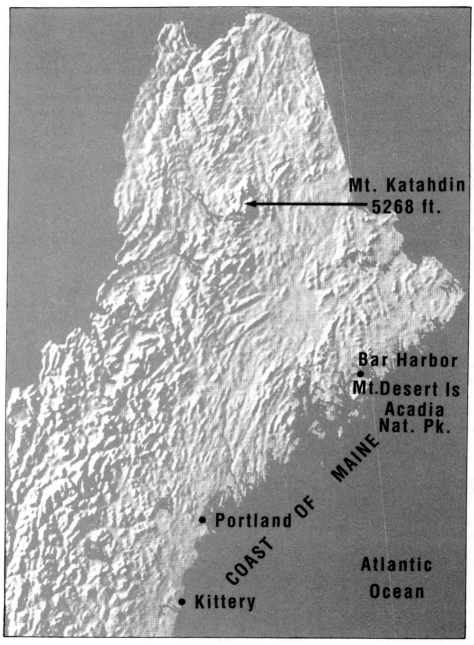

Mt. Katahdin
5268 ft.

Bar Harbor
Mt. Desert Is
Acadia
Nat. Pk.

MAINE

Portland

OF

COAST

Atlantic
Ocean

Kittery

TOPOGRAPHY OF MAINE

on Mount Desert Island or places further Down East. Herring gulls are common, as are terns, great cormorants, snowy egrets, blue herons, sandpipers, osprey, and Canada geese. Mergansers dive in the ocean for fish. Teals swim on the rivers. Puffins, nicknamed "sea parrots," and once near extinction, nest on Matinicus. Visitors also frequently meet with other Maine wildlife, including black bears, deer, and moose.

Hundreds of wildflowers are found along the coast and its islands, including the spiky purple wild lupine, white Queen Anne's lace, yellow goldenrod, orange Turk's-cap lily, pink rhododendron and laurel, and pale green jack-in-the-pulpit. Wild blueberries stain the hillsides and coastal mountaintops from Ellsworth to Eastport (in the fall, the blueberry barrens Down East turn bright red).

There are 76 species of trees in Maine. Softwoods like the white pine, balsam fir, white spruce, and hemlock account for only 14 of the different species of trees, but make up more than 80 percent of the forest. And, even today 89 percent of the state is forested.

Geese flying south over the coast.

Herb Swanson

The most famous of the state's trees is the white pine. Maine takes its nickname, "The Pine Tree State," from the tall and stately coniferous tree that grew in abundance near the shore when the first Europeans arrived in the 1600s. The British crown government had all pines more than 74 feet tall with a diameter 24 inches and greater marked with the King's Arrow and reserved for use in the making of masts for his navy. The colonists often — in defiance of the crown — exploited the white pine for their own purposes, and in Pre-Revolutionary Maine homes you often could find broad white pine beams, floor boards, and clapboards. Later, paper manufacturers cut the pine for use in pulp mills. As a result, few of these great trees, many of which measured 6 feet around and stood 200 feet tall, remain today. The pine that do exist are not the abundant virgin forests the early explorers saw lining the coast, but second and third growths on land once cleared by coastal farmers.

Fishing the rich waters Down East. The barrel contains sea urchins, one of the many edible forms of sea life found off the coast of Maine.

The balsam fir is an easily recognized denizen of the coastal forests. It is the tree seen most often growing in the thin topsoil on the islands and near the coast. On a cool, moist day in late summer or early fall you can smell its fragrant aroma as you drive or walk through a grove of balsams.

The white birch grows in the state's northern reaches and along the easternmost shore. Coastal Native Americans used to make their canoes from birch bark. Coast white cedar and butternut is found in York County, but as a rule not further north. Maples and fast-growing aspens are abundant. The American elm was once so plentiful around the city of Portland that it was called "Forest City." The trees, which had survived two devastating fires that raged through the city, fell prey to Dutch elm disease during the middle of this century.

Maine's waters are home to hundreds of species, including cod, haddock, flounder, whiting, yellowtail, pollock, lobster, mussels, oysters, and clams. Wild Atlantic salmon occasionally are found in the waters of Merrymeeting Bay near Bath. More often the salmon one finds has been farm-raised in aquaculture pens near Vinalhaven and Eastport. Whales also frequent the coast.

Pilot whales sometimes become stranded near the South Coast's beaches, because they follow squid too far into shore. Humpbacks and finbacks visit late in summer after warmer water temperatures lure the fish they feed on close to shore. Seals are as numerous as boats in many Maine inlets.

Tidal Pools

The importance of tidal pools cannot be underestimated. They are a miniature saltwater empire that reveal a great deal about life in the ocean at large. The food chain in a tidal pool is much the same as it is in the ocean. Hermit crabs take over empty snail shells and dine on smaller animals. Clams bury themselves in the sand and at low tide you can see airways leading down to their hiding places. Mussels and barnacles cling to rocks and ocean debris with periwinkles, starfish, kelp, rockweed, Irish moss, and hundreds of other plants and animals.

The Maine coast has an abundance of tidal pools, from the small puddles left at low tide to Biddeford Pool, which is a mile in diameter. Another great place to observe the ocean community at work is at Two Lights Park in Cape Elizabeth, where the receding waters expose hundreds of small saltwater pools and the marine organisms that make them hop.

Discovering nature in a tidal stream, Washington County.

Herb Swanson

SOCIAL HISTORY

RED PAINT AND OYSTER SHELL PEOPLE

Remains from the first known inhabitants of Maine date from approximately 4000 B.C. to 3000 B.C., well after the glacier's ice began to recede from the coast. These early Native Americans were well developed in their ability to make and use implements. Spears, knives, and fire-starting tools fashioned from stone indicate that the first known human residents of Maine were hunters who eventually evolved into farmers and fishermen. Found among their remains were heavy woodworking tools, including adzes, gouges, and axes. They had elaborate rituals, including the practice of burying their dead in graves lined with a mix of clay and iron oxide. For that they have been named the "Red Paint People." To collect the iron oxide, they had to travel inland to Katahdin, Maine's highest peak. Their grave sites have been found near Blue Hill and Ellsworth, as well as at several locations inland.

The Red Paint People have provided the basis for a great deal of speculation and romanticizing among historians and archaeologists. For a long time it was believed they were a lost race washed away by a huge tidal wave or erased by some other natural catastrophe. While scholars speculated, no archaeological record was uncovered to support the theory. Today most historians believe the Red Paint People are ancestors of the Native American tribes Europeans found when they first came to Maine. It is believed that their burial rituals — like their reliance on wildlife and game for food — changed with time.

The next archaeological record of Maine's native population occurs around A.D. 80 to 350. Giant piles of oyster and clam shells were left in waste heaps near rich oyster-breeding grounds. The largest of these middens, or collections of everyday "kitchen" waste, was called the "Whaleback Heap," and was removed in the 1900s. Today several smaller middens remain, measuring up to 400 feet in length and almost 25 feet high. They can be seen near Damariscotta on Rte. 1 in the Midcoast region.

Few Native American artifacts have been found among the oyster, clam, and mussel shell mounds. The implements that were discovered — spoons of copper and well-formed pottery — indicate that the Oyster Shell People, like their predecessors the Red Paint People, were sophisticated in their use of tools and natural resources.

THE FIRST SUMMER VISITORS

By the time of the Oyster Shell People, life had developed a rather peaceful rhythm for Maine's natives. They summered in relatively large colonies on

Members of the Micmac tribe in Bar Harbor at the turn of the century.

Courtesy of Penobscot Marine Museum

the coast and sometimes on its islands. When the cold weather arrived, they dispersed to smaller communities inland. That seasonal way of life was carried on by the Oyster Shell People's successors, the Abenakis, or "people of the dawn."

The Abenakis, a branch of the Algonquin nation, were divided into four distinct tribes: the Androscoggins, the Kennebecs, the Penobscots, and the Passamaquoddies. In summer they tended gardens of beans, squash, and corn. They also picked wild berries and harvested and dried fish and shellfish. During the winter they hunted game, fished the rivers and inland lakes and made maple syrup.

When the Europeans "discovered" the New World in the 15th century, historians estimate there were approximately one million Native Americans living in North America. Some 3,000 of the more fortunate of those — the Abenakis — lived along Maine's coastal region.

FROM AWAY

About A.D. 1000 Vikings may or may not have sailed down Maine's coast. They even may have landed, but contrary to popular opinion, there is no proof they did.

The first European documented to have landed on the Maine coast was an Italian in the service of an English king during the late 1400s. King Henry VII hired Italian navigator and explorer John Cabot (his unAnglicized surname was "Caboto") to sail up and down the northeastern seaboard and explore endless rivers to find a passage to the Indies. All Cabot found was dense forest, much of it in Maine, but he drew a map later used by England as the basis for its claim to North America.

After Cabot, the exploration of the land was left mostly to the French. They were not only interested in treasure, but also in the establishment of a New France. King Francis I of France hired another Italian explorer, Giovanni da Verrazano, to explore and chronicle the prospects of the new world. Although Verrazano reached Maine's coast in 1524, he had no great interest in what he found. On a subsequent trip Verrazano was eaten by natives on a beach in Guadeloupe.

Maine also held little attraction for the Spanish explorer Gomez, who arrived one year later. Nor did it promise enough riches to hold the interests of several other explorers who set ashore here during the 1500s. The Frenchman Jean Allefonsce did stay long enough to explore a cape and river he called "Oranbega," which in native Abenaki means "stretch of quiet water between two rapids." He probably described the land near the mouth of the Penobscot River.

Sometime during the 1500s, "Norumbega" achieved notoriety in Europe as a city filled with precious minerals and gems and inhabited by wealthy, regal Indians. One of the first to write extensively about Norumbega was David

Ingram, an Englishman who in 1568 sailed to the New World on a pirate ship. He was left ashore in the Gulf of Mexico, and claimed to have walked to Maine, where he said he saw the fabled city. He found a ride home on a French trading ship and wrote a book documenting his adventure and perpetuating the myth.

Several other Frenchmen came and went, but the team of Samuel de Champlain, Pierre du Gast and the Baron de Poutrincourt left the era's most notable mark. In 1604, after Champlain and du Gast already had spent considerable time exploring the Atlantic coast, they established a settlement with de Poutrincourt on an island at the mouth of the St. Croix River (which now forms the border between Maine and Canada).

While his partners built their new town, Champlain toured the nearby coast. He sailed into what is now known as Frenchman Bay, saw an island with ancient treeless mountains and named it *L'Isle des Monts Deserts*, or Mount Desert Island. Today it is the most visited spot in all of Maine.

A WEALTH OF FISH

Ironically, European fishermen looking to fill their nets had been rummaging about the Gulf of Maine for years. They camped ashore for months at places such as Pemaquid Point, drying their catch and co-existing peacefully with the Abenakis. These fishermen didn't keep records. Finding a good fishing hole is not something a smart fisherman boasts about, and the Gulf of Maine may have been the best fishing spot in the known world. In 1604, Champlain claims to have met one industrious boat captain along the coast who had made more than 40 fishing trips across the Atlantic. By the 1600s more than 300 fishing boats were harvesting Maine fish to feed Spain, Italy, France, England, Portugal, and Scandinavia.

In 1605, Captain George Waymouth explored the New England coast. Returning home, he convinced King James I of England of what the French already knew. This was a region worth more than gold; it was worth developing. To make the king feel a part of the exploration, Waymouth kidnapped five Native Americans and brought them with him to England. This did not endear the English to the Native Americans. More of that later. The king backed Waymouth's bid for future colonization.

FRENCH AND ENGLISH SETTLERS

The French and English were eager to colonize the coast, although the French at first were less aggressive than the British. The French tended to learn the languages and try to fit in with the local tribes in order to foster a profitable fur trade. A few Frenchmen came to spread their religion. In 1613, nine years after Champlain gave Mount Desert its name, a group of Jesuits established a religious community there.

One month later, the British razed the Mount Desert settlement and set the

Jesuits out to sea. This marked the beginning of a long and bloody feud between the two nations. The region that is now Maine was, in fact, part of two overlapping territorial claims established by both nations. The territory played heavily in the struggle for supremacy that continued until the Peace of Paris in 1763, when France gave up its claim to the vast timberlands, excellent deep-water harbors and potential fur trade.

DREAMS FOR "THE MAIN"

In 1606, James I granted a charter for southern Maine to the Plymouth Company. In 1607, the same year the British established a permanent settlement at Jamestown, Virginia, a group of British settlers established the Popham Colony (they called it St. George) at the mouth of the Kennebec, in what is today Phippsburg. This was the start of British colonization in New England (the Popham Colony preceded the settlement at Plymouth, Massachusetts, by 13 years). Although the colonists endured only one long and unusually harsh winter, this is where Maine's famed shipbuilding history began. In 1608 the colonists built the fifty-foot pinnace *Virginia* to take them back to England. The *Virginia* was much hardier than the colonists who had built it; it sailed the Atlantic for many years.

The first permanent European settlements in Maine were at Monhegan in 1622, Saco in 1623 and Agamenticus (later York) in 1624. In 1629 the Pilgrims of the Plymouth Colony in Massachusetts established a trading post at Bagaduce, on the Penobscot peninsula. From there they sent their English sponsors furs and other goods to pay off the debt for their New World voyage. The French didn't like the English being in what they considered their territory. Forty years later Baron de St. Castin took it by force.

In 1635 King Charles I of England, assuming it was his to give, gave Maine to Sir Ferdinando Gorge and named him "Lord of New England." Sir Gorge chose Agamenticus, which had grown into a small village, as the center of his empire. Five years later, he named it after himself, Gorgeana. Sir Gorge's hopes to develop "the main" — or the mainland and later "Maine" — were never realized. His heirs sold out his dream in 1677, and Gorgeana was reorganized as the town of York.

PRELUDE TO THE FRENCH AND INDIAN WARS

Uneasy relations between the French and English continued for years before formal war was declared. The coastal lands of Maine, particularly those east of the Penobscot River, were in a fairly constant state of dispute.

Although the French controlled most of the area east of the Penobscot, the English had managed to establish two trading centers there — one at Machias and one at Penobscot village. The French raided the posts in 1634 and 1635, and the English retook them in 1654. In 1664, the Duke of York was granted the lands between Pemaquid Point and the St. Croix River. In 1667, the English

Archaeological dig done in the late 19th century under the direction of antiquarian John Henry Cartland uncovered British officers' quarters at Fort William Henry, Pemaquid Point, first built in 1692.

R.L. Bradley. Courtesy, Maine Historic
Preservation Committee

King Charles II surrendered his claim on lands including Nova Scotia, Acadia and Penobscot to the French under the Treaty of Breda. At that time, Baron de St. Castin established himself in Penobscot and proceeded to protect France's interest while trading with both the English and the Native Americans. He remained there until Sir Edmund Andros, the governor of New York and Massachusetts, forcibly took the town for the English.

Official hostilities between the two countries lasted from 1675 to 1763. In the British colonies it was known as the Indian War. Saco, Scarborough and Casco were the first towns to be attacked in September 1675. The Native Americans perhaps were still angry with Waymouth's kidnapping of their five kinsmen 70 years earlier. Certainly they were threatened by the English colonials' encroachment on their land. They sided with the French, who largely had left them and their ancestral claim to the land alone. The acrimonious 88-year struggle preoccupied the small native and colonial populations of Maine and was the reason why colonization nearly halted during that time. Following the defeat of the French at Quebec in 1759, English colonists began to settle on the coast in larger numbers.

By 1790 the few Native Americans who had survived the French and Indian Wars were made wards of the Commonwealth and confined to two reservations — one at Old Town, near Bangor, and the second at Perry, near Eastport. They had no documents on which to base their claims to the land, no guns, and were highly susceptible to diseases that had crossed the ocean with the Europeans. "In the end," writes historian James MacGregor Burns, "the less numerous and less sophisticated [Native American] society crumbled before the aggressive expansion of history's largest migration."

In 1953, Native Americans were given voting rights. In 1977 the Penobscot, Passamaquoddy, and Maleseet Indians sued the state claiming that all treaties granting land to Maine were null and void, because they were never ratified by Congress. They asked for $25 billion and 12.5 million acres of land. In 1980 they received a settlement of $81.5 million, but no land.

THE REVOLUTIONARY WAR

In the mid-18th century, Maine was still very much a part of Massachusetts. Whereas Bostonians threw tea into the harbor, a Falmouth (now known as Portland) mob seized the Imperial tax stamps in 1765. Still many residents along the coast of northern Massachusetts were actively doing business with the British. Although Boston was the capital of Maine, Mainers valued above all their independence from London and Boston.

Once the Revolutionary War started, Mainers refused to ship their highly prized masts to the British fleet. The Royal Navy bombarded the city then called Falmouth and burned much of it to the ground. Even before that, zealous Maine patriots claimed the first naval victory of the war when in 1775 colonists captured the British cutter *Margaretta* in Machias Bay, a battle James Fenimore Cooper called the "Lexington of the seas."

The first colonial warship, Ranger, was built at Kittery in 1777. Two years later the colonies suffered a disastrous setback when 19 armed ships and 24 transports with more than 1,300 soldiers and marines were lost to the British at Castine. At the war's end in 1783 the Treaty of Versailles established Maine's most easterly border at the St. Croix River.

POSTWAR PROSPERITY AND THE WAR OF 1812

After the Revolutionary War, Maine prospered and grew. The era of logging began. Maine became a center for production of lumber for houses, barrels for trade, masts for ships, and wood for fuel. Ships from safe harbors all along the coast established trade routes around the world. Maine began to think about breaking away from Massachusetts.

Then France declared war on England in 1793. Short of men, England's navy began boarding American ships and impressing sailors with naval duty under pretense they were still subjects. For this reason President Jefferson finally ordered an embargo in 1807 disallowing trade with any foreign country. The embargo was particularly tough on the people and ports of Maine.

Many of the region's maritime businesses turned to smuggling. Eastport, just south of Canada, became the busiest port in the country. When the United States went to war against England in 1812, Mainers at first offered little resistance to the British, who were their best customers. People along the coast also continued trading with their own government. Worse, for the British, they continued building ships used by the American navy. The British set up a blockade and captured Castine and the surrounding towns.

With the Treaty of Ghent in 1814, the war ended as did England's blockade. The people of Maine started thinking again about breaking off from Massachusetts. In 1820, Maine was granted statehood as part of the Missouri Compromise.

The separation papers were signed at the Jamestown Tavern in Freeport (the tavern still operates today down the street from L. L. Bean). The 23rd state to join the union established its current-day capital inland at Augusta 12 years later.

Fish drying on a pier in Friendship during the mid-19th century.

Courtesy of the Penobscot Marine Museum

WOODEN SHIPS

"There are still any number of working lobster boats, plenty of yacht yards, and even a few deep-sea fishermen. . . . These are inadequate compensations, though, for anyone brought up in the knowledge of Maine's deepwater supremacy, those great times when Maine skippers were admired from the Elbe to the Amazon, and Maine-built ships were the world's criteria of seaworthiness. In those days, local prodigies like the stupendous six-masted schooner *Wyoming* were legends of the sea," wrote Jan Morris in *New England Monthly* magazine.

By 1850, Maine was considered the preeminent shipbuilding capital of America. By 1860, one fifth of the state's population were mariners, 759 of them masters of ships. Ten percent of the nation's deepwater shipmasters lived in Searsport at the top of Penobscot Bay. Bath, midway up the coast, was the United States' fifth busiest port. A little farther up the coast, Wiscasset was the busiest international port north of Boston.

Maine's romantic era of wooden shipbuilding ended with a complex set of economic events that came just before the Civil War. The invention of ironclad ships didn't help. Foreign trade moved to other ports. Maine businessmen began looking for other industries to bank on; they didn't have to look far. Forests that once supplied timbers for masts and lithe hulls now are devoted almost entirely to the production of paper.

Fisheries were among the industries that flourished, with fishermen reaping a bounty from the cold waters off northern New England, including the fish-rich St. George's Bank. At its peak in 1902, the state landed and processed 242 million pounds of cod, cusk, hake, haddock, ocean perch, mackerel, halibut, pollock, crabs, clam, shrimp, mussels, lobster, herring, and sardines. Canneries built during the height of this fishing boom, now abandoned, are still in evidence from Yarmouth to Eastport. The canning industry fell on hard times. The nation's hunger for canned herring and sardines slaked with the advent of refrigeration and the easy transport of fresh fish at the turn of the century. Other popular whitefish species, such as cod, halibut, haddock, and pollock, have become scarcer as fishermen have overfished the waters off Maine's coast.

ARTISTS "DISCOVER" MAINE'S COAST

Painting the landscape near Somesville on Mount Desert Island.

Herb Swanson

In 1844, Thomas Cole, founder of the Hudson River School of painting, visited Bar Harbor, loved what he saw and spread the word around the art community. He also told his wealthy patrons. More than 200 lavish summer "cottages" were built. Grand hotels appeared. Developers were quick to claim Mount Desert Island's thick fogs were "as healthy for the body as basking in the sun." Bar Harbor became as well known as Newport, Rhode Island.

The Maine Almanac, compiled by the *Maine Times*, reported in 1870 that "Tourists begin arriving in Maine." Not only did they come to see Maine's rocky coast, they came to see and be near the rich people who lived on the coast. Then in 1912 Leon Leonwood Bean invented the Maine Hunting Shoe, an ugly duckling of a shoe, half-leather, half-rubber that nevertheless has made many a hunter happy. "L. L.," as Freeport residents and shop clerks still call him, might as well have invented shopping. The shoe, and the store that grew up around it, eventually turned the little village of Freeport into the second most popular place in Maine.

Somesville on Mount Desert Island.

THE BIRTH OF ACADIA

The most visited place in Maine was also being established about the same time. A group of wealthy Mount Desert "rusticators" decided to donate large parcels of land to be used for a national park. Today Acadia is a public toe-hold on a coast that is 98 percent privately owned. In 1947 much of Bar Harbor was destroyed in a forest fire. The French paper *Le Figaro* mistakenly reported the peasants of Maine had struck a blow against feudalism. The town's year-round residents did not like being called peasants.

The fact is there are no aristocrats in Maine. It is a place where millionaires and lobstermen — Yankees who above all value self-reliance — talk about politics, the weather, and their boats over pie and coffee in homespun diners. The beauty of the coast and the ocean is considered more important to the people who live and visit here than what is being worn on the streets of Boston or New York. "We are hardly fashionable," wrote Frances Fitzgerald, whose family members have been longtime summer residents of Northeast Harbor, in the August 1989 *Vogue*. "You might say we are consistent to the point of atavism."

> Come one, come all.
>
> There are many facets of the promotional spirit which beguile us, but our favorite is the promotion of states of the Union by their development commissions. It is common practice for a state to recommend itself as a sanctuary to people of other states, extending a blanket invitation to all to come and romp in the peculiar sunlight within its borders. Maine, conscious of its paradisiacal quality, doggedly advertises its 'unspoiled wilderness,' presumably in the hope that millions will shortly arrive to cry in it. This is an odd quirk. Obviously, if a state valued its wildness, it would keep silent and not let the secret out among the tame. The very idea of 'development' is inconsistent with natural beauty, and there is, of course, little likelihood that the Maine woods will be thoroughly appreciated by Maine until after they no longer exist, except in the joists and rafters of the wayside soft-drink parlors. . .
>
> — E. B. White, *Writings from* The New Yorker, *1925-1976*

A JOURNEY UP THE COAST

Today there are many destinations on the coast that could be described as still having the "wild" feeling of a place barely settled. Throughout Washington County far Down East, there are long stretches of shoreline without summer cottages where the homes of year-round residents lie hidden within a dense, second-growth forest of spruce and pine. Even in the populated Midcoast section, there are meandering peninsulas punctuated with small fishing villages that seem to have only a tenuous hold on the landscape.

The coast also is home to several cities where a seat at the symphony can be hard to come by, and where the pastrami on rye is almost as satisfying as that found on Second Avenue in New York. There are the bustling old summer resorts, many of which have expanded their seasons during the past decade and now host visitors year round. Visiting the Maine coast can be a matter of choosing between more than 200 towns and villages, each of which is a small, distinct world unto itself.

KITTERY AND THE YORKS

Depending on what direction you're coming from, Maine begins or ends in Kittery, Maine's first city, incorporated on Oct. 20, 1647. The Warren Lobster House, on the banks of the Piscataqua River, displays the first or last of many giant red lobster signs used to woo visitors along a several hundred mile long strip.

Ships for the Civil War were built here; so was the nation's first submarine. The shipyard, which is open to the public and sits on Seavey Island in the middle of the Piscataqua River, is actively functioning today.

Recently Kittery has shifted to a retail economy that is based around factory outlet and discount designer stores. This is the beginning — or end — of a long stretch of what could be called the "shopper's coastline." The oldest residential part of town is in the pretty area called Kittery Point, which can be reached by Rte. 103, a winding, wooded state road that intersects with U.S. Rte. 1 and leads on toward Rte. 1A and York.

The Yorks are a group of small villages — York Village, York Harbor, York Beach and Cape Neddick — that were among the first areas of the coast to be settled during the 1600s.

York has a well-preserved historical district. The Old Gaol Museum at the heart of York's "living history district" is the earliest example of stone architecture in the U.S. For most people, though, the Yorks have other charms. Some of the coast's best beaches are right here. Cape Neddick was one of the state's first summer resorts. Today York's coastal routes and shoreline are marked by an eclectic mix of stately homes, antique shops, working lobster boats and striking stretches of fine white sand.

OGUNQUIT AND WELLS

During the high season in July and August, these two towns have almost a carnival-like atmosphere and are packed with visitors from New York,

The broad stretches of sand at York Beach make it a favorite on the South Coast for families.

State Development Office

Boston, Montreal and Quebec who c
restaurants, a healthy cultural calendar
quit together have about seven miles o
as Old Orchard.

Once a fishing village, Ogunquit,
place by the sea," was discovered by
These days, you still can see painters
road trying to capture the elusive sou
Cliff, which rises a sheer 100 feet from
tion spot for artists of all kinds and tou
Cove and walk Marginal Way, the mile-

While Ogunquit caters to an art-min
with shops and family-style restaurant
children. Birders and naturalists also
Wildlife Refuge, 1600 acres of fragile co
number of migrating birds during sprin

THE KENNEBUNKS

*Surfers and families enjoy the water at Kennebunl
houses in the town.*

Until George Bush was elected presid
ative obscurity. Now Bush's stone
drop. Judging from the queue of cars
tripods across from the Bush estate, t
Kennebunkport. Once the most popular
dramatic 30-foot spray of water that a
ranks a pale second to the Bush family c

This affluent community has all the
country roads, acres of coastline, state
restaurants, shops, boutiques and gallerie

boutiques — and don't sell T-shirts
You Fish, It's How You Wiggle The

following for Old Orchard Beach
pins, 120 restaurants, and 15 arcades.
most spectacular and well-groomed

ke French Canadians feel at home —
esidents of Old Orchard and nearby
stry. Everywhere is the sign, "Ici on
gual menus. You can buy a cup of cof-
n nearby Biddeford and hear fellow
he weather — in French. St. Margaret's
olds a mass in French every Sunday.
nguage newspapers from back home in

speaking Canadians have another reaping. The exchange rate has been very
the "TPS," or "GST" — 7 percent tax
sed in Canada since 1991. Visitors from
percent sales tax on top of the TPS, mak-
em quite reasonable, indeed.
at many Canadians can't get enough of:
n's center strip, has at least nine elec-
o here — in its several downtown blocks.

Y ISLANDS

t is an anomaly, it is Portland. Outsiders
s at first. To the rest of Maine, Portland is
than the state's largest city and home to
ne million inhabitants.
y ways. Boutiques. Ethnic food and more
ne other U.S. city (San Francisco). A full-
estra. The I. M. Pei–designed Portland
erry (to Nova Scotia) and an international
rt, the old waterfront commercial district
cca for shoppers and business people who
w York Times once described it as the "San

y peninsula framed by the Fore River to the
e east and Casco Bay to the north. With its
ath its big city ways (only a Mainer would
est incarnation of a 19th-century seaport.

THE COAST OF MAINE BOOK

There are hundreds of islands large and small in Casco Bay, several of which have become bedroom communities for working Portlanders. They are interesting to explore, as well as good swimming, biking, and walking ground.

FREEPORT

A newcomer to Freeport will certainly note that this town was built for shopping. Rte. 295 off the Maine Turnpike deposits the traveler on a two-lane road leading right through town. For the most part, the view from the car window is good enough to eye the buttons on a Ralph Lauren shirt or catch the winsome line of a canoe bow at L.L. Bean.

Way back before there were factory outlets, and before there was even an L. L. Bean, this was a favored stopping place for the British navy. His Majesty's ships would berth and pick up the famous Maine white pine the Royal Navy used to make their masts. Even today, two major landmarks commemorate this early trading route — Upper Mast Landing and Lower Mast Landing — where the mast pines were collected before being shipped.

Until 1981, there was L. L. Bean and the kind of stores you'd find on Main St. in any small town. Now it is wall-to-wall factory outlets. But the true beauty of Freeport isn't in the great bargains to be found there. It's that the town has retained much of its feel as a New England village and knowing that only two minutes' drive east on Bow St. and you're out in the country. There you get a sense of the way this part of the coast used to be: hilly, green pastures, tidy 18th- and 19th-century farmhouses, country lanes, pines, and firs.

BRUNSWICK AND WISCASSET

B owdoin College is the overwhelming presence in Brunswick, but there's much more here than just the school, including the Peary-MacMillan Arctic Museum and the Maine State Music Theatre. This is also where Harriet Beecher Stowe wrote *Uncle Tom's Cabin*. For most visitors, this town is a place to get serious about their visit. This is the point in the coast where little-known detours can often be more rewarding than the better-known vacation destinations like Bar Harbor, Portland, and the South Coast beaches. Brunswick is certainly the place where one has to start picking and choosing.

For example, just a little to the southeast of Brunswick are the Harpswells, skinny fingers of land that stretch into Casco Bay and are connected by bridge to the rounded and rocky terrain of Sebascodegan, Orrs, and Bailey islands. Making your way to the edge of Mackerel Cove on Bailey Island is only a matter of about 15 miles, but it can seem like time-traveling through decades. There's also Cundy's Harbor off on its own, a fishing village so heavily populated with photographic subjects that local stores do a brisk business selling film.

Bath is a city of ships and shipbuilding that hugs the shores of the Kennebec, a deep and navigable waterway that has an ocean-like feel to it — as if it were capable of handling any oceangoing vessel large or small. During World War II, Bath built more destroyers than all the shipyards in the entire Japanese empire. Not far from here is the Phippsburg peninsula, the cradle of Maine civilization and its shipbuilding industry.

Across the Kennebec is Georgetown Island, a sprawling network of summer communities and fishing villages with names like Robinhood, Five Islands, Marrtown, and Arrowsic. Robinhood Cove, which cuts into the island's northeastern side, is often filled with the yachts of summering residents, and Reid State Park at the outermost reaches of the Sheepscot River is a wonderful family park with one of the better beaches in the Midcoast.

Wiscasset has billed itself as the "prettiest village in Maine." That title is disputable, but the town's location where Rte. 1 crosses the Sheepscot River makes the town's charm readily visible to anyone traveling up the coast. Adding to Wiscasset's romance are two old schooners lodged haphazardly on the west bank of the river. The *Hesperus* and the *Luther Little* once carried cargo between Boston, Haiti, and Portugal. They were two of thousands of ships that plied the seas until well into the 1920s. Today they are one of the most photographed sites in Maine.

BOOTHBAY HARBOR

Formerly a trading center, and later a hub of shipbuilding activity, Boothbay Harbor today is mostly about boats, activities attached to boats and people who find the boating way of life appealing. The shady streets of the town, at the tip of a rocky peninsula, are lined with summer-people-minded shops and a wealth of art galleries. The pretty harbor is jam-packed with boats to rent, boats to hire, boats to envy, and boats to drool over and make one consider Captain Kidd's occupation. (The notorious pirate also liked to summer here and reportedly left a buried treasure on nearby Damariscove Island. Treasure hunters are still trying to locate the fabled store.) This is also the port of call for Windjammer Days, a famous Maine boaters' event.

Within half an hour's drive you can see the great boats being built in East Boothbay. Nearby are the summer retreats of Newagen on Southport Island to the west and Ocean Point to the east.

NEWCASTLE/DAMARISCOTTA TO PEMAQUID POINT

For centuries Native Americans summer camped here and left behind giant piles of oyster shells, a feat which today is celebrated at the annual Damariscotta River Oyster Festival. Not far off Rte. 1, you can still see one of the great shell heaps where the Damariscotta River and the inland Great Salt Bay meet.

Here is another one of those famous coastal junctures, where travelers can push on toward Rockland and Camden or veer off the main road onto picturesque Rte. 129. This road runs down the Pemaquid peninsula along the river to South Bristol, a fishing village, and Christmas Cove, a yachting basin so named by Captain John Smith, who anchored here on Christmas Day in 1614. Rte. 130 picks up in the fishing village of New Harbor and meanders on through the historic peninsula to Pemaquid Point, where there is one of Maine's most stunning lighthouses — Pemaquid Light. This spot shows off the Maine coast at its stormy best with the power of the ocean pounding against the rockbound coast. Rte. 32 takes you back up along Muscongus Sound through pretty Round Pond to Waldoboro.

WALDOBORO TO ROCKLAND

Waldoboro was settled by Germans in the mid-18th century, and today is famed for two of the state's culinary landmarks — Moody's Diner and Morse's Sauerkraut. The first five-masted schooner was built here in 1888.

From here, Friendship is just a short trip down Rte. 220, which skirts the western shore of the Medomak River. It's hard to believe Friendship exists. Where are the shops, the hotels, the gas stations, restaurants? Here on beautiful, isolated Hatchet Cove are a few summer homes, a handful of lobster boats and a Friendship sloop or two, that famous gaff-rigged working boat now prized by wealthy modern-day sailors. Rte. 97 leads past Cushing, another quiet fishing village, made famous by painter Andrew Wyeth.

From Thomaston, home of the state prison, you can veer off onto Rte. 131, which leads down yet another peninsula filled with history. Tenant's Harbor looks simple, but look again. Those are mighty big yachts anchored so casually in the harbor. Southwest from here is Port Clyde, once called Herring Gut. Port Clyde is the point of departure for the hour-long boat ride to Monhegan, eleven miles off the coast. Measuring only one mile by $^1/_2$ mile, Monhegan literally is besieged with painters, and the salt breezes alternately smell of turpentine. The dark forests and dramatic cliffs make the island a hiker's paradise as well.

Once known for its quarried limerock that was shipped to the four corners of the earth, Rockland today bills itself as the lobster capital of the world. It is the Penobscot Bay region's central working town, and its harbor is filled with lobster boats and commercial fishing boats that regularly fish the waters of the Grand Banks. Rockland is a bustling town that in recent years has become gentrified with artists' studios, galleries, and moderately expensive restaurants that clearly aim to serve tourists. It also is a hub of the windjammer trade, and from here ferries regularly travel to Vinalhaven, Matinicus, and North Haven.

Sitting fifteen miles out in Penobscot Bay, Vinalhaven flourished when granite was quarried here. Today the island has a tenacious year-round population of lobstermen and fishermen and a dedicated coterie of summer residents who seem to like keeping the secret of this island to themselves. To the north is the small and exclusive summer community of North Haven on North Haven island. Windjammers and large pleasure boats often anchor in Pulpit Harbor where passengers can catch a glimpse of the large seaside estates owned by the island's reclusive summer residents.

In striking contrast there is the quiet, tiny island of Matinicus. Approximately 100 people make their living here, most of them lobstering and fishing the outer waters of Penobscot Bay. It takes about two hours by ferry to ply the 23 miles of water to the island. Dedicated birders often opt to charter a local boat and keep going another five miles to Matinicus Rock, where nesting puffins often can be seen.

CAMDEN

Just off Rte. 1 before Camden is Rockport, a pastoral village where Galloways munch in green meadows and actors, photographers, and boatbuilders live in mansions by the sea. Rockport was also the home of Andre the Seal; today a statue on the harbor commemorates him.

The storybook beauty of Camden was captured in the film Peyton Place. Today it's considered the shoppers' resting place between Freeport and Bar Harbor. Expensive shops cram the old-fashioned town center. The town is part of a miniature filmmaking boom and movie stars and movie crews frequently can be seen at work or relaxing over lunch at Camden's restaurants.

This pretty town is a worthwhile destination, although it can be a hard town in which to find a parking space. Space in the harbor is also scarce. Luxury yachts moor next to giant windjammers that ferry passengers on week-long cruises; and on a busy summer day it seems possible to walk from boat to boat from one side of the harbor to the other. When here, be certain to visit Merryspring, a breathtaking public garden and one of the most famous horticultural sites of New England.

Lincolnville Beach just to the north offers an expansive view of Penobscot Bay. This is also where you catch the ferry to Islesboro, the exclusive summer community three miles off shore.

BELFAST TO BUCKSPORT

The towns along this part of the coast keep promising to be the next Camden. The fact each is still waiting to be discovered makes this a wonderful place to visit. Antiques and sea captains' homes abound. Beautiful old houses with ocean views are still more than reasonably priced. There are art galleries, theater groups, and restaurants for big city palates in Belfast.

The deepwater port of Searsport at the head of Penobscot Bay was once known in ports around the world. The town still has the grand waterfront houses to prove it, many of them now converted to inns and bed and breakfasts. Today it bills itself as the antique capital of Maine.

A mooring in beautiful Camden Harbor is one of the most valuable pieces of real estate on the coast.

Tom Hindman

BLUE HILL PENINSULA

Rte. 175 off Rte. 1 just past Bucksport takes you down to Castine. This former trading post is one of the most attractive towns on the coast, with its tree-lined streets, grand homes, and spectacular views of Holbrook Island Sanctuary, Islesboro, and Cape Rosier, where authors Helen and Scott Nearing built their own Walden. The Maine Maritime Academy is in Castine and so is its training ship, the *State of Maine*, which is open for tours when in port. Rte. 15 to Stonington on Deer Island at the end of the peninsula is a good hour and a half off Rte. 1 and prefers it that way. The fishing industry is very much alive here. The mail boat leaves here for Isle au Haut, Acadia National Park's least-visited outpost shared with a small community of fishermen and farmers.

Blue Hill, named after the nearby blueberry-crested mountain, has abundant views of Mount Desert Island. This is obviously ample inspiration, because it is a thriving center for artists and writers who live here and in nearby villages including Brooklin and Sedgwick. It is also the site of the annual Blue Hill Fair, made famous by local writer E. B. White in *Charlotte's Web*. Surry, on pretty Rte. 172, which leads up to Ellsworth, may be the only village of its size with its own opera company.

MOUNT DESERT ISLAND AND THE SCHOODIC PENINSULA

If only the French explorer Champlain had known what he had discovered when he first set eyes on this island of rounded mountains almost 400 years ago. Today Mount Desert, which includes Bar Harbor and most of Acadia National Park, is the most visited place in Maine. Visitors come here to walk the famed carriage trails that were built in the early part of this century as a kind of social lifeline connecting the homes of summer residents like the Rock-efellers and the Pulitzers. They also drive the twenty-mile Park Loop Road along Frenchman's Bay and the road to the top of Cadillac Mountain to watch the sun go down at Sunset Point, which has been renamed Blue Hill Overlook by park officials to help reduce overcrowding at dusk. The hike up Cadillac is usually a lovely, lonely climb.

Mount Desert Island is also home to Bar Harbor, a lively, unabashedly tourist town that somehow manages to keep its dignity. Maybe the stately Victorian townhouses lining the streets, many converted to small inns and bed and breakfasts, keep check on the proliferating T-shirt and souvenir stores. Maybe also because the people who get the most out of their visit here only stop mountain climbing, biking, canoeing, and kayaking long enough to grab a bite and a good night's rest. If you like it quieter, there are the civilized charms of tea at the Jordan Pond House in Acadia and the famous Mount Desert gardens bursting in bloom at the height of summer. There also are more secluded island spots like Northeast Harbor, Hulls Cove, Southwest Harbor and Bass Harbor, and the islands — including Little Cranberry Island, the lovely home of the tiny village of Isleford. Or do what many Mainers do, and visit in the spring, fall, and winter — when the island is less crowded.

Just east of Mount Desert is the Schoodic Peninsula, the tip of which is part of Acadia National Park, a smaller, wilder version of the main portion of the park. The rest of the peninsula is characterized by an anything goes feeling. Lobstermen rub elbows with the sons of captains of industry and movie stars. Army personnel venture about, caring for a secretive military installation on the point. Year-round residents like to tell the story of one neighbor who bought a whole fleet of little wooden sailboats and every year rounded up family and acquaintances to compete in friendly regattas.

EAST OF SCHOODIC

For the majority of coastal Maine visitors, the world ends at Bar Harbor. Washington County (also known as Sunrise County) is thought to be dirt poor, flat and endless. It's not. In fact, it has a beauty all its own, stark as a blueberry barren, religious, pure — probably thanks to the fact that developers have largely ignored it during the last 50 years.

Everything up here is out in the open, exposed to the elements, and here they seem more, well, elemental. Like Jonesport. It's terrifyingly close to the sea. In the hilly fishing village, weather-beaten clapboard and shingled houses huddle together as if to draw comfort from one another. There's also Dennysville, tucked into the countryside on the Dennys River where stately Georgian homes rise up from the rolling landscape and make this look more like the manor-strewn countryside of England than Down East.

MACHIAS TO LUBEC AND EASTPORT

A few years ago, tourism officials decided to rename the region that stretches down east to the Canadian border, "Sunrise County" to capitalize on the fact that this is the easternmost land in the United States. Yet despite the modest hype, this beautiful region is among the least visited areas of the coast — and for that reason a good place to explore, scramble over the rocks of the rocky coast, search for rare bald eagles and puffins or just get away from the hubbub of points south.

Machias, which is Indian for "bad little falls," is the most businesslike of towns. It's a get-em-in-get-em-out place where waitresses wait on busloads of people headed out of town almost as quickly as they drive in, no questions asked. Settled by the English in 1633, this was a favorite repair and refueling spot for pirates in the late 17th century. For those American history students who thought the Revolution was a unanimous undertaking by all colonists, think again. Prosperous lumbermen, who understood quite well that England was their best customer, argued for a long while about whether or not to support the revolt. They did, and a few months later nearby Machiasport was the site of the first naval battle of the Revolutionary War. Stalwart Mainers, you'll be glad to know, won the skirmish, captured the British armed schooner the *Margaretta* and inspired leaders in Philadelphia to establish a navy.

Lubec sits on a narrow strip of land that juts into Cobscook Bay and is a quiet town with tree-lined streets and wonderful views of the bay. Just down the road is West Quoddy Head, the easternmost point of land in the United States and site of a beautiful state park and a lighthouse that is enshrouded by fog 59 days of the year. Lubec is also the only auto route (via bridge) to Campobello Island, the summer home of President Franklin D. Roosevelt. To get there, you have to go through customs — Campobello is within Canadian territory — although the presidential landmark is operated jointly by the U.S. and Canadian governments. The island is also a birdwatcher's haven, part of the famous Quoddy Loop that extends through northeastern Maine and southeastern Nova Scotia.

Eastport has been described as a city of dreamers, and there are ample examples of the city's saga of boom-and-bust. During the early 1800s, when trade between the United States and England was embargoed, Eastport gloried as a smuggler's port. It was certainly far enough down east to escape diligent enforcers.

Fishing was, and remains today, the city's main industry. Cod, pollock, haddock, halibut, and herring once flourished in the cold offshore waters, but during the past 25 years have dwindled. During the late 1800s to mid-1900s, sardines were big business, and canneries lined the waterfront (sardines are actually small herrings). During the 80s, the bay's sweeping tides and deep coastal waters were discovered as ideal for farming salmon in offshore pens. Now, every year the town celebrates the domesticated Atlantic salmon with a festival in early September. To the outsider this hillside town, with a startlingly minimal number of gift shops and art galleries, has almost a Wild West feel and is a great place to make home base when exploring the beautiful country that surrounds it.

CHAPTER TWO
How to Get Here and Get Around
TRANSPORTATION

Sections of coastal U.S. Rte. 1 in Maine, which today runs from Kittery to Fort Kent by way of Rockland, Ellsworth, and Machias, follow ancient Native American trails. Settlers marked the trails during the 1600s and named the resulting road the King's Highway. The route first was used by mail couriers traveling from Boston to Machias; later, as settlements grew up along the coast, the public highway was traversed by horse-drawn vehicles.

Herb Swanson

Swans Island Ferry leaving from Bass Harbor on Mount Desert Island.

The first stagecoach began operating between Portland and Portsmouth in 1787. The 90-mile journey took three days. Keep that slow crawl in mind as you're creeping across the Carlton Bridge east of Bath. (Later we will tell you about some of the most famous bottlenecks along the coast, including the Carlton Bridge; we'll also suggest ways to avoid them.)

Despite the early full-fledged "highway," most of the coast was serviced by roads that were muddy and impassable during much of the year. Because this is a coast, the preferred method of travel then was by sea; ships and shipping were the industries that made Maine.

By the 1850s, 246 sailing vessels and 12 steamships called regularly on the port of Portland while 31 different railway lines carrying lumber and passengers crisscrossed the state. At the turn of the century electric trolleys carried tourists from Boston up the coast to Kennebunkport and Bar Harbor.

With the creation of the Interstate Highway System during the 1950s, suddenly half the populations of the United States and Canada were within a day's drive of the Maine coast. Today, most visitors come by highway.

The biggest change on Maine's transportation scene since we last wrote is a state-of-the-art automatic toll taking system on the *Maine Turnpike*. Hopes are it will help eliminate toll booth bottlenecks on busy summer days. The turnpike also has *a new exit at Scarborough (Exit 6)*, which makes getting to the coast north of Saco and south of South Portland easier.

Plans for eliminating one frequent traveler's jam spot, on *Carlton Bridge over the Kennebec River in Bath*, are under discussion and, despite ongoing discussions to determine the best course of action, chances are Bath will get a new, wider bridge soon. Until then, check out "Shortcuts" at the end of this chapter where we show how to avoid the bridge altogether.

In other transportation news, the train still doesn't come to Portland but local businesses and individuals are still lobbying for an extension of the *Amtrak* line that will connect the southern coast of Maine to Boston. Reports are that despite cutbacks in Amtrak's budget, the train will stop in Portland — eventually.

Finally, we'd like to mention that smoking is no longer allowed on *Casco Bay Lines*, the ferry service that connects Portland to the nearby islands. Ahh, the island air feels cleaner already.

TRANSPORTATION TODAY

Airports at Boston, Portland, and Bangor service domestic and international airlines with direct flights from Canada and Europe. Smaller airports, including Rockland and Bar Harbor, serve as connecting points for air travelers. Passenger train service to Maine ended during the 1950s, and as we mentioned at the beginning of this chapter, the battle continues to open an extension of Amtrak that would connect Portland with Boston and New York. Car ferries run regularly between the maritime provinces of Canada and Bar Harbor and Portland.

GETTING TO THE COAST

BY CAR

From Connecticut, New York, New Jersey and South: I-95 goes right across the Piscataqua River separating New Hampshire and Maine and into Kittery, the first and oldest town on the coast.

From New York: I-95 runs along the coast of Connecticut, up through Providence, Boston, and Portsmouth. For a more direct route take I-95 to New Haven, I-91 north to Hartford, I-84 northeast until you get on the Mass. Pike at the Sturbridge entrance. Take the Westborough exit and follow I-495 northeast to where it joins I-95, just south of the New Hampshire border.

From Boston: Although this route adds a few more miles, it is faster than fighting your way up Rte. 1. Take I-93 north to Rte. 128 east until it rejoins I-95. On the way home there's also the added benefit of saving the Tobin Bridge toll — and avoiding traffic.

From Montreal: AAA recommends you take Rte. 10 to Magog; 55 south to the international border just north of Derby Line, Vermont. Pick up I-91 at the border and follow to Rte. 2 in St. Johnsbury. Continue east on Rte. 2 through Gorham, New Hampshire, and on to Bethel, Maine.

If your destination is the Midcoast, Casco Bay or South Coast region, pick up Rte. 26 in Bethel and follow to Portland.

For the Down East/Acadia and East of Schoodic regions, continue on Rte. 2 from Bethel to I-95 near Newport, Maine, and follow to Bangor. From there you can take Alternate Rte. 1 to Stockton Springs and Belfast. Or you can take Rte. 1 south to Ellsworth and points east.

Trolleys like this were a popular form of transportation. This one and many others from around the world may be seen at the Seashore Trolley Museum in Kennebunkport.

Courtesy of Maine Historic Preservation Commission

From Quebec City: Take Rte. 73 to Rte. 173 and the border, about 10 miles south of Armstrong. Pick up Rte. 201 at the border and follow all the way to Skowhegan, Maine. To access the South Coast, Casco Bay and Midcoast regions, continue on Rte. 201 to Waterville where you pick up I-95 south. If you're headed to the Midcoast or Down East, pick up Rte. 2 east of Skowhegan. It connects with I-95 near Newport, Maine, and goes to Bangor. From there you can take Alternate Rte. 1 to Stockton Springs and Belfast. Or you can take Rte. 1 south to Ellsworth and points east.

From Saint John or Fredericton: Take Rte. 1 from St. John to the international border at St. Stephen, then south to Calais, Maine. Continue on Rte. 1 toward Machias and points south. Rte. 190 in Perry veers off toward Eastport. An alternate route to the Midcoast, Casco Bay, and South Coast regions is to follow Rte. 1 to Rte. 9 near Calais. Follow Rte. 9 to Bangor.

From Toronto: You have the choice of traveling north or south of Lake Ontario. Both routes take approximately the same amount of time. The southern route is super highways — and tolls — most of the way. The northern route is smaller roads and no tolls.

Traveling north around the lake, take Rte. 401 east to Cornwall, just north of the international border. Pick up Rte. 37 in Rooseveltown, New York, and follow that east to Malone. Take Rte. 11 East to Swanton, Vermont, where you get onto I-89 south. Take this highway to Montpelier. Pick up Rte. 2 east and follow all the way through St. Johnsbury on to Bethel, Maine.

If your destination is in the Midcoast, Casco Bay, and South Coast regions, pick up Rte. 26 in Bethel and follow to Portland.

For the Down East/Acadia and East of Schoodic regions, continue on Rte. 2 from Bethel to I-95 near Newport, Maine, and follow to Bangor. From there you can take Alternate Rte. 1 to Stockton Springs and Belfast. Or you can take Rte. 1 south to Ellsworth and points east.

Traveling south around Lake Ontario, take the QEW to the international border. Take 190 through Niagara Falls, New York, to I-90. Follow I-90 to the connection with the Mass. Pike. Take the Mass. Pike to the Westborough exit and follow I-495 northeast to where it joins I-95, just south of the New Hampshire border.

BY BUS

*G*reyhound (800-231-2222) will take you as far as Boston, but from there **Vermont Transit** (207-772-6587 or 800-451-3292) goes as far north as Bar Harbor. From Boston, the bus stops in Portsmouth, NH; Portland, Brunswick, Lewiston, Augusta, Waterville, Bangor, and Bar Harbor. Sticking to the coast, **Concord Trailways** (207-828-1151 or 800-639-5505) leaves from Boston for Portland, Brunswick, Bath, Wiscasset, Damariscotta, Waldoboro, Rockland, Camden, Rockport, Lincolnville, Belfast, Searsport, and Bangor. Concord also offers an express bus from Boston to Bangor with one stop in Portland. If you need to reach the coastal towns between the New Hampshire border and Portland, they

One of the best ways of exploring coastal waters.

Tom Hindman

will refer you to *C+J Trailways* (800-258-7111), which makes one trip daily from Boston to Concord's Portland terminal via Hampton Beach, Ogunquit, Kennebunk, and Biddeford. There is no direct bus link to points in Canada.

BY PLANE

If you are not traveling by car, you most likely will arrive in Maine via plane. There are major airports in Portland, Augusta, and Bangor, all with connecting flights to smaller airports in Rockland and Bar Harbor. Many choose to fly into Boston's Logan Airport, only 1.5 hours to Kittery and 2.5 hours to Portland by car. All of the large airports are served by the major airlines. In addition, there are several small coastal and island airports with independent air services that have connecting regular and charter flights.

Augusta State Airport — 207-626-2306; Continental Connection.

Portland International Jetport — 207-874-8300; Business Express, Continental, Continental Express, Delta, United, US Airways.

Bangor International Airport — 207-947-0384; Business Express, Continental Express, Delta, Northwest, US Airways Express.

Knox County Regional Airport, Owls Head (near Rockland) — 207-594-4131; Continental Connection.

Hancock County/Bar Harbor Airport, Trenton (near Bar Harbor) — 207-667-7329; Continental Connection.

Maine Turnpike

To find out what the weather or traffic is like on the turnpike, call 800-675-PIKE. Following is a list of Maine Turnpike interchanges and their numbers.

Exit No.	Location
1	Kittery, York
2	Ogunquit/Wells
3	Kennebunk
4	Biddeford
5	Old Orchard, Saco
6	Scarborough
6A	Portland/I-295
7	South Portland
8	Portland/Westbrook
9	Falmouth Spur, Freeport, Yarmouth
10	Portland north
11	Gray
12	Auburn
13	Lewiston
14	Gardiner
End	Augusta

MAINE ACCESS

The chart below gives miles and approximate driving times from the following cities to Portland:

City	Time	Miles
Albany	5.5 hours	237
Boston	2.5 hours	109
Hartford	4 hours	200
Montreal	6 hours	255
New York	7 hours	317
Philadelphia	9.5 hours	424
Quebec	6.5 hours	278
St. John	7 hours	309
Toronto	14 hours	621
Washington, D.C.	12.5 hours	557

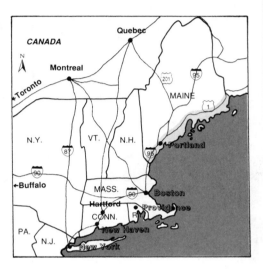

The chart below gives you miles and approximate driving times from the following cities to Bangor.

City	Time	Miles
Montreal	7.25 hours	306
Quebec	5.75 hours	236
St. John	3 .5 hours	163
Toronto	13.25 hours	609
Yarmouth	19 hours	850
Boston	5.5 hours	249
New York	9 hours	452

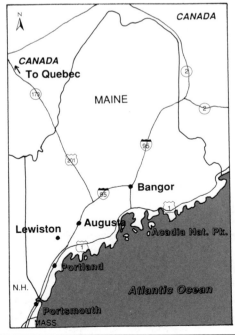

This ferry carried passengers between the island of Vinalhaven and Rockland during the 18th century. Ferry service is still the island's most vital link to the mainland.

Courtesy of the Penobscot Marine Museum

GETTING AROUND THE COAST OF MAINE

BY CAR

There are three ways to drive up the coast: the fast way on I-95; the medium-fast way on U.S. Rte. 1; and the slow-and-easy way on smaller state highways and roads that often turn out to be the fastest of all. Which route you take depends on your destination — or how serendipitous you want to be.

The three most-visited spots in Maine and on the coast are: Acadia National Park, L. L. Bean in Freeport and Old Orchard Beach. Depending on your intentions and schedule, you may wish to see — or avoid — all three.

Acadia is one of the most beautiful parks in the national park system. To get to Acadia, take Rte. 1 or Rte. 1A to Ellsworth, which is in the center of the Down East/Acadia region. From Ellsworth take Rte. 3 to Bar Harbor. The park is less than a mile from Bar Harbor. Bar Harbor is 211 miles from Kittery, 122 miles from Eastport, and 46 miles from Bangor. The portion of Acadia on the Isle au Haut can be reached by ferry from Stonington. Most of Acadia's 5 million yearly visitors speed up or down I-95 to Augusta or Bangor before heading coastward along Rte. 3 or Rte. 1A. Once they arrive, they drive the famed Park Loop Road, a 20-mile winding road through the 35,000 acre park, which culminates at the top of 1,530-foot Cadillac Mountain with views of Blue Hill, Penobscot, and Frenchman Bay. In recent years, the number of vehicles on the loop has been so heavy that there have been traffic jams.

To reach Freeport, most visitors opt for Exit 17 or Exit 19 off I-95 (the coastal extension that begins as Rte. 295 in South Portland and leads to Topsham before rejoining the Maine Turnpike). The signs from the highway lead directly into Freeport, home of L. L. Bean and a growing community of factory outlets from Ralph Lauren to Maidenform lingerie (see Chapter Seven, *Shopping*).

To get to Old Orchard Beach, most travelers take Exit 5 off I-95, which leads to Rte. 5 and Old Orchard Beach. The town is home to a seven-mile long beach — one of the state's most significant sand beaches and the closest to Canada. During July more than 80 percent of the vacationers in Old Orchard Beach are French Canadian.

Then there is the rest of the coast. A small road sign leading off Rte. 1 on the right reads "Friendship." The whole Penobscot peninsula gets a similar simple sign or two. If you opt to heed one of these signs and turn off —and deciding which one or two to take can be the hard part, since any one could be considered a vacation destination — most likely you will find other tourists. You won't find nearly as many tourists as you will find in Acadia, Freeport, and Old Orchard Beach. You could also find a place like Jonesport, where fishermen's houses are piled around the waterfront like lobster traps.

The best way to see the area is by car. Given the relatively long distances between towns on the coast be sure to plan carefully before you leave. Many secondary routes that access towns along the coast are narrow, two-lane roads, and they make travel slower than you might expect. For example, it takes a full hour to get from Rte. 1 at Orland to Stonington via Rtes. 175 and 15.

If you want help getting around the coast, and you're a member, check in with AAA. They can map various routes to your particular destination. Their offices on the coast are:

Portland — AAA Maine
425 Marginal Way
207-774-6377
Mailing address:
P.O. Box 3544
Portland, ME 04104

South Portland — AAA Maine
443 Western Ave.
So. Portland, ME 04106
207-775-6211

CAR RENTALS

If you are flying into Boston, Portland, Bangor or Bar Harbor, chances are you will rent an automobile to explore the coast. It is best to call well ahead of your visit to reserve a rental car, particularly during the busier season between Memorial and Labor days.

Alamo Rent A Car: 800-327-9633 (9 Johnson Rd., Portland, 207-775-0855). Pick up at the airport.

Avis: 800-331-1212 (Portland Jetport, 207-874-7500; Bangor Airport, 207-947-8383).

Budget: 800-527-0700 (Portland Jetport, 207-772-6789; Bar Harbor Airport, 207-667-1200; Augusta Airport, 207-622-0210; Bangor Airport, 207-945-9429; Rockland Airport, 207-594-0822).

Enterprise: 800-736-8222 (Portland Jetport, 207-854-0560; Bangor Airport, 207-990-0745; with other offices in Portland, Saco, Brunswick, and Augusta).

Hertz: 800-654-3131 (Portland Jetport, 207-774-4544; Bar Harbor Airport, 207-667-5017; Bangor Airport, 207-942-5519).

National Interrent: 800-227-7368 (Portland Jetport, 207-773-0036; Bangor Airport, 207-947-0158; Rockland, 207-594-8424).

Thrifty: 800-367-2277 (Portland Jetport, 207-772-4628; Bangor Airport, 207-942-6400).

BY PLANE

A fast way to get around the coast is by air. Following is a list of air charter services that fly on the coast.

Maine Aviation Corporation, Portland Jetport   207-780-1811
Down East Flying Service, Portland Jetport   207-774-2028/800-290-9401
Penobscot Air Service, Rockland Airport   207-596-6211/800-780-6071
Acadia Air Inc., Bar Harbor Airport   207-667-5534
Snug Harbor Airways, Bangor Airport   207-947-0824
Ace Aviation, Belfast Airport   207-338-2970
Lands Ending Air Charter, Knox County Airport   207-594-5311

COASTAL TOWN ACCESS

Here are approximate distances between selected cities and towns within the state. The time it takes to travel these distances varies widely, depending on time of year, traffic conditions and the route traveled. The highway speed limit in Maine is 55 mph in populated areas, 65 mph in rural regions.

From Kittery to:	Miles	From Eastport to:	Miles
Old Orchard Beach	37	Machias	44
Portland	50	Bar Harbor	122
Freeport	66	Belfast	141
Brunswick	76	Camden	160
Augusta	107	Rockland	167
Boothbay Harbor	109	Boothbay Harbor	207
Rockland	131	Brunswick	217
Camden	135	Freeport	227
Belfast	153	Portland	243
Bangor	183	Old Orchard Beach	262
Bar Harbor	211	Kittery	293
Machias	249		

Others:	Miles
Bangor to Bar Harbor	46
Augusta to Rockland	42
Augusta to Belfast	47

BY FERRY

One of the advantages of visiting the coast of Maine is that you have so many opportunities to ride a ferry. Island residents live with their inner clocks set to the ferry schedule, and so will you when you plan to visit one of the coastal outlands. For information on ferries statewide, write to or call the *Maine State Ferry Service*, P.O. Box 645, 517A Main St., Rockland 04841; 207-624-7777. Their Rockland number is 207-596-2202. Find them on the Internet at www.state.me.us/mdot/mainhtml/feryinfo.htm.

Rockland to Vinalhaven: Year-round service between Rockland and Vinalhaven on the *Governor Curtis* and the *Charles Philbrook* (207-863-4421); 15 miles; crossing time: one hour and 15 minutes.

To North Haven: Year round on the *Captain Neal Burgess* (207-867-4441); 12.5 miles; crossing time: one hour and 10 minutes.

To Matinicus: Ferry service one day a month in winter; three days a month in summer. The ferry carries supplies to the islanders as well. Best to call in advance. For a taste of Maine (and whether you go or not), it's a phone call well spent. On the *North Haven* (207-596-2202); 23 miles; crossing time: two hours and 15 minutes.

Lincolnville to Isleboro: Year-round service on the *Margaret Chase Smith* (207-789-5611 or 207-734-6935); 3 miles; crossing time: 20 minutes.

Bass Harbor to Swans Island: Year-round service on the *Captain Henry Lee* (207-526-4273); 6 miles; crossing time: 40 minutes.

To Frenchboro: Year-round service on the *Captain Henry Lee* (207-244-3254); 8.25 miles; crossing time: 50 minutes.

Portland to Peaks, Great Chebague; Long, Great and Little Diamond, and Cliff islands, with seasonal service to Bailey Island: Year-round service on *Island Holiday, Island Romance, Maquoit II, Machigonne II* and on their newest boat, the *Quickwater*, by Casco Bay Lines, P.O. Box 4656 DTS, Portland 04101 (207-774-7871; www.cascobay.com/islands/ferry/ferry.htm); 17 minutes to Peaks; 30 minutes to Long Island; one hour and 15 minutes to Chebeague. Ferry leaves Ferry Terminal at Commercial and Franklin streets. This is America's oldest ferry service.

Portland to Eagle Island: Daily service from late June to Columbus Day. Leaves Long Wharf on Commercial St., Portland. Eagle Tours (207-774-6498); 90-minute stopover on island.

Freeport to Eagle Island: Ferry service runs daily between Memorial and Columbus Day. Atlantic Seal Cruises, 25 Main St., South Freeport 04078 (207-865-6112); one-hour stopover on island.

Portland to Yarmouth, Nova Scotia: Regular car and passenger service on the *Scotia Prince* from May through October with occasional "no-sail days." Prince of Fundy Cruises, P.O. Box 4216, Portland, 04101-0416 (207-775-5616 in Portland; 800-341-7540 in U.S.; www.princeoffundy.com); 11 hours. Leaves from the International Ferry Terminal, Commercial St., Portland. Children under 5 travel free. Vehicle and cabin rates extra. Tractor-trailer trucks often

Waiting to cross the border into Canada at Calais.

Herb Swanson

take this boat to save driving 850 miles. Once offshore you can gamble and shop duty free. Proof of citizenship required.

Cousins Island to Great Chebeague Island: Year-round service on the *Big Squaw* and *Islander*; Chebeague Transportation Co., Chebeague Island 04107 (207-846-3700). No transient parking available at Cousins Island. Parking and shuttle bus service available from Cumberland Center.

Boothbay to Monhegan: Daily service early June to late September on the *Balmy Days II* with Capt. Bob Campbell, P.O. Box 535, Boothbay 04538 (207-633-2284); one round trip per day. Weekends, off season. Leaves from Pier 8, Commercial St., Boothbay.

Port Clyde to Monhegan: Daily service from May through October on the *Laura B* and the *Elizabeth Ann* with Capt. James Barstow, P.O. Box 238, Port Clyde 04855 (207-372-8848; www.monhegan.boat.com); one hour, 10 minutes. Ferry operates three times a week in winter.

New Harbor to Monhegan: Daily service mid-June through October 1, less frequentiy in winter, on the *Hardy III*, Capt. Al Crocetti, PO Box 326, New Harbor 04554 (207-677-2026 or 800-278-3346). Reservations recommended.

Stonington to Isle au Haut and Duck Harbor: Five trips daily from mid-June through early September on the *Mink*, or *Miss Lizzie* with Capt. George Aldrich, RR 1, Box 3636, Stonington 04681 (207-367-5193); 45 minutes. Leaves from Seabreeze Ave. Dock, Stonington.

Northeast Harbor to Sutton Island (on request), Great Cranberry Island, and Islesford: Six trips daily late June through Labor Day on the *Sea Queen* and *Double B*, operated by Beal & Bunker, P.O. Box 33, Cranberry Isles 04625 (207-244-3575).

Bar Harbor to Yarmouth, Nova Scotia: Daily service June through mid-October on the *M.V. Bluenose*, operated by Bay Ferry, 121 Eden St., Bar Harbor (207-288-3395 or 888-249-7245, in continental U.S.); 6 hours. Leaves Ferry Terminal, Bar Harbor. Car and passenger ferry. Children under 5 travel free.

SHORTCUTS

Bottlenecks are common on the coast because there is one main thorough-fare, Rte. 1, that stretches the entire length. (I-95 follows the coast only between Kittery and Brunswick.) Rte. 1 in Maine is a two-lane highway, with few exceptions, and often it becomes packed.

Sometimes traffic jams are unavoidable. Freeport is intolerable on a rainy day. Shop, if you can, when the sun shines. Rte. 1 between Kennebunkport and Ogunquit is almost always busy. The Park Loop at Acadia National Park is packed during the summer and empty before Memorial Day and after Labor Day. (The loop closes at the first snowfall and reopens in late spring. Cross-country skiers "own" the loop during the winter.) If you want to travel through Bath on your way up coast, the slowdown at the Carlton Bridge is inevitable, particularly when workers change shifts at Bath Iron Works. (We give you a good alternate for this area, below.) The bridge over the Sheepscot River at Wiscasset is another trouble spot. Traffic here is often halted by a single, unyielding light.

Below are some shortcuts we've found. They are routes that will take you off the beaten track — and most of the time get you back on your way faster. If you don't want to miss the action, take Rte. 1 one way and the shortcut the other. Many of these shortcuts are just as scenic as, if not more than, more heavily trafficked routes.

South Coast

- To avoid downtown Ogunquit en route to Perkins Cove. As you travel north on Rte. 1 take a right onto Pine Hill Rd. Follow to Shore Rd. and take a left. You'll come out at Perkins Cove.

Midcoast

- To avoid bottlenecks at Carlton Bridge to the east of Bath, as well as the Wiscasset bridge. Take I-95 north to the Gardiner exit. Go east on Rte. 126 until you reach Rte. 32. Follow Rte. 32 south until you reach Rte. 1 in Waldoboro.
- To eliminate the heavily trafficked section of Rte. 1 through Rockland. Take Rte. 90 off Rte. 1 in West Warren. It leads you into Rockport, just south of Camden, and can save you up to 30 minutes on a busy summer day.

East of Schoodic

- To avoid the long jog in Rte. 1 through Hancock, Sullivan, Gouldsboro, Steuben, and Milbridge. Take Rte. 182, 4 miles east of Ellsworth, to Cherry-field. It is a few miles shorter than Rte. 1 and the Rte. 1A section from Milbridge to Harrington and is faster and much less crowded. It winds through the hills and is one of the most scenic roads in New England.

CHAPTER THREE

Where Sea Captains Slept
LODGING

Romantic is the word that best describes the coast's lodging industry. Centuries of seagoing travelers made their homes here. Many of these grand houses have been turned into inns and bed and breakfasts, and are now used by travelers who live in faraway places. There are so many of these stately homes with widow's walks and the wonderful carpentry of renowned Maine ships' carpenters that all the sea lore can seem a bit passé to year-round and

Samoset

Set on 230 acres, the Samoset is a great resort for those who prefer an active holiday.

returning seasonal residents. A surprising number of these lodging houses are run by people from away — men and women who have visited the coast and found innkeeping a good opportunity to come back and enjoy it full time.

Equally romantic are the old summer resorts from the turn of the century, when Maine was discovered by prosperous New Yorkers and Bostonians. These well-heeled havens still appeal to old money vacationers, and are often both expensive and spartan. To paraphrase local art critic Edgar Allen Beem, this is a place where moderation and tradition — the hallmarks of Yankee pragmatism — are valued above all.

The lodgings we recommend in this survey represent places we either have stayed at, visited and toured, or that have been recommended and written up by well-traveled friends and family. They are by no means the only places to stay on the coast (there are more than 300 inns and B&Bs in Bar Harbor alone), but a reliable list of those places we know that provide a good resting place. Some are quiet and beautiful enclaves where it might be worth staying for two or more nights to absorb all the peace the place has to offer. Others are well situated for sightseeing and recreational opportunities. Several inns listed have restaurants. When possible, we have provided reviews of their dining rooms in the restaurant chapter. If we didn't eat there and the food is good, we let you know.

For alternative listings, you can contact the **Maine Publicity Bureau** (P.O. Box 2300, Hallowell, ME 04347; 207-623-0363 in Maine; 800-533-9595 out-of-state and Canada). Every year they publish the *Guide to Inns & Bed & Breakfasts*, a list of inns and B&Bs by region. All of the listings are written and paid for by the owners, so you should take them with a grain of salt. The **Machias Bay Area Chamber of Commerce** (P.O. Box 606, Machias, ME 04654; 207-255-4402) distributes a pamphlet for member inns and B&Bs in coastal Washington County. The **Maine Innkeepers Association Food & Lodging Guide**, with advertising from hotels, motels and inns throughout the state, is available at most tourist information centers, or from the association (305 Commercial St., Portland, ME 04101; 207-773-7670).

MAINE COAST LODGING NOTES

Rates: Rates can vary widely off season and in season. They generally increase close to Memorial Day and are highest from July through the leaf season in mid- to late October. Special packages are often available for two or more nights stay, and frequently there are even better values during the off season. If breakfast and/or dinner is included with the price of a room, we do not alter the rate category, we just note that the room rate includes one or more meals.

Inexpensive	Up to $65
Moderate	$65 to $125
Expensive	$125 to $180
Very Expensive	$180 and up

These rates exclude Maine state lodging tax or individual hotel service charges that may be added to your bill.

Credit Cards: Several lodging places we recommend in this book do not take plastic. If they do not, they almost always take personal or travelers' checks. Following are credit card abbreviations:

AE — American Express	DC — Diner's Card
CB — Carte Blanche	MC — MasterCard
D — Discover Card	V — Visa

Minimum Stay: Many inns and B&Bs require a minimum stay of two or more nights during the summer season. We have noted minimum stays when possible, but it's best to check when making room reservations.

Deposit/Cancellation: To reserve a room on the Maine coast, it is generally necessary to make a deposit to cover the first night of your stay — and some places may require up to 50 percent of the cost of the intended stay. Cancellations often must be made at least seven to 10 days in advance. Ask about the inn's policy when you make reservations.

Handicap Access: Many of the inns and B&Bs in this book have yet to comply with federal regulations regarding handicap access. We have noted handicap access is available in inns, B&Bs, and hotels where the owners can guarantee at least one room with access.

Other Options: For information on camping, from tents to RVs, see the section entitled "Camping" in the *Recreation* chapter. If you plan to camp with an RV, be sure to make reservations well in advance. If you plan on tent camping, most of the national and state parks and national forests campgrounds are available on a first-come, first-serve basis, although some advance reservations may be made for Acadia National Park during the summer season.

Another alternative for a stay in the Bar Harbor area is the *American Youth Hostel* (Kennebec St., Box 32, Bar Harbor, ME 04609; 207-288-5587). Members may find lodging there during the summer season for a minimum fee. Reservations are suggested. From September to mid-June the hostel moves to 122 Cottage St., Bar Harbor 04609; 207-288-3855.

LODGING — SOUTH COAST

ATLANTIC BIRCHES INN

Innkeepers: Dan and Cyndi Bolduc.
207-934-5295 or 888-934-5295.
20 Portland Ave., Old Orchard Beach 04064.
Open: All year.
Price: Inexpensive to Moderate.
Credit Cards: AE, CB, D, MC, V.

This homey inn set in a 1910 Victorian seems out of place among the strip motels that populate Old Orchard Beach. The Bolducs have made many additions and improvements to the inn, ensuring a more spacious and comfortable stay. They recently renovated a small neighboring house, boasting three additional rooms with private bath. The inn also has added two one-bedroom kitchenette apartments, for a total of ten bedrooms. An in-ground pool has also been a welcome addition to keep guests cool in the hot summer months. The Atlantic Birches is located on one of the town's few tree-lined streets. Guests can relax on the big porch, read, or watch passersby coming and going from nearby Old Orchard Street, the town's main strip. The rooms have flowered wallpaper, oriental rugs, and a smattering of antique touches. Fresh-baked muffins, fruit salad, cereals, and juices are served every morning in the dining room (breakfast is included in the room rate). Children are welcome. Smoking isn't.

CAPE ARUNDEL INN
Owner: Ann Fales.
207-967-2125.
P.O. Box 530A, Ocean Ave.,
   Kennebunkport 04046.
Open: Memorial Day week-
   end to Columbus Day.
Price: Moderate to
   Expensive.
Credit cards: AE, MC, V.
Handicap Access: Limited.

Set on a hillside with handsome trees and shrub-beries, this forest-green-shingled inn makes the most of its aerie over the Atlantic. The common areas, dining room, and guest rooms (seven at the inn, six at the motel, one in the carriage house) have dramatic panoramas of the sea. Curved windows and turrets add to the cachet. Rooms are decorated in pale tones—cream spreads with dark wood antiques and reproductions. A few of the bathrooms are on the small side, but many have vintage sinks and clawfoot tubs. Country wicker and antiques fill the parlors, while the dining room leans toward early American. Not so the food, which is modern and inventive. Children in the motel only. No pets. No smoking in the dining room.

**CAPTAIN LORD
   MANSION**
Innkeepers: Bev Davis and
   Rick Litchfield.
207-967-3141 or
   800-522-3141.
P.O. Box 800,
   Kennebunkport 04046.
Corner of Pleasant and
   Green Sts.
Open: All year.
Price: Expensive.
Credit cards: D, MC, V.
Handicap Access: Limited.

This is one of the coast's great inns. Seven generations of Lords lived in grand style here before this was made an inn. As inn lore goes, old Nathaniel Lord, the captain, built this stately home to keep his ships' carpenters busy during the British blockade in the War of 1812. Today it is an elegant stopping place in the historic district of this handsome seaside town. There are 16 bedrooms on three floors, all with private bath, 14 with gas fireplaces. Most have king- or queen-sized beds. A suite has been added to the mansion, featuring a grand bath with a double Jacuzzi and fireplace. The suite has two pieces of workout equipment and a king-sized canopy bed. The inn is filled to the brim with lovely antiques, most from the Federalist period, oriental rugs, and art. The beautifully restored woodwork and staircases are knockouts. A three-course breakfast includes muesli, fresh fruit and yogurt; homemade muffins, and either French toast, fresh fruit pancakes, quiche or Belgian waffles. The innkeepers are more than willing to accommodate a guest's special diet with advance notice. The inn offers guests beach parking passes, beach towels, umbrellas, and mats. They also serve afternoon tea. Children over six. No pets. Totally non-smoking.

**DOCKSIDE GUEST
   QUARTERS**
Innkeepers: Eric Lusty.
207-363-2868 or
   800-270-1977.
P.O. Box 205, York 03909.

This hideaway compound offers Yankee austerity in spite of recent renovations and million dollar views. Harris Island is actually a peninsula that sticks out into York Harbor with the Dockside taking up the better half. Vacationers tend to come back with their families year after year. The Dock-

Harris Island Road just off Rte. 103.
Open: All year.
Price: Moderate to Expensive.
Credit Cards: D, MC, V.

side Restaurant is a short walk. People living aboard their boats sometimes move here for the winter. There's a shuffleboard court, croquet, and a sandbox. There are five guest bedrooms in the main house, an elegant white clapboard summer cottage with black shutters. Most have a bath, a porch and direct access to the level, well-kept lawn. The four cottages are clean and neat. Some have apartments suitable for two to four people. Others are studios for two or three. All of the apartments have private baths and private decks.

ECONO LODGE
207-985-6100; out-of-state 800-336-5634.
Rte. 1 south, Kennebunk 04043.
Open: All year.
Price: Inexpensive.
Credit Cards: MC, V, D, AE.
Handicap Access: Yes, but call ahead during the off-season.

Set against a backdrop of pines minutes away from downtown Kennebunkport, this Econo Lodge has more appeal than most chain motels. That's particularly appreciated in a town where lodging during the high season can be hard to come by and expensive. Wood balconies lend a rustic air to the low-slung brick-and-stucco building, and the rooms are, for the most part, tastefully decorated. Color cable TV, phones, air conditioning, and continental breakfast are among the perks, and there is an outdoor pool. Smoking and non-smoking rooms. No pets.

EDWARDS' HARBORSIDE INN
Innkeeper: Tracy Piquette.
207-363-3037 or 800-273-2686.
Stage Neck Rd. just off Rte. 1A.
P.O. Box 866, York Harbor 03911.
Open: All year.
Price: Inexpensive to very expensive.
Credit Cards: MC, V.

Come by boat and tie up at the pier. Take advantage of fishing rods made available to guests. This three-story, turn-of-the-century, sprawling, gabled inn looks like a mass of sails in a brisk wind. Inside, the house is immaculately kept, open, airy, and quiet, and opens onto a great stairway. Most of the 10 rooms have a view, TV, and air conditioning. Some have fireplaces, some share baths; others, including the suites, have private baths. All are furnished simply and elegantly. Out front, the well-tended lawn leads to Little Harbor Beach. Breakfast is continental, and a nice feature is afternoon wine and cheese, a great relaxer after a hard day at the beach. No pets. No smoking.

GREEN HERON INN
Owners: Charles and Elizabeth Reid.
207-967-3315.
P.O. Box 2578, Kennebunkport 04046.

Less than a mile from Dock Square, the Green Heron is a homey stop, just the thing for families. Rooms (there are 10 of them plus a cottage with kitchenette) are cozy with pastel quilts, extra pillows, modern motel-style bathrooms, TV, and

On Ocean Ave.
Open: All year, except
January.
Price: Inexpensive to
Moderate.
Credit Cards: None.
Handicap Access: Yes.

air conditioning. Each sleeps four (there's a double plus a trundle). So what if the parlors are a mish-mash of summerhouse wicker and hunting camp castoffs? The inn has many of the comforts of home — local and big city newspapers, books, jigsaw puzzles, cards, and games. Breakfast is included with the room, and it's an elaborate one with homemade English muffins, buttermilk biscuits, vegetable frittatas, blueberry pancakes, orange French toast, and Welsh rarebit. Smoking in rooms only. Pets allowed but not in the common rooms. Children accepted.

GUNDALOW INN
Innkeepers: Cevia and
George Rosol.
207-439-4040.
6 Water St., Kittery 03904.
Open: All year.
Price: Moderate.
Credit Cards: D, MC, V.
Handicap Access: Limited.

This is a very civilized place to stay just across the New Hampshire border and not far from Maine's first shopping mecca. This carefully reno-vated brick Victorian offers travelers excellent views of the Piscataqua River from the dining room and four of the six well-appointed guest rooms. All have private baths with lovely restored bathroom fixtures. We recommend breakfast on the patio — if the weather's good. You can watch boats on the river. No pets, children under 16, or smoking.

HARTWELL HOUSE
Innkeepers: Jim and Trisha
Hartwell; Christopher
and Tracy Anderson.
207-646-7210 or
800-235-8883.
P.O. Box 393, 118 Shore Rd.,
Ogunquit 03907.
Open: All year.
Price: Moderate to
Expensive.
Credit Cards: V, MC, AE,
D.
Handicap Access: Yes.
No children under 12.

With 16 rooms in its two houses, Hartwell House is among the largest B&Bs in Ogun-quit. Modeled after the English country inns of Europe, it is also one of the most elegant. In keeping with the theme, they serve a lovely "European" tea every day at 4:30. The rooms are large, full of light, carefully decorated, and furnished with Early Amer-ican or English antiques. All are equipped with air conditioning and have private baths, and many of the rooms have decks, patios, or balconies, and views of the water. Several extremely large suites include a kitchen and a living area, and are good for families or groups traveling together. Unlike many of the town's inns, the Hartwell has a good bit of property. Its two buildings flank Shore Rd., and this assures privacy and plenty of greenery and gardens to enjoy. No TV or tele-phones in the rooms. No pets. No smoking in the inn. No children under twelve.

THE TRELLIS HOUSE
Innkeepers: Jerry and Pat
Houlihan.

The Trellis House is the sort of place that becomes familiar quickly, where guests feel at home soon after arriving. Originally a summer cot-

207-646-7909.
P.O. Box 2229, 2 Beachmere
  Pl., Ogunquit 03907.
Open: All year.
Price: Moderate.
Credit Cards: AE, D, MC,
  V.

tage, the gray-shingled house with the large screened porch looks friendly, comfortable, and homey. Inside, the rooms are filled with a mixture of antiques and collectibles. A fireplace in the living room encourages conversation and mingling, and there are many private nooks in the house. There are six guest rooms, including a two-room suite, all with private baths. There is also a carriage house near the main house that has recently been renovated to hold four new rooms, all with private baths. Three of the rooms feature fireplaces. Best of all, the Trellis House is within walking distance of the village, the beach, Perkins Cove, and the Marginal Way. So there's no worry about where to park while doing the rounds. Full breakfast included. No smoking.

WHITE BARN INN
Innkeeper: Jonathan Wise.
207-967-2321.
P.O. Box 560 C,
  Kennebunkport 04046.
Beach St., off Rte. 9.
Open: All year.
rice: Moderate to Very
  Expensive.
Credit Cards: AE, MC, V.

It's hard to imagine this as a boardinghouse in 1800. It's too grand: lush landscaping, antiques, and English country floral fabrics. Fresh flowers, robes, and comfortable beds are a given in the 24 rooms, all with air conditioning, telephones, and private baths. Seven suites also have fireplaces, sitting areas, marble baths with whirlpools, and TVs. The parlor, with its claret walls, elegant wing chairs, and garden views, is an ideal spot for an aperitif. The inn now features an outdoor pool for guest use in the summer months. And the restaurant is arguably the best (and most expensive) in town. The local rumor mill tells us that Barbara Bush likes meeting her pals there when she's in town. Breakfast is included in the room rate, along with afternoon tea (dinner is separate). Special off-season packages with dinner are available. Smoking at the bar only.

**THE WOODEN GOOSE
    INN**
Innkeepers: Jerry Rippetoe
  and Anthony Sienicki.
207-363-5673.
P.O. Box 195, Cape
  Neddick 03902.
Open: All year, except July.
Price: Moderate to
  Expensive.
Credit Cards: None.

This warm six-bedroom inn envelopes you. It gives you the cozy feeling that comes from being at your grandmother's house. Handsome antiques, exquisite fabrics, elegant furnishings against a backdrop of interesting, rich colors like persimmon, dark teal, and sage. It's beautiful here, but anyone who visits will admit that breakfast is really the thing. If you choose, you can be awakened in the morning by a light knock on the door, with a tray bearing tea and coffee left behind. Or you can wander down to the dining room for an inventive breakfast that takes the innkeepers five and a half hours to prepare —lobster quiche, poached pears with Grand Marnier custard sauce, potato pancakes with poached eggs and Hollandaise sauce, date bread, and orange-pineapple muffins. An equally extravagant tea is served every afternoon, where you may be offered paté, homemade tarts, and other baked wonders. We know innkeepers in the area who not only tell their guests to stay here, but when they have a chance, go themselves. Rippetoe and Sienicki, the owners of The Wooden Goose, don't advertise. They don't have to. They also have a controversial new policy of closing at the peak of the season. "It's too hectic here in July, and none of our regulars will come." You'll want to become one of their regulars, no doubt. No smoking in the inn.

LODGING — CASCO BAY

The elegant and intimate Atlantic Seal Bed & Breakfast.

Atlantic Seal

ATLANTIC SEAL BED & BREAKFAST
Innkeeper: Captain Thomas Ring.
207-865-6112.
Main Street, Box 146, South Freeport 04078.
Open: All year.
Price: Moderate to Expensive.
Credit Cards: None, but they accept personal and travelers' checks.
Handicap Access: None.

The tiny, picturesque village of South Freeport sits on the water; so does the Atlantic Seal. It has since the mid-19th century. Capt. Tom Ring, a tugboat captain who has worked around the world, grew up in this old Cape, and generations of his family have gone to sea and returned with furniture. The house is filled with Ring family treasures, including wonderful seascapes. The three rooms, all named after ships, have pumpkin pine floors, hand-hooked rugs, beds with homemade quilts, and private baths. One comes with a private whirlpool bath. Another has a window seat overlooking the harbor. A new chimney was recently added, and soon there will be another fireplace in one of the rooms. Breakfast is served on Sunday-best blue Camilla Spode with a silver setting. Breakfast can include lobster omelets or something called "stuffed" French toast, and the mahogany dining table it's served at has been all over the world on a sailing vessel. Tom also offers cruises out to the neighboring islands on the *Atlantic Seal* and the *Arctic Seal*. Ask and he'll give you a short course on lobstering. No smoking. No pets.

CAPTAIN DANIEL STONE INN
Innkeeper: William R. Bennett.
207-725-9898 or 800-267-0525.
10 Water St., Brunswick 04011.
Off Rte. 1.
Open: All year.
Price: Moderate to Expensive.
Credit Cards: AE, DC, MC, V.
Handicap Access: Yes.

The Captain Daniel Stone Inn mixes old and new to appealing effect. The "old" is the Federal-style home from which the inn gets its name (Capt. Daniel Stone owned it). The "new" refers to the wings that have been added in recent years. Rooms and suites have modern conveniences like cable TV, VCRs, and cassette players. Furnishings are period reproductions. No two of the 34 rooms are alike. Some are done in pine, others in mahogany. Several have whirlpool baths and brass beds. The inn also has a popular restaurant, the Narcissa Stone (named for the captain's daughter) and serves lunch and dinner, in the summer on an outdoor veranda. A light breakfast is included in the price of the room.

CAPTAIN'S WATCH BED AND BREAKFAST AND SAIL CHARTER
Innkeepers: Donna Dillman and Ken Brigham.
207-725-0979.
2476 Cundy's Harbor Rd., Brunswick 04011.
Open year round; by reservation in winter.
Price: Moderate.
Credit Cards: MC, V.
Handicap Access: Limited.

Perched atop a high bluff, this former Civil War "Union Hotel" affords long views over a small working harbor and beyond to ledge, islands, rivers, and bays. The Captain's Watch is an elegant, unpretentious Greek Revival home decorated with family antiques and collections of old china and quilts. All five bedrooms have private bath and overlook the water or secluded woods. Breakfast is included. Outside smoking only. We vow to one day take advantage of the B&B's sail charter on *Symbian*, Donna and Ken's 37-foot sailboat. Ken is a Coast Guard licensed captain and takes guests out for day trips and week-long cruises. Limited availability for children.

CHEBEAGUE INN
207-846-5155.
Box 492, South Rd., Chebeague Island 04017.
Open: Mid-May to late Sept.
Price: Moderate.
Credit Cards: AE, D, MC, V.

On a gently sloping hill overlooking Casco Bay, the Chebeague Inn is the sort of old-style seaside hotel that's fast becoming extinct. The 21 rooms — some are on the small side — are simply done in pale tones. Many have ocean views, as does the dining room, which serves breakfast, lunch and dinner (See Chapter Five, *Restaurants and Food Purveyors*). While there's a public golf course right next door, beaches nearby and plenty of spots on the island to walk or bike to, more sedentary types will set up camp on the expansive porch with its cane-backed rocking chairs. There's also a comfortable living room with loungers and a stone fireplace should the weather turn chilly. Chebeague Island is a 15-minute ferry ride from Cousin's Island and an hour's ride from Portland.

THE DANFORTH
Innkeeper: Barbara
  Hathaway.
207-879-8755.
163 Danforth St., Portland
  04102.
Open: All year.
Price: Moderate to
  Expensive.
Credit Cards: MC, V.

The Danforth is the newest of Portland's small inns, an 1823 Federal-style yellow brick mansion with polished wood floors, spacious rooms, and grand staircases. Opened in late 1994, it was still a work-in-progress when we visited, with finishing touches yet to be completed on some of the common rooms and one third floor room as of yet unrestored. The nine guest rooms have been fully restored and furnished. Seven have private baths and working fireplaces. Most have deep white carpeting and follow rich color schemes (cool sea green, navy blue, and gold). Rooms No. 5 and 6 are former servants quarters, and are small, but ample, pretty and share a bath, a good choice for a traveling family. A full breakfast is included with the room and is served in your room or in the sun room. Health club passes are available for the guests. No smoking.

The Harraseeket Inn, comprised of old and new buildings, is luxurious throughout.

Michael Loomis

HARRASEEKET INN
Innkeepers: The Gray
  Family.

With 54 rooms and suites, a health club as well as other features, the Harraseeket Inn offers

207-865-9377 or
800-342-6423 out-of-state.
162 Main St., Freeport
04032.
Open: All year.
Price: Expensive to Very
Expensive.
Credit Cards: AE, CB,
D, DC, MC, V.
Handicap Access: Yes.

the kind of amenities you would expect to find in most big hotels. But this is Freeport, and everything here has to be bigger because there's so much shopping going on. Right on the village's main drag, this elegant black-shuttered inn is really a series of connecting buildings. The newest was built in 1989; the other two in 1798 and 1850. At the time we are writing this, the inn has plans to add 30 more rooms and an indoor/outdoor pool. Many of the rooms have fireplaces, jacuzzis, steam baths, and canopied beds. All have air conditioning and cable TV, and are decorated in tasteful muted florals. The parlor has cushy wing chairs and couches and is accented with gleaming old silver and dark wood antiques — reminiscent of a country estate's drawing room. The dining room has a solid wine list, a growing reputation for inventiveness, and a commitment to using local seafood and produce (See Chapter Five, *Restaurants and Food Purveyors*). The tavern is more casual. Breakfast is included with the room rate, as well as afternoon tea and hors d'oeuvres. Dinner is additional. Special packages available.

HARPSWELL INN

Innkeepers: Susan and Bill
Menz.
207-833-5509 or
800-833-5509.
141 Lookout Point Rd.,
RR1, Box 141, Harpswell
04079.
Open: All year.
Price: Moderate.
Credit Cards: MC, V.
Handicap Access: Partial.

A shipbuilder built this home for himself, his family, and the raft of shipwrights busily building boats not far from his door. It's a beautiful old home with white clapboards, black shutters, and more windows than anybody would ever want to clean. Susan and Bill Menz moved here from Houston. Bill is a Bowdoin alumn and many alumns as well as parents of Bowdoin students stay here. The downstairs is filled with furniture they've picked up in their travels to China and Europe. There are 14 bedrooms, eight with private bath. There's the Bowdoin Room, of course. There are also two luxury suites in the cottage—one with a jacuzzi and both with kitchens (breakfast is not included with these rooms). Breakfast in the main house may include quiche, homemade muffins, and French toast. Children over ten in the main house; children of all ages welcome in the cottages. Smoking on the porch or grounds.

INN AT PARKSPRING

Innkeeper: Judi and Bob
Riley.
207-774-1059.
135 Spring St., Portland
04102.

The ParkSpring was the first of the city's small, first-rate inns to serve what is Maine's most cosmopolitan city. In a renovated 1839 townhouse on a busy city street, the inn is quiet and private. Each of the seven rooms is different. Five have pri-

Open: Year round.
Price: Moderate.
Credit Cards: AE, MC, V.

vate baths; one has a "European-styled" bath with a toilet and shower behind a partition in the room. The walls of the Courtyard room — our favorite — are painted a pretty French blue and a door leads to a city garden where guests may breakfast alone. Otherwise breakfast is at a long table in the sunny breakfast room. There is no working kitchen at the inn, but the Riley's bring home-baked sweet breads, fresh squeezed juice, and granola from home. The ParkSpring is two blocks from the Portland Museum of Art and not far from galleries, shops, and the Old Port. No children under 12. No smoking.

INN BY THE SEA
Innkeeper: Maureen
  McQuade.
207-799-3134.
40 Bowery Beach Road
  (Rte. 77), Cape Elizabeth
  04107.
Open: All year.
Price: Expensive to Very
  Expensive.
Credit Cards: AE, D, MC,
  V.
Handicap Access: Partial.

This modern day, grey shingled inn is not far from where Portland goes to the beach and comes to pick their own during strawberry season. It is a 43-suite complex, each suite featuring Chippendale furniture, TV and VCR packed away in a cherry armoire, and terry-cloth robes in the closet. Many have ocean views. There are four cottages with rocking chairs on their porches. Amble down to Crescent Beach on the wooden walkway bordered by rose bushes. There are tennis courts, shuffleboard courts, a swimming pool, and a restaurant — the Audubon, which looks out on Casco Bay and provides the setting for a romantic interlude. No pets. No smoking at the inn.

INN ON CARLETON
Innkeepers: Phil and Sue
  Cox.
207-775-1910 or
  800-639-1779.
46 Carleton St., Portland
  04102.
Open: Year round.
Price: Moderate to
  Expensive.
Credit Cards: D, MC, V.

This is a lovely bed and breakfast in a stately Victorian-style brick townhouse that is within walking distance or a short drive to nearly all of Portland's sights, restaurants, and shopping. Sue Cox is a southerner who has lived in Maine for a dozen or so years, and since she and her husband Phil bought the inn a couple of years ago, they have shuffled the period furnishings, uncovered, and refinished wide pine floors in several of the tall-ceiling guest rooms. They've also hung painting and pastels by Maine artists on almost every wall and added a gorgeous English garden out back. The service is still friendly and accommodations remain comfortable. There are seven guest rooms; four of the rooms have private baths; one bath is a mere postage stamp, and guests will marvel that both a toilet and a shower fit inside. Don't worry, you can apply makeup and shave at the ample sink in the room. The shared baths are all roomy and have clawfoot tubs. A full breakfast — usually homemade waffles or blueberry pancakes with real maple syrup or quiche — is served in the formal dining room. After dinner in town, stroll along the Western Prom, just down the street. Children are welcome ages eight and up. No smoking; no pets, although there is a resident marmalade cat named Kitty.

ISAAC RANDALL HOUSE
Innkeepers: Jim and Glynrose Friedlander.
207-865-9295 or 800-865-9295.
5 Independence Dr., Freeport 04032.
Open: All year.
Price: Inexpensive to Moderate.
Credit Cards: D, MC, V.
Handicap Access: Very Limited.

Just down the block from what is now the outlet center of Freeport's shopping district, descendants of Mayflower passengers built this farmhouse which later was a stop on the Underground Railway and still later a speakeasy during Prohibition. The ten rooms all have private bath, telephones, and air-conditioning. Five of the rooms have fireplaces. They share an upstairs sitting room and a common-area kitchen, stocked with cheese, crackers and soft drinks and a VCR . Travelers on a tight budget can cook dinner here. There's a Honeymoon Suite with a king-size wicker bed; a Southwestern room with exposed beams, prints of New Mexico and an antique copper captain's tub in the bathroom — something male visitors seem to take to; and an Aqua room with a king-sized bed and two twin beds. Kids love the twin set in a small alcove. There's a full breakfast. Items include homemade granola, pancakes, and raspberry coffee cake. There's also a pond out back. In the winter they encourage people to bring skates. There's also a caboose out back which has been converted into guest quarters with a queen-sized bed, two stacked singles, and bath with shower. Pets allowed in two of the rooms. No smoking.

THE POMEGRANATE INN
Innkeepers: Isabel and Alan Smiles.
207-772-1006.
49 Neal St., Portland 04102.
Open: All year.
Price: Moderate to Expensive.
Credit Cards: AE, D, DC, MC, V.

Near Portland's Western Prom, this stucco Georgian looks proper from the outside, but one step over the threshold and the visitor will be left breathless. Isabel Smiles was an antiques dealer and interior designer before she and her husband turned their efforts to innkeeping. The Smiles have created an entertaining, offbeat small inn that always offers the visitor an eyeful. Guest and common rooms feature handpainted walls with *trompe l'oeil* and other imaginative motifs, along with the Smiles' collection of original paintings, sculpture, and highly unusual antiques. There are eight rooms, each decorated differently and each with a private bath. Four of them have fireplaces. The carriage house has been recently renovated and is now a separate, private suite with a kitchen for travelers who might want to cook

The Pomegranate, with contemporary hand-painted walls and its striking collection of antiques, is one of Maine's most unusual inns.

Michael Loomis

their own dinner or merely make coffee or tea. Below the suite is a room with a private garden. Breakfast is included.

PORTLAND REGENCY
207-774-4200 or
  800-727-3436.
20 Milk St., Portland 04101.
Open: All year.
Price: Expensive.
Credit Cards: AE, D, DC,
  CB, MC, V.
Handicap Access: Yes.

Right in the heart of the Old Port with its boutiques, restaurants, and nightlife, the Portland Regency has a lot of charm for what used to be an old armory. A brick-paved circular drive, marble floors in the lobby and parlors with Oriental rugs and antiques give this turn-of-the-century, block-long brick building the aura of luxury. The 95 rooms, some of them a little cramped, are done in antique reproductions and muted florals. Several have four-poster beds and standing mirrors. There's also a restaurant, lounge, and health club on the premises.

WEST END INN
Innkeepers: John Leonard
  and Lynn Whitney.
207-772-1377 or
  800-333-1377.
146 Pine St., Portland
  04102.
Open: All year.

This small inn in an immaculate 1871 brick townhouse is located on a quiet residential street in Portland's historic West End. There are six tastefully appointed guest rooms, each with its own modern, spacious bath and cable TV. A full, hot breakfast is included. The inn is within walking distance of the Western Prom and views of the Fore

Price: Moderate to
Expensive.
Credit Cards: AE, CB, DC,
MC, V.

River and the White Mountains. It's also a longer walk (or a short drive) to downtown and the city's Old Port. No children; no smoking.

LODGING — MIDCOAST

BELFAST HARBOR INN
Innkeeper: Cindy White.
207-338-2740 or
800-545-8576.
Rte. 1, Belfast (mailing
address: RR # 5, Box
5230, Belfast 04915).
Open: All year.
Price: Moderate to
Expensive.
Credit Cards: AE, CB, D,
DC, MC, V.
Handicap Access: Very
limited.

We stumbled on this inn by accident and were pleasantly surprised. It is just the thing for weary coastal travelers. Large — 61 rooms — comfortable and clean, this is an efficiently run roadside inn just about midway between Belfast and Searsport. We liked it because 24 of the rooms are non-smoking, and because the deck right outside our back door was a great place to convene for a gin and tonic after long day (there's no restaurant or bar here; its BYOB). Best of all, the inn sits at the edge of a large expanse of green lawn that leads all the way down to the shore of Penobscot Bay. Ask for a room on the waterside of the inn. Children stay free. Dogs are welcome, but should not stay in rooms alone.

THE BRADLEY INN
Innkeepers: Warren and
Beth Busteed.
207-677-2105 or
800-942-5560.
Rte. 130, HC 61 Box 361,
Pemaquid Point, New
Harbor 04554.
Season: Year round.
Price: Moderate to
Expensive.
Credit Cards: AE, MC, V.

Built more than 100 years ago as an inn, the building was "literally gutted" a few years ago, brought up to the standards of the modern leisure traveler, and filled with nautical pictures, charts, and huge ship models. There are 16 rooms, all with private bath. There's also a cottage across the croquet court. From the top floor, the cathedral-ceilinged rooms look out onto John's Bay and the gardens. A hearty continental breakfast is included. Dinner, additional, is open to the public. So is the pub which boasts a granite-topped bar and attracts a mix of guests and local residents. Non-smoking rooms available.

**CAPTAIN DRUMMOND
HOUSE B&B**
Owners: Donna Dillman
and Ken Brigham.
207-389-1394.
P.O. Box 72, Parker Head
Rd., Phippsburg 04562.
Season: May –Oct.

High on a wooded bluff called Parker Head, the Captain Drummond House looks down onto the Kennebec River. The lodging house was built in 1792, a snug Federal-style residence that once was home to a ship captain, a shipbuilder, and later served the residents of nearby Phippsburg as a local tavern and stagecoach stop. It was moved to

Price: Moderate.
Credit Cards: MC, V.
Handicap Access: Limited.

its current location, with its spectacular view, in 1977. There are three rooms with period furnishings, two of them with private bath. A modern furnished "suite" with queen bed has a private entrance. While the owners are at their other B&B (see Casco Bay, Captain's Watch B&B), the entire Drummond House is available for guests to rent on a weekly basis with full efficiencies. Full breakfast included. No smoking. **(Note: As we were on press, we learned that this inn has closed. The owners now own and operate the Captain's Watch Bed & Breakfast and Sail Charter in Brunswick; see page 52.)**

CAPT. LINDSEY HOUSE INN
Innkeeper: Leslie Oster.
207-596-7950 or
   800-523-2145.
5 Lindsey St., Rockland
   04841.
Open: Year round.
Price: Moderate to
   Expensive.
Credit Cards: AE, D, MC,
   V.
Handicap Access: Yes.

This is the place to stay if you're off on a windjammer cruise (the owners offer discounts to windjammer passengers) or ferrying to the islands from Rockland Harbor. A mustard-painted 1837 brick house on a quiet side street, this was first a sea captain's home. Since then it has housed the local water company (the water company's giant safe, too big to remove, remains as a topic of conversation in one of the sitting rooms). Today it is an inn, owned by two sea captains, Ellen and Ken Barnes — former theater folk who also offer cruises on their schooner *Stephen Taber* or their motor vessel *Pauline*. Right next door is the Waterworks, a pub owned by the Barnes and worth checking out. Local windjammer crews like to hang out in between cruises, and you can sample the best Maine microbrews on tap. The inn has a pleasant, professional air about it, and it seems bigger than it is — big enough to give guests plenty of elbow room and privacy. There are nine rooms, all freshly decorated with unusual lamps and furnishings collected from around the world and covering a range of styles from masculine plaids and stripes to Art Deco. All the beds are big and firm with down comforters and tapestry bedspreads. Every room has a private bath, air conditioning, television, and telephones. If you've borrowed one of the inn's paperbacks from their library and haven't finished it, they insist you take it with you. No smoking. Children over ten welcome.

DARK HARBOR HOUSE
207-734-6669.
P.O. Box 185, Main Rd.,
   Islesboro 04848.
Open: Mid-May to
   Mid-October.
Price: Expensive to Very
   Expensive.

The Dark Harbor House is a yellow clapboard Georgian mansion built for a wealthy banker on an Islesboro hillside at the turn of the century. The inn has spacious, summer-elegant rooms, and a well-deserved reputation as a restful staging ground from which to explore Islesboro, enclave of the rich and famous. The inn has ten guest rooms and two suites; all rooms have private baths and several have balconies. Antiques are everywhere. The service is impeccable. The dining room offers a creative menu. A full breakfast is included; dinner is additional.

EDGEWATER FARM B&B
Innkeepers: Bill and Carol Emerson.
207-389-1322.
Rte. 216, Small Point 04565.
Season: Year round.
Price: Moderate.
Credit Cards: MC, V.
Handicap Access: Yes

The Emersons have converted this 1800 farm-house into a lovely bed and breakfast, and because the owners have green thumbs, the breakfast table and afternoon snack often include bounty from their orchards and organic gardens. The five guest rooms are comfortable and pretty; one has a private bath. This is a good place to stay for bicyclists and kayakers touring the peninsula. There are several great white sand beaches nearby including those at Popham Beach State Park. If you prefer warmer water however, the B&B has a new enclosed swimming pool. No smoking.

EAST WIND INN
207-372-6366 or 800-241-8439.
P.O. Box 149, Tenants Harbor 04860.
Open: Early April–late Nov.
Price: Inexpensive to Expensive.
Credit Cards: AE, D, MC, V.

The main house of the East Wind is a former sea captain's home, and most of the rooms in the inn and its downstairs restaurant and wide porch offer fine views of Tenants Harbor. The inn is a staple for regular visitors. The 15 guest rooms in the main house are filled with antiques and have a spartan Yankee quality. Six of those rooms have private baths. There are 10 more rooms in the modern "meeting house," and all of those have private baths. The East Wind recently built a new cottage that houses three apartments. One is a full apart-ment, another a two bedroom, and still another a studio. All three have kitchens. The restaurant, Windows, serves breakfast and dinner, and is a favorite among local residents and business people.

FIVE GABLES INN
Innkeepers: Mike and Dee Kennedy.
207-633-4551 or 800-451-5048.
P.O. Box 335, Murray Hill Rd., East Boothbay 04544.
Open: Mid-May through late Oct.
Price: Moderate to Expensive.
Credit Cards: MC, V.

Recently restored, this cream-colored inn is perched on a hillside overlooking pretty Line-kin Bay near Boothbay Harbor. Airy, uncluttered, and made cozy with country craft accents, the Five Gables is a restful retreat in an otherwise bustling tourist region. All 16 rooms have private baths and water views; five have working fireplaces. Borrow the inn's golf clubs and hit a few. Or take after-noon tea on the porch overlooking the lush cottage garden. No smoking. Children over eight wel-come.

THE FOX ISLAND INN

Innkeeper: Gail Reinertsen.
207-863-2122 or in winter
 904-425-5095.
P.O. Box 451, Carver St.,
 Vinalhaven 04863.
Open: Mid-June–mid-Sept.
Price: Inexpensive.
Personal checks accepted.

This once was an island home; now it is a small village inn that offers guests comfortable lodging in a homelike setting. There are four lovely, clean single and double rooms with shared baths and a restored three-room suite with a private bath. Gail serves breakfast and lets guests use the kitchen — a nice option for picnickers and those made hungry by the sea air. There are also bikes for guest use. Children over six welcome.

GOSNOLD ARMS

Owners: The Phinney
 Family.
Summer 207-677-3727;
 winter 561-575-9549.
Northside Rd., Rte. 32, New
 Harbor 04554.
Open: Mid-May to
 mid-Oct.
Price: Moderate to
 Expensive.
Credit Cards: MC, V.

The Gosnold Arms is the type of old Maine inn that people like to visit again and again. In its first incarnation this was a saltwater farm. It has also served as a summer boarding house for Smith College students (it still has a Please No Men Permitted Upstairs sign), and it's easy to imagine the exuberant voices of Smith women ringing in the hallways and across the inn's broad green lawn. The Gosnold sits at the entrance to New Harbor, not far from splendid Pemaquid Point and its lovely lighthouse. There are accommodations for 40 to 50 guests (every room has its own bath) spread out among the farmhouse, the three-story barn, and 10 separate cottages. One of the cottages is a former steamboat freight office; another is a steamboat cabin. The dining room seats 80 — or you can take your meal on the porch and watch as working and pleasure boats pass by. Dinner is real Yankee fare — fresh seafood, beef, and homemade desserts. We haven't eaten here, but with this view, you almost can't lose. Breakfast included, dinner additional. Smoking in the cottages and on the ground floor. Children welcome.

THE HICHBORN INN

Innkeepers: Nancy and
 Bruce Suppes.
207-567-4183 or
 800-846-1522.
P.O. Box 115, Church St.,
 Stockton Springs 04981.
Open: All year.
Price: Inexpensive to
 Moderate.
Credit Cards: None;
 travelers' and personal
 checks accepted.

It is quiet around this carefully restored former shipbuilder's house that is on the National Register of Historic Places. With high ceilings, handsome Victorian furniture, fireplaces, down quilts, fine linens, and fresh-ground coffee, this is a wonderful home base for those exploring nearby Fort Point State Park (a great spot for biking), antiquing in the as- of-yet undiscovered Stockton Springs or enjoying a nice quiet stop outside busy Mount Desert Island. The inn is small. There are five guest rooms with private and shared baths and views of Stockton Harbor. You can have breakfast in your room, or venture downstairs for Belgian waffles with real maple syrup, homemade bagels, or "Dutch babies" — eggy, oven-baked pancakes that guests fill with fresh fruit in season or the Suppes' homemade raspberry jam. Breakfast included. No smoking.

HOTEL PEMAQUID
Owners: Skip and Cindy Atwood.
207-677-2312.
3098 Bristol Rd., New Harbor 04554.
Season: Mid-May to mid-October.
Price: Inexpensive to Moderate.
Credit Cards: None, but personal and travelers checks are accepted.
Handicap Access: Yes.

This Victorian inn sits almost at the very end of the Pemaquid peninsula, not far from the famous lighthouse. The main house is an old-style hotel with eleven rooms; seven with private baths. The inn's parlors are jam packed with dark period furniture, flowered curtains and upholstery, and an idiosyncratic collection of Victoriana and other "stuff" including a check signed by glamor goddess Marilyn Monroe. Our favorite room is the Chauffeur's Quarters, a sunny ground floor guest room with a private bath that has been recently redecorated in not-to-fussy shades of rose. The hotel annex offers a comfortable suite with a kitchen, living room, and cable TV. The hotel also rents four-unit bungalows and operates a five-unit motel with clean, nicely appointed rooms for budget-conscious travelers. Cottages can be rented on a weekly basis. Breakfast is not included, although the coffee pot is always on. No smoking in the main house, but smoking allowed in one of the bungalows and in the motel.

INN AT BATH
Innkeeper: Nicholas Bayard.
207-443-4294.
969 Washington St., Bath 04530.
Open: All year.
Price: Moderate to Expensive.
Credit Cards: AE, D, MC, V.
Handicap Access: Partial.

This old house was built in 1810 when Bath was a booming shipbuilding town. One of the most striking characteristic of this handsomely restored Greek Revival home is the twin parlors with a marvelous marble fireplace and filled with antiques and striking family pieces. There are seven comfortable and roomy guest rooms, all with private bath, TVs, VCRs, air-conditioning, and telephones. Several have fireplaces and king- or queen-sized beds. Two new double Jacuzzis can be found resting next to wood-burning fireplaces in two of the guest rooms. Two of the rooms adjoin and can be made into suites. Our favorite is the River Room, formerly a hayloft in the attached barn, which now has exposed old wood beams and a woodburning fireplace to take the chill off an autumn evening. A full breakfast is included. Children over five welcome. Pets welcome. No smoking.

LODGE AT CAMDEN HILLS
Innkeepers: The Burgess Family.

The Lodge at Camden Hills offers modern, quiet, clean, efficiently run lodgings to travelers who want a location close to Camden, but away

207-236-8478 or
 800-832-7058.
P.O. Box 794, Rte. 1,
 Camden 04843.
Open: Year round.
Price: Moderate to Very
 Expensive.
Credit Cards: AE, D, MC,
 V.
Handicap Access: Yes.

from the traffic and bustle. The Lodge is a small, comfortable motel with several efficiency cottages that sit on a landscaped hillside north of Camden. It's been here for years, although the Burgess family undertook a major renovation and modernization of the lodge during the early 1990s. Everything is spanking new and rooms now provide the amenities that are increasingly in demand by upscale travelers. Many of the private cottages have their own decks, jacuzzis, and fireplaces. All of the 20 rooms have private baths, cable TV, air conditioning, telephones, and refrigerators. No smoking. Children welcome. No pets.

MAINE STAY INN
Innkeepers: Peter and
 Donny Smith and Diana
 Robson.
207-236-9636.
22 High St. (Rte. 1),
 Camden 04843.
Open: All year.
Price: Moderate.
Credit Cards: AE, MC, V.

The Maine Stay is one of our favorite inns. Intimate, trim and quiet, the inn is an early 18th-century farmhouse that sits on two acres in the heart of Camden's historic district. There are eight bedrooms in the main house and the attached carriage house; six have modern, private baths; two share a bath. The largest room now has a wood-burning stove, and two guest rooms have fireplaces. One is located in the inn's new suite, complete with a large sitting room and queen-sized bed. Out back there is a majestic four-story barn and gardens which the innkeepers expand and improve every year. Capt. Peter Smith is a retired navy pilot, and the house is full of things the Smiths have picked up on their travels — including a tonsu, a 300-year-old Samurai warrior's chest. There are two parlors, each with a fireplace with matches on the mantel and wood and paper ready to be burned when you want to take the chill off. Every morning, breakfast is cooked on an old Queen Atlantic black stove and served on Spode china at a long pine farm table. Usually it's "something eggy one day, something not the next," says Donny. Tea is served in the afternoon. No smoking. Children seven and older.

**NEWAGEN SEASIDE
 INN**
Innkeepers: Peter and
 Heidi Larsen.
207-633-5242 or
 800-654-5242.
P.O. Box 68, Rte. 27
 South, Cape Newagen
 04552.
Open: Mid-May through
 late Sept.

Pronounced "new wagon," this resort inn sits on 85 acres at the southern tip of Southport Island six miles from Boothbay Harbor. The inn retains a '40s look and feel that makes you think of Bing or Bob on the set of a favorite old movie. Almost any good day in season you can hear that quiet, comforting pock pock of the ball being batted back and forth. On inclement days you can hear the foghorn — one guest said if it wasn't turned off he was leaving. (One person's romance is another's night-

Price: Moderate to
   Expensive.
Credit Cards: MC, V.
Handicap Access: Yes.

mare.) Most of the 26 rooms have an ocean view; all have private baths. During the day you have a choice of activities — tennis, horseshoes, badminton, volleyball, rowboats, fishing, swimming in the saltwater pool or heated freshwater pool. The dining room serves all three meals, and the owner recently screened in a portion of the porch so you can dine *al fresco*, sans bugs. Breakfast included; other meals additional.

THE NEWCASTLE INN
Innkeepers: Rebecca and
   Howard Levitan.
207-563-5685.
60 River Rd., Newcastle
   04553.
Open: All year.
Price: Moderate to
   Expensive.
Credit Cards: MC, V.
Handicap Access: Limited.

This handsome inn and restaurant is just off Rte. 1 as you drive into Damariscotta and head down the road for Pemaquid Point Lighthouse. It is also a great stopping point on the route up the coast to Camden, Bar Harbor, and beyond.

The 14 rooms are well-appointed and comfortable, all with private bath; eight are in the main house, while six are in the carriage house. The Newcastle recently changed innkeepers and has since undergone major renovations. There are now two upscaled rooms with king beds. One has a fireplace while the other holds a Jacuzzi. A new suite with a queen canopy bed also has a new Jacuzzi. In several of the rooms you can lie on your pencil-post bed and gaze at the Damariscotta River. Five of the guest rooms have fireplaces. The kitchen turns out three- and five-course meals that have won so many fans that the inn now has two dining rooms. The common room, with its stenciled floor, fireplace, and high-backed antique wing chairs, is a great place to relax with fellow guests. There's also a sunporch with comfortable lawn chairs and views of the Damariscotta River. Children over 12 welcome. No smoking. Breakfast is included. People also come here to cross-country ski.

NORUMBEGA
Innkeeper: Murray Keating.
207-236-4646.
61 High St., Camden 04843.
Open: All year.
Price: Expensive to Very
   Expensive.
Credit Cards: AE, D, MC,
   V.

The Norumbega is a stone castle on a hill by the sea that was built about a century ago. Since it opened as an inn a few years back it has become a favorite of honeymooners — perhaps because of its brooding, romantic presence, strong colors, and Victorian antiques scattered everywhere on lovely birds-eye maple floors. Or maybe it's the kitchen where hungry romantics will find a constant supply of fresh-baked cookies, fresh fruit, and other surprises. Altogether there are 13 guest rooms, including the penthouse. (It's really the attic done over into a luxe suite. It offers the best views in the house; it is also the most expensive room at the inn — and perhaps in the entire state.) All rooms have private baths. Almost all the beds are king-sized. Five of the rooms have fireplaces and impressive views. The library suite is just that —

The Norumbega, with its brooding castle-by-the-sea looks, is a favorite among honeymooners and Texans.

Michael Loomis

with books lining the shelves of the balcony which skirts the bedroom. Outside there are stately elms and well-kept gardens. For those who love theatrics, the inn hosts "Murder by the Sea" some weekends. Guess whodunit, and you could win two nights for you and a friend. The manager told us Texans also like to stay here, and we can understand why. Everything here seems scaled to suit a Texan's grand style. No smoking.

Owl & Turtle

Each of the Owl & Turtle's three rooms has a view of the water and the promise of plenty of bedtime reading.

THE OWL AND THE TURTLE HARBOR VIEW GUEST ROOMS
Innkeepers: The Conrads.

This small bed & breakfast is on the floors above Camden's favorite bookstore, right on the harbor in downtown Camden. There are three rooms, each with bath or shower, and million-dollar

207-236-9014.
P.O. Box 1265, 8 Bay View,
    Camden 04843.
Open: All year.
Price: Inexpensive to
    Moderate.
Credit Cards: D, MC, V.

mountain or harbor view. The accommodations are modest, but a good value. Breakfast includes homemade muffins. No smoking

At the Roaring Lion the owners cater to travelers on special diets — lo-cal, vegetarian and macrobiotic.

The Roaring Lion

ROARING LION
Innkeepers: Bill and Robin
    Branigan.
207-832-4038.
P.O. Box 756, 995 Main St.,
    Waldoboro 04572.
Open: All year.
Price: Inexpensive.
Credit Cards: None.

In a town that's world famous for sauerkraut and sausage, this very inexpensive inn is an anomaly. It has built a reputation for accommodating vegetarians and other people on special diets. Built at the turn of the century, this was originally a tourist home that once refused to give breakfast to traveling salesmen. There are four rooms at the inn. One has a private bath and a queen-sized bed; two have double beds and one has twin beds. One of the double-bed rooms has a fireplace. The rooms without a private bath share a private bath and a half bath. Downstairs there are four tables in the dining room, and every morning they serve fresh coffeecake, muffins, and other homemade breads to their guests, all with healthy sides of homemade jams and jellies. Ask for the sourdough pancakes — made from sourdough starter nurtured for more than 22 years. The Branigans are big on gardening, and homegrown flowers are everywhere. No smoking. Children of all ages are welcome.

THE SAMOSET RESORT
General Manager: James H.
    Ash.

The Samoset is one of the places where Mainers like to stay — quite possibly because the resort offers so much for a population that tends to be

207-594-2511 or
800-341-1650.
220 Warrenton St.,
Rockport 04856.
Off Rte. 1.
Open: All year.
Price: Moderate to Very
Expensive.
Credit Cards: AE, D, DC,
MC, V.
Handicap Access: Yes.

physically active. Ten kilometers of great cross-country skiing in the winter; golf in the summer on an 18-hole course which was extensively revamped in 1994 and 1995. Year round there is tennis (indoor and outdoor courts), racquetball, indoor and outdoor pools, bicycles, basketball, fitness room with Nautilus, croquet, badminton, volleyball, and horseshoes. How do they fit all this in? The resort sits on an ample 230 acres that stretches to the water. Although the resort was established more than 100 years ago, few vestiges of the old Yankee inn remain. The rooms are modern, and comfortable after a hard day at play. There is a restaurant on the premises called Marcel's, or you can venture into Rockport, Rockland, or Camden to give yourself a break from all that activity. While everything's deluxe, including the rooms, off-season package deals make it affordable for everyone. Meals are additional.

The Samoset, Rockport, summer of 1917.

Samoset

SEBASCO HARBOR RESORT
Owner: Bob Smith.
207-389-1161 or
800-225-3819.

Sebasco Lodge is a friendly, oddball collection of structures situated on 600 acres at the southeastern tip of the Phippsburg peninsula near Popham Beach State Park. It offers families and

Rte. 217, Sebasco Estates 04565.
Off Rte. 209 near Phippsburg.
Season: May through October.
Price: Moderate to Very Expensive.
Credit Cards: AE, D, MC, V.

recreation-minded travelers a feeling for how people relaxed — and socialized — 40 years ago. In fact, the Lodge calls the busy months "our social season," and daily activities center around meals served in the large spit-and-polish dining room where jackets are suggested, but not required. Twice a week, everyone moves their socializing outdoors, weather permitting. There's the Sunday pool-side blueberry pancake breakfast. Tuesday, everyone's outside again for the weekly lobster picnic. In between, there's plenty of appetite-building activities for guests of all ages: nine holes of golf, swimming in the saltwater swimming pool, playschool for the kids, tennis, shuffleboard, canoeing, lawn bowling, sail and motor boat rental, bingo, and evening dance socials with live music. The cottages and lodge are clean and comfortable, but not luxurious. Major renovations have begun since a new owner has taken over here. A gazebo is already a welcome new fixture at the Sebasco. The meals are wholesome and plentiful. Rates for the modified American plan (breakfast and dinner) are available.

SQUIRE TARBOX INN
Innkeepers: Karen and Bill Mitman.
207-882-7693.
1181 Main Rd., Westport Island 04578.
Open: May through late Oct.
Price: Moderate to Very Expensive.
Credit Cards: AE, D, MC, V.

Karen and Bill Mitman met while working at the Copley Plaza Hotel in Boston, and although this handsome, beautifully kept farmhouse inn with its pastoral setting may seem charmingly rustic, there is nothing less than polished about the service. The main house has wide colonial floorboards, an interesting mix of antiques, and four guest rooms with private baths and working fireplaces (two are not air conditioned); the barn has seven romantically removed bedrooms and private baths. The barn dates from 1763 and includes a homey common room and a woodstove. Breakfast and dinner, served in a simple paneled and brick dining room with fireplace, are excellent. Beyond hospitality and good food, the primary products here are distinctive goats' milk cheeses — the inn and its restaurant (see Chapter Five, *Restaurants and Food Purveyors*) operate in the midst of a working dairy farm complete with its own herd of purebred Nubian goats. Borrow the inn's bikes and pedal off to explore the rolling countryside. No pets — they would disturb the goats; no children under 12.

TRAILING YEW GUEST HOUSE
Innkeeper: Marian Choiffi.
207-596-0440.
Monhegan Island 04852.

Monhegan is an island famous for its simple way of life, its views, and the number of renowned artists who for more than a century have stayed on the island, hoping to capture and carry away the island's peculiar light on canvas. The

Open: Mid-May to mid-
Oct.
Price: Inexpensive.
Credit Cards: None;
personal and travelers'
checks accepted.

Trailing Yew fits right in, a spartan collection of rustic white clapboard houses clustered around a lawn where guests gather before dinner to play horseshoes. The 37 rooms are clean and well kept. Minimal electric lighting is provided by generator to most rooms through part of the day and evening; after the generator is turned off, you can read or play cards by oil lamp or candle. Breakfast and a hearty family-style dinner are included with the cost of the room. Limited smoking. Children and pets welcome.

WHITEHALL INN
Innkeepers: The Dewing
family.
207-236-3391 or
800-789-6565.
P.O. Box 558, 52 High St.,
Camden 04843.
Open: Late May to late
October.
Price: Moderate to
Expensive.
Credit Cards: AE, MC, V.

This is a fine, sprawling old Yankee inn with an interesting history. The main house began as a fine white Greek Revival sea captain's home built in 1834. It became an inn in 1901, and with many additions has become a favorite coastal retreat. Camden born poet Edna St. Vincent Millay was "discovered" here by a guest. Between the main inn and two smaller "cottages" across the street, there are 50 guest rooms; 42 with private baths. (All three buildings are on the National Register.) Guest rooms and spacious common areas, decorated in colonial colors, are quiet, gracious, and comfortable but not deluxe. There are no televisions, but there are books, games, puzzles, a piano, and tennis on the inn's private courts. Tea is served at 4 p.m. We imagine this is how our Yankee ancestors sought relaxation in simpler days, and it feels pretty good. The dining room offers a good wine list and a good menu which changes daily (jackets required). Full breakfast included; dinner additional. Modified American plan available. Children welcome.

**THE WILLIAM & MARY
INN**
Innkeepers: William and
Mary Sweet.
207-548-2190.
Rte. 1, Searsport 04974.
Open: All year.
Price: Inexpensive to
Moderate.
Credit Cards: None;
personal and travelers'
checks accepted.

In 1774 Capt. Perry Pendleton sailed into town and built a log cabin just across the street from what is now the William & Mary Inn. More than 50 years later, the captain's granddaughter, Prudence, moved into this elegant home on a hill just two miles northeast of Searsport center. The inn is named for its owners — former history teacher Bill and his wife Mary Sweet. They have redone the house to emphasize its architectural features — including the wonderful six-on-six windows. There are three guest rooms with pencil-post beds and reproduction wallpapers; each has its own bathroom tucked into former closets. Breakfast every

The William & Mary Inn sits high on a knoll overlooking Penobscot Bay.

William & Mary Inn

morning is served in a style befitting this elegant New England home at the Chippendale table in the dining room.

LODGING — DOWN EAST/ACADIA

The Asticou Inn in Northeast Harbor on Mount Desert Island.

Herb Swanson

ASTICOU INN
Manager: Joseph Joy.
207-276-3344 or
  800-258-3373.
Northeast Harbor 04662.
Open: Mid-May to mid-
  Oct. Cottages are open
  all year.

The Asticou Inn is in the low key, wealthy summer town of Northeast Harbor, and it has all sorts of charms — simple furnishings, courteous bellmen, ties and jackets suggested for dinner, unadorned, locally caught halibut, and Grapenut pudding for dessert. It is a sage and weathered-looking place — with 44 rooms it looks like a over-

Price: Moderate to Very
Expensive.
Credit Cards: D, MC, V.
Handicap Access: Yes.

grown summer cottage that is set in the middle of beautiful, well-groomed lawns and gorgeous gardens. Guests are welcome to the heated pool and the inn's tennis court. Some rates in the summer include breakfast and dinner, while others offer a B&B style breakfast. No children under six. Smoking is allowed, but discouraged. There's a non-smoking area in the dining room and you may smoke in your room.

THE BLUE HILL INN
Innkeepers: Mary and Don
Hartley.
207-374-2844 or
800-826-7415.
P.O. Box 403, Union St. (Rte.
177), Blue Hill 04614.
Open: Mid-May to late
Nov.
Price:Expensive to Very
Expensive.
Credit Cards: MC, V.
Handicap Access: Limited.

This place is no newcomer to innkeeping; the lovely old clapboard and brick building framed by stately elms and handsome gardens has been an inn since 1840 (before that it was a private residence). It is, in fact, the oldest continuously operating inn in the state and, like much of the rest of Blue Hill, is listed on the National Register of Historic Places. There are 11 guest rooms, all furnished with period antiques, many with fireplaces. Every one has a private bath. A suite with a king-sized canopy bed, cathedral ceiling, raised hearth, large bathroom, and full kitchen is a new addition to the Inn. Also, two bathrooms have been upgraded with ceramic tile floors. You might as well plan to take advantage of the works while staying here. Dinner (see Chapter Five, *Restaurants & Food Purveyors*) is so good, you will regret it if you don't eat here at least once while you're in town. Breakfast and *hors d'oeuvres* are included and served year round. There is a rate that does not include dinner.

BREAKWATER 1904
Owners: Tom and Bonnie
Sawyer.
207-288-2313 or
800-238-6309.
45 Hancock St., Bar Harbor
04609.
Open: Mid-April to
early November.
Price: Expensive to Very
Expensive.
Credit Cards: AE, MC, V.
Handicap Access: Yes.

Only a few blocks from downtown Bar Harbor, and right on the shore, this English Tudor estate feels miles and eras away. On the National Register, this is the former summer cottage of John Innes Kane, great-grandson of John Jacob Astor. (The Astors still can be seen around town.) This was how the wealthy "rusticators" must have vacationed in Bar Harbor — in the grand style to which they were accustomed. The parlors and game rooms offer the decor and furnishings one would expect at a private, turn-of-the-century hideaway: substantial, overstuffed sofas; broad, open hearth fireplaces; wood paneling; gleaming wood floors, and a grand pool table. The guest rooms are impressive — all of them large enough to spread out in and furnished with antique and reproduction furniture and great beds — sleigh beds, mansion beds, iron valanced canopy beds — every one big and comfortable. All six chambers have their own fireplaces and private baths. Four have ocean views. Abigail's Chamber has views of the courtyard and rose garden. Breakfast is included and is served in the formal dining room. A complimentary tea hour and hors d'oeuvres are provided in the afternoon.

CASTINE INN
Innkeepers: Tom and Amy
   Gulow.
207-326-4365.
P.O. Box 41, Main St.,
   Castine 04421.
Open: Early May through
   mid-Dec.
Price: Moderate to
   Expensive.
Credit Cards: MC, V.
Handicap Access: Yes.

Bright, airy and welcoming, the Castine Inn is the more relaxed of two inns in Castine, and it offers all a visitor could want by way of lodgings in this pretty seaside town — a fine restaurant, harbor views from many of the 20 rooms and a perfect location. Perched half-way up the main street that ascends from the town's bustling port, the inn is a good example of the many late-Victorian structures that grace this historic area. There are plenty of spots where you can relax after a walking tour of the historic town: on the lovely front porch among the flowers and rocking chairs; out back in the gardens; in the sitting room with a wood-burning fireplace; or in the sauna. Contemporary and older seascapes and harbor views hang on every wall. The dining room walls have been painted with a mural of the region that is something of a local tourist attraction. The pub is a good place to have a nightcap and maybe meet a captain from one of the many windjammers that anchor in the bay. Breakfast included; dinner additional. No children under five.

CLAREMONT HOTEL
Owners: The McCue
   Family.
800-244-5036.
P.O. Box 137, Southwest
   Harbor 04679.
Open: Mid-June–
   mid-October.
Prices: Moderate to
   Expensive.
Credit Cards: None.
   Personal checks
   accepted.
Handicap Access: Limited.

This is a wonderful old place, listed on the National Register, with its great, green lawn, clay tennis court, and a pier extending out into the sheltered, yacht-dotted harbor. There are 30 simple rooms in the main building and Phillips House, as well as 12 cottages. This is a traditional summer hotel where you can expect to hear the sound of slamming wooden screen doors and kids, many of whom probably know each other from previous visits. Downstairs in the main house, hanging next to the life preservers, is an eclectic collection of dinner jackets to borrow. These jackets and the fact there are men willing to wear them bear witness to a certain devil-may-care sense of Yankee propriety that can be experienced on the coast of Maine. Ties are not required. The Claremont is renowned for its croquet tournaments. Smoking outside only.

LE DOMAINE
Owner: Nicole Purslow.
207-422-3395 or
  800-554-8498.
Box 496, Rte. 1, Hancock
  04640.
Open: Late May to
  mid-Oct.
Price: Very Expensive.
Credit Cards: AE, MC, V.

As one might guess from the name, Le Domaine is less a New England inn and more an *auberge*. From the small parlor with its wicker and floral settees and tiny bar to the handsome dining room dominated at one end by a huge walk-in fireplace, the inn has the look of a Provençal hideaway. There are seven rooms divided between the main inn and a modern annex . All rooms have private baths and most have small balconies or terraces. The inn rooms are smaller and stylishly done with good Italian reading lamps, small libraries, crisp new linens, lounge chairs and lovely modern baths. Breakfast is a French-American hybrid — crisp, buttery croissants, homemade granola, yogurt, cream, fresh fruit, and honey from the inn's own hives. The inn's restaurant, with an extensive wine list and excellent cuisine, is we believe the finest in all of Maine (See Chapter 5, *Restaurants & Food Purveyors*). Breakfast and dinner are included in the room rate.

THE HARBOURSIDE INN
Owner: The Sweet Family.
207-276-3272.
Rte. 198, Northeast Harbor
  04662.
Open: Mid-June to Mid-
  September.
Price: Moderate to Very
  Expensive.
Credit Cards: None;
  personal and travelers'
  checks accepted.
Handicap Access: Yes.

According to one guest, this inn has a "monastic quiet" to it. The Sweet family likes it that way. The inn was built in 1888, and retains much old-time character. Rooms are furnished with 19th century pieces and show distinctive touches such as Wedgewood patterned wallpaper, a Wallace Nutting bed, and Gustave Stickly rugs. Each has a private bathroom; most have working fireplaces; some have king- or queen-size beds; some have kitchenettes. Telephones were recently installed in all of the guest rooms. There are three suites with adjoining rooms to accommodate larger families. A short walk from the village, the woods behind the inn are honeycombed with hiking trails that extend into Acadia National Park. Breakfasts are simple: homemade blueberry muffins and coffee or tea. Many visitors come here for extended stays. No smoking.

INN AT CANOE POINT
Innkeepers: Tom and
  Nancy Cervelli.
207-288-9511.
P.O. Box 216, Bar Harbor
  04609.
Off Rte. 3.
Open: all year.
Price: Moderate to Very
  Expensive.
Credit Cards: D, MC, V.

Closeted away in the garret room of the Inn at Canoe Point on Hull's Cove, one is apt to feel like the heroine of a Brontë novel. Despite its Tudor trappings and the pounding surf below, the five rooms are stylishly modern. Lots of pillows, sleek subdued fabrics, white walls, and beds as comfortable as the one at home. The master suite has a gas fireplace. Down in the parlor, the look is polished as well — dark wood floors, a flickering

The Inn at Canoe Point on the shore of Frenchman Bay in Hulls Cove is a quiet spot on busy Mount Desert Island.

Inn at Canoe Point

fireplace, handsome chairs. In summer, a substantial and delicious breakfast is served on the porch: homemade blueberry pancakes, quiches, muffins. Later in the afternoon, refreshments are served as well. Set in a wooded area on the edge of a small cove, the inn has a commanding view of Frenchman Bay, and exploring the rocky outcropping is a favored pastime among guests. Though the feeling is remote, Bar Harbor is minutes away. We would love to come stay here with our cross country skis in the winter. No smoking. No young children.

JEANNIE'S PLACE B&B
Innkeepers: Llewellyn and
    Jeannie Joyce.
207-526-4116.
Box 125, Swans Island
    04685.
(Off Bar Harbor).
Open: All year.
Price: Inexpensive.
Credit Cards: None;
    personal and travelers'
    check accepted.

A 45-minute ferry ride from Bass Harbor on Mount Desert Island, this simple gabled home has three guests rooms that share a single bath — all with double beds. Two rooms overlook Burnt Coat Harbor. The look is plain, homey and clean, and everyone is treated as part of the family. Guests are just as likely to answer the phone when you call to book your room. The Joyces also rent a housekeeping cottage with a kitchen. It's available for weekly visits or for the night. There's a full breakfast for those who want it that includes home-made bread and muffins, cereal, eggs, and bacon. They also serve dinner, "if need be." No smoking. No alcohol. Children welcome.

JOHN PETERS INN
Innkeepers: Rick and
    Barbara Seeger.
207-374-2116.
P.O. Box 916, Peters Point
    Rd., Blue Hill 04614.
Open: May to Nov.

Just a mile out of Blue Hill village, the John Peters is on a sparsely inhabited peninsula known as Peters Point. The inn, built in 1810, is on the National Historic Register. Over the years, there have been changes to the building's exterior and modern conveniences added, but the original struc-

Price: Moderate to
Expensive.
Credit Cards: MC, V.

ture possesses a great deal of old time charm. It has eight rooms in the main house and six in the carriage house, many with fireplaces, all with warm, country furnishings. Several of the rooms offer a view of the bay. Some have outside decks; all have private baths. Four have kitchens. Breakfast often includes fresh crabmeat or lobster prepared in various ways, including the Seegers' lobster omelette. For those guests who can tear themselves away from the comfort of the inn, a sailboat and canoe are available. No smoking allowed. Children over 12 welcome.

THE KEEPER'S HOUSE
Innkeepers: Jeff and Judi
Burke.
207-367-2261.
P.O. Box 26, Lighthouse
Point, Isle au Haut 04645.
Open: May through Oct.
Price: Expensive to Very
Expensive.
Credit Cards: None, but
they accept personal and
travelers' checks.

Isle au Haut is the best kept secret of Acadia National Park, and the Keeper's House is a wonderful place to enjoy this national treasure. Guests ride the mail boat from Stonington — the innkeepers ask you to either amuse yourself all day on the island shore and trails or take the later boat. The stone cottage used to be the home of the lighthouse keeper before it was converted to an inn in 1986, and today the lighthouse, the "oil house" and the "woodshed" have six guest rooms, three shared baths, and are furnished with antiques and comfortable beds with down comforters for cool island evenings. There is no electricity — which makes the candle-lit Keeper's House romantic and cozy. You eat and relax after dinner in candlelight. There is a kerosene lantern in the common room for reading, but usually there's too much talk among guests to concentrate. The room rate includes tea, an exquisite dinner cooked by Ms. Burke (bring your own wine and don't expect red meat), as well as a hearty breakfast and a bag lunch to take with you as you explore the island the next day. Be sure to make your reservations early. Aside from the park lean-tos, this is the only lodging on the island and fills up quite rapidly. If you're lucky enough to book your stay in late August, look for the wild blueberries and raspberries that grow in abundance on the island. Two-night minimum during July and August.

THE LEDGELAWN INN
Owner: Nancy Cloud.
207-288-4596 or
800-274-5334.
66 Mount Desert St.,
Bar Harbor 04609.
Open: Mid-May to late Oct.
Price: Moderate to Very
Expensive.
Credit Cards: AE, D, MC, V.
Handicap Access: Some of
the rooms in the Carriage
House.

A short walk from downtown, this large, red-shingled Victorian summer cottage is homier and more inviting than many of the Bar Harbor "cottages" we have visited. But this 1904 mansion seems as if it were built to accommodate company and lavish parties. All the ornately decorated rooms in the inn and the Carriage House next door provide the proper retreat. Most of the beds are queen-sized, several are kings. Some have whirlpool tubs, sauna, fireplaces, and sitting areas.

They all have private baths and mostly original furnishings. The sweeping staircase says come on up, and there are bowls of red apples in the common room. There's a pool out back and bar in one corner of the living room (open 4 p.m. to midnight). The inn also offers a breakfast buffet for a nominal fee. No smoking. Pets and children are welcome.

LINDENWOOD INN
Innkeeper: James King.
207-244-5335 or
   800-307-5335.
118 Clark Point Rd., Box
   1328, Southwest Harbor
   04679.
Open: April 1 to Jan 1.
Price: Inexpensive to Very
   Expensive.
Credit Cards: AE, MC, V.

The Lindenwood has been extensively remodeled, expanded, and now has three very private cottages and a piece of the shore. The main house of the inn, located in one of Mount Desert's small, quiet island communities, was a sea captain's home at the turn of the century. The house is flooded with light, while the 16 rooms all have an off-to-themselves feel. Most have harbor views. All have private baths. Some have balconies. The Lindenwood has a heated pool and hot tub for guests to enjoy, as well as a restaurant with fine dining. Breakfast is included for guests staying in the house. No smoking. No pets. No children under 12 in the inn. Younger children are welcome in suites and cottages.

**MIRA MONTE INN &
   SUITES**
Owner: Marian Burns.
207-288-4263 or
   800-553-5109.
69 Mount Desert St., Bar
   Harbor 04609.
Open: Early May through
   late October.
Price: Moderate to
   Expensive.
Credit card: AE, MC, V.
Handicap Access: Yes.

A recent winner of Maine's innkeeper of the year award, Marian Burns has restored this gracious 1865 mansion to its former glory and filled it to the rafters with antiques. There are thirteen spacious and elegant rooms, all with private baths, air-conditioning, televisions, and telephones. Nine of the rooms have fireplaces. Two additional suites have double whirlpool baths, queen canopy beds, fireplaces, bay windows with window seats, and cooking units. These suites can be rented for the week during the winter. The grounds are beautifully kept, and the library is a good place to relax after a day scouring the island for fun. This is a restful place — and one of our favorite stopping places on the coast. The Mira Monte offers a glimpse of what Bar Harbor must have been like during the grand old days. Full breakfast buffet is included. Smoking allowed on the room balconies only.

**OCEANSIDE MEADOWS
   INN**
Innkeepers: Sonja
   Sundaram and Ben
   Walter.

Set on the Schoodic Peninsula near the farthest reaches of Acadia National Park, this 19th-century sea captain's home is still one of the best bargains on the coast. Spacious, immaculate and quiet,

207-963-5557.
Box 90, Rte. 195, Corea Rd.,
 Prospect Harbor 04669.
Open: May to Nov.; by
 reservation the rest of
 the year.
Price: Moderate.
Credit Cards: AE DC, MC,
 V.

the inn has undergone many renovations since we first visited. Every one of the rooms now has a private bath, and the owners, Sonja Sundaram and Ben Walter, have restored and updated the building. A separate old stage coach inn at the head of the bay has seven rooms, all with private baths, two rooms for receptions, and a full country kitchen. It's perfect for large families and longer term guests. Family reunions are popular here. The main house sits on a beautiful 200-acre preserve just yards away from a lovely private cove and sand beach. The sound of the surf is a great lullaby. Well-behaved children and amiable dogs are welcome. Breakfast and tea included. No smoking.

PENTAGOET BED & BREAKFAST

Innkeepers: Lindsey and
 Virginia Miller.
207-326-8616 or
 800-845-1701.
P.O. Box 4, Main St.,
 Castine 04421.
Open: May to October.
Price: Moderate.
Credit Cards: MC, V.

The Pentagoet, a lovely three-story Victorian, sits right across the street from the Castine Inn and right down the street from the water. There are 15 rooms in the main building and an older colonial structure. There are turrets, balconies, tea rose prints, and a flower-decked porch with rockers. Pentagoet is Old Breton for "on a hill lined with trees leading to the water," an apt description. A full breakfast is included. Afternoon and high teas, hors d'oeuvres, and drinks are usually available to guests; inquire ahead to confirm.

PILGRIM'S INN

Innkeepers: Jean and Dud
 Hendrick.
207-348-6615.
Deer Isle 04627.
Open: Mid-May to mid-
 Oct.
Price: Very Expensive.
Credit Cards: V, MC.

There are 13 wide pine-floored guest rooms in this wonderful 18th-century National Register house about 15 minutes' drive from Stonington. Eight have private baths and all are furnished with antiques and Laura Ashley fabrics. There are two parlors where you can read in front of the fire until *hors d'oeuvres* are served and people gather for dinner. Dinner is served in what once was a goat barn. The Hendricks also rent "Ginny's," a cozy vintage house adjacent to the Inn. It has two separate units, each with a bedroom with queen bed, living room (with a pull-out sofa), cable TV, gas stove, kitchenette, and dining area. Ginny's is great for families who seek privacy but still wish to take part in the activity of the inn. They've also added a gift shop — The Rugosa Rose — filled with local products. The food is good, country inn fare served by well-trained waiters in white jackets. Breakfast may include homemade granola, cheddar omelets, or pancakes. Breakfast and dinner included. Children ten and up are welcome.

**SUNSET HOUSE BED &
BREAKFAST**
Owners: Kathy and Carl
    Johnson.
207-963-7156 or
    800-233-7156.
HCR 60 Box 62, Rte. 186,
    West Gouldsboro 04607.
Open: Year round.
Price: Moderate to
    Expensive.
Credit Cards: AE, D, MC,
    V.

This family-run bed and breakfast offers ocean views from the front bedrooms and views of a freshwater pond and an old millstream from the rear bedrooms. The six rooms, three with private bath, are small and cozy. There is also a full kitchen on the third floor which can combine with three bedrooms to become a suite. The breakfasts are fortifying: French toast from fresh homebaked bread; sourdough waffles; fresh herbed goat cheese omelets. Book your winter stay in advance, and you may be asked to stay for a homestyle dinner cooked by Carl, who is an executive chef during the summer at a big deal restaurant in nearby Bar Harbor. In 1994, Carl was named Maine's Chef of the Year by the American Culinary Federation. No pets are allowed. There is one cat in residence. The Johnson family also keeps goats, and guests are invited to the morning milking. No smoking. Bikers take note: the Sunset House is located near the 27-mile bike trail through the Acadia region.

LODGING — EAST OF SCHOODIC

*The Lincoln House in
Dennysville.*

Herb Swanson

**LINCOLN HOUSE
COUNTRY INN**
Innkeepers: Mary Carol
    and Jerry Haggerty.
207-726-3953 or
    888-726-3953.

The lemon-yellow Georgian-style inn lords over the surrounding rural landscape from a dramatic hillside perch above the Dennys River. Mary Carol and Jerry Haggerty, a professional carpenter and antique restorer (who worked for the Smith-

R.R.1, Box 136A, Rte. 86 and Rte. 1, Dennysville 04628.
Open: Late May to October.
Price: Inexpensive to Moderate.
Credit Cards: MC, V.

sonian), bought the 200-year old home during the mid-1970s, and have fashioned it into an immaculate and handsome showcase for antique lovers and history buffs. Many of the original features of the National Register home are still intact. The inn has six rooms, two with private baths. Guests may roam the adjoining 100 wooded acres. A stay at the inn includes a full breakfast.

PEACOCK HOUSE BED & BREAKFAST INN
Owners: Chet and Veda Childs.
207-733-2403.
27 Summer St., Lubec 04652.
Open: May through October.
Price: Inexpensive to Moderate.
Credit Cards: D, MC, V.
Handicap Access: Yes.

This modest white clapboard house sits on a quiet corner near the far end of Lubec's main street. Step over the threshold and you find yourself at a crossroads where Texas meets New England. The bed and breakfast is named for five generations of the Peacock family who once lived there. It was converted to a lodging house by two Southerners — Chet and Veda Childs who serve up expansive breakfasts of homemade Texas-size muffins, blueberry crepes or "rum-runners" French toast. Five small to large rooms, all with private baths, are decorated with a mix of comfortable, modern, and reproduction furniture. The smallest, the Captain's Cabin, is a cozy single named for Capt. William Trott, who built the house for his bride in 1860. The largest — the Margaret Chase Smith — is named after the Maine senator who was a friend and frequent guest of the previous owners. This room has cable TV. No pets. Children over seven welcome. No smoking.

RIVERSIDE INN & RESTAURANT
Owners: Carol and Tom Paul.
207-255-4134.
P.O. Box 373, Rte. 1, East Machias 04630.
Open: All year.
Price: Inexpensive to Moderate.
Credit Cards: AE, MC, V.

Dinner at this tiny inn has become so popular, the Pauls have added two dining rooms to accommodate guests six days a week. The inn itself is a pretty 1820 cape-style sea captain's home overlooking the Machias River. There are three guest rooms, each with private bath. Two are in the main house, while the third is in a neighboring carriage house. The owners have also added a suite with its own kitchen and living room also in the carriage house. The main house rooms are small but elegantly appointed with antique furniture and old linens collected over the years by the Pauls who used to own an antiques store in Newport, Rhode Island. The prix-fixe dinner here, friends tell us, is one of the best and tastiest bargains way Down East (BYOB). Breakfast included, dinner by reservation, is additional.

TODD HOUSE
Owner: Ruth McInnis.
207-853-2328.
1 Capen Ave., Todd's
    Head, Eastport 04631.
Open: Year round.
Price: Inexpensive to
    Moderate.
Credit Cards: MC, V.
Handicap Access: Yes.

After a career in Portland teaching and collecting antiques, Ruth McInnis returned home to Eastport where she bought and restored this classic Cape farmhouse, now on the National Register of Historic Places. It was built during the Revolutionary War on the shore of Passamaquoddy Bay. The owner, a storehouse of local history, gladly will take you on a tour and has opened up her library of Maine, Revolutionary, and Civil War history books. The six rooms vary greatly in feel: one has a working fireplace; several are packed with carefully chosen antiques and brimming with historical significance; two are strictly modern with queen-sized beds, cable TV, private modern baths and kitchenettes. A simple, but ample, breakfast is served in the common room: cranberry muffins, fancy breads, cereal, and some very welcome fresh fruit. Children and pets are welcome. No smoking.

WESTON HOUSE
Owners: Jett & John
    Peterson.
207-853-2907 or
    800-853-2907.
26 Boynton St., Eastport
    04631.
Open: All year.
Price: Inexpensive to Moderate.
Credit Cards: None.

The Weston House is a civilized place. The formal parlor, with comfortable sofas and wing chairs, odd lamps, and a dish of pistachios on the coffee table, is the perfect place to curl up with a book as the afternoon wanes. There's also a cheerful back room for watching TV. Breakfast, served in the handsome dining room, is a gourmet affair: pancakes with fruit syrup, fresh baked breads and whatever else Jett Peterson — a prodigious cook — fancies (Mrs. Peterson will also pack box lunches and make dinner on request). Five comfortable guest rooms are furnished with handsome antiques, floral fabrics, and oriental rugs; some have fireplaces and four-poster beds as well.

CHAPTER FOUR
What to See, What to Do
CULTURE

On the 26th of December, 1950, on the evening of freezing cold and in the almost polar silence of Mount Desert Island, off the Atlantic shore, I was striving to live again through the smothering heat of a day in July, in the year 138 in Baiae, to feel the weight of a sheet on weary, heavy limbs, and to catch the barely perceptible sound of that tideless sea as from time to time it reached a man whose whole attention was concentrated upon other murmurs, those of his approaching death. I tried to go as far as the last sip of water, the last spasm of pain, the last image in his mind. Now the emperor had but to die.

—Marguerite Yourcenar, *Reflections on the Composition of Memoirs of Hadrian*

Herb Swanson

The light at West Quoddy Head, the easternmost lighthouse in the United States.

The Maine coast has long attracted artists and writers like Brussels-born author Marguerite Yourcenar, who in the latter part of her life made her home on Mount Desert Island. Many have found the coast a place from which they could advance their art and gather inspiration. Others found it a good place to look out at the Atlantic Ocean stretching eastward to Europe, with everything filtered through a hard, cool northern light. For many the Maine coast has been a great place to get away from the hectic pace of New York or Boston for a few months every summer — yet still be close enough to their wealthy patrons' summer homes to make the solitude profitable.

The earliest painters to record life in Maine were itinerant limners or portraitists who traveled the roads between Boston, Portsmouth, Kittery, and

Since our last edition, the cultural life of Maine has continued to flourish. A new museum dedicated to the history of the lighthouse was commissioned in Cape Elizabeth at the site of *Portland Head Light* (see Lighthouses, below). The *Children's Museum of Maine* opened in a grand new space in downtown Portland, next door to the *Portland Museum of Art*; check out the Camera Obscura at the very top of the museum for a bird's eye view of the Casco Bay. Also, the *Farnsworth Museum* in Rockland completed a major renovation of the Greek Revival building that houses this extraordinary collection, making it even more appealing (see Museums, below).

Aficionados of the grand old opera houses should visit the **Camden Opera House** and the **Rockport Opera House**. Both theaters have been restored recently and are home to two coastal cultural institutions — the **Camden Civic Theater** and Rockport's **Bay Chamber Series**.

Finally, the blues have come to the region, greatly adding to the nightlife with **Morganfield's** and **The Big Easy**.

points north. They painted portraits of ships' captains, merchants and their families. But the true boom in Maine painting came with the arrival of the summer artists. The first were from the Hudson River and Luminist movements. They were at once transfixed by the coast's rugged beauty and the quality of its sunlight. In 1844, Thomas Cole came to Bar Harbor and Mount Desert Island in search of a picturesque reality to idealize. Cole found a virtual Eden, and he kept coming back, often bringing with him fellow painters including his premier student Frederic Church. His style, which became the cornerstone of the Hudson River School, became popular with his wealthy patrons as did the idealized works of Fitz Hugh Lane, the leader of the Luminist movement, who first painted Mount Desert Island four years later.

Painters, sculptors, musicians, poets, and writers all have found the coast a place to concentrate on their art. Edgar Allen Beem, a local art critic, has described the attraction of Maine for artists who have always been "mavericks and loners seeking privacy and freedom from influence." The coast, he writes, offers "a sense of authenticity that occurs only when nature and culture are in right relation with each other." That relation has become an elusive balance in most other parts of America these days.

During the late 1800s, Winslow Homer painted at Prouts Neck, a 112-acre point of land stretching into the Gulf of Maine south of Portland (his mother was born in Bucksport). Realists Robert Henri, Rockwell Kent, and George Bellows painted on Monhegan during the early 20th century. Soon after the turn of the century, painter Charles Woodbury and modernist Hamilton Easter Field established two competing and sometimes feuding painting schools at Perkins Cove in Ogunquit. Their presence drew other artists there through the mid-1900s, including Alfred Stieglitz, Georgia O'Keeffe, Maurice Stern, and Stefan Hirsch. Walter Kuhn, one of the greatest American painters of the 20th century, made his home in Ogunquit, too, although he kept himself aloof from the sometimes raucous antics of the local art colony.

Sculptor Louise Nevelson lived near Rockland for many years. Andrew Wyeth painted his famous canvas *Christina's World* on the site of an old farm near Cushing. In 1991, the Olson family, who owned the three-story farmhouse with gray weathered clapboards, donated the saltwater farm on Hawthorne Point Rd. to the Farnsworth Museum in Rockland. Neil Welliver, whose landscapes hang in the Metropolitan Museum of Art and Museum of Modern Art in Manhattan, has a farm in Lincolnville, northeast of Camden.

The most American of poets, Henry Wadsworth Longfellow was born in Portland in 1807, and immortalized the town in his poem "My Lost Youth." He and novelist Nathaniel Hawthorne were classmates at Bowdoin College in Brunswick, both graduating in 1825. Essayist and author E. B. White summered on the Blue Hill peninsula and found inspiration for his famous children's story, *Charlotte's Web*, at the Blue Hill Fair, now almost 100 years old. Before him, there were a long line of American authors who wrote in and about the coast. Henry David Thoreau contemplated nature here; abolitionist and novelist Harriet Beecher Stowe (whose husband taught at Bowdoin) wrote *The Pearl of Orr's Island* here; Sarah Orne Jewett, who was born and lived much of her life in South Berwick, wrote her fine novel, *The Country of the Pointed Firs*, in Maine.

Edna St. Vincent Millay was born at 198 Broadway in Rockland (the house, a private residence, still stands) and spent much of her childhood in Camden, the subject of many of her poems. For one long and painful year, novelist Jean Stafford *(The Mountain Lion)* and her husband, poet Robert Lowell, lived in Damariscotta Mills. Their marriage hit the rocks there. Later Stafford wrote *An Influx of Poets*, about poets and their quarreling wives and mistresses who came to visit them during their short residence. Author and environmental activist Rachel Carson, who summered in the South Coast, found Maine a wonderful laboratory for her study of the environment. She wrote *The Edge of the Sea* here.

Today there are dozens of artists and writers who live here year round, many lured by the relatively low cost of living. There are so many writers on the coast that ships arrive with cargoes of Xerox toner and depart laden with manuscripts, cracked humorist Garrison Keillor on a recent stopover in Portland. A thriving crafts community is centered near the Haystack Mountain School of Crafts in Deer Isle, and a talented group of photographers live in the midcoast region stretching from Bath to Rockland. Novelist Anne River Siddons has summered near Blue Hill and used the coast as a setting for her novel *Colony*.

The result of all this history of artistic activity is a public that has a deep and healthy appreciation for the visual, written, and spoken arts. In this chapter we have tried to give you an idea of the people and organizations that give shape to the coast's cultural community. Still it has not been possible to list every historic site and arts organization. For a more complete listing for the area you plan to visit, contact the chamber of commerce for that region (See Chapter Eight, *Information*).

ARCHITECTURE

The earliest buildings built by Europeans making their homes on the coast are believed to have been turf and thatch huts similar to those in England of the same period. It is thought that soon after their arrival settlers began using the abundant lumber from local forests.

Few examples of the structures built by European settlers prior to 1760 remain. Farmhouses, forts, and other early buildings were victims of the ongoing French and Indian Wars, which lasted from 1675 to 1763. One exception is the *Old Stone Gaol* in York, a stone building built in 1653. The old jail house is now a museum and is the oldest stone building still in use in the United States.

Wood continued to be the most popular building material throughout most of the state. Brick became popular in Portland after two fires, in 1775 and 1866, tore through streets lined with wooden structures. Native granite, quarried inland and on several islands off the coast, was primarily used for decorative facades.

The earliest surviving wood-built houses on the Maine coast are similar to those found to the south in New Hampshire and Massachusetts. The design focused on a central chimney and entranceway. A parlor and a dining room usually flanked the entranceway. The kitchen was situated at the rear of the chimney with a small room to either side filling out the basic rectangular shape of the building. Upstairs there were two main bed chambers at the front of the house and two smaller rooms to the rear. Many of the old houses were expanded throughout the years with rooms and a covered walkway connecting to a barn at the back of the house. The exterior of the houses were finished with clapboards (a few were built from brick), and the earliest houses were devoid of outside decoration.

Many examples of the Federal and Georgian styles have survived and seem to have been the preferred architecture for well-to-do residents during the late 1700s and early 1800s. The Greek Revival took hold of Maine during the mid-1800s, a time when the coast was experiencing a great influx of wealth from the shipbuilding and shipping trade. Many of the newly wealthy were ships' captains, and their houses that line the coast are rich with elegant woodworking and flying staircases. A good example of the Greek Revival is the *Sarah Orne Jewett House* in South Berwick. The Gothic Revival movement was not as popular, although there are several fine examples that have survived. In Brunswick, there are two Gothic Revival churches: the *First Parish Church* is the more ornate of the two; *St. Paul's* is a more austere example of the trend.

Machias today is an historical center of the coast. The first naval battle of the American Revolution was fought near here.

Roy Zalesky

In Kennebunk, the **Wedding Cake House** is perhaps the state's most conspicuous example of the Gothic. Portland is home to the state's most outstanding example of the Italianate phase of the Gothic Revival. The **Victoria Mansion**, also known as the Morse-Libby House, was built in 1859 and is rich in Italianate detail.

After the Civil War, the coast became a summer playground for wealthy Bostonians and New Yorkers. Thus the predominate style of architecture during the late 1800s was the grand "cottage," summer homes that were the size of small mansions. Boston architect William R. Emerson made a great impact with the cottages he designed for wealthy patrons on Mount Desert Island — rambling wooden shingled buildings with large airy rooms that also incorporated native granite and stone. Portland architect John Calvin Stevens expanded on Emerson's principles and lined streets throughout the state with stately shingled cottages for both summer and year-round residents.

Since the mid-1600s, the predominant trend in coastal architecture has been simplicity and practicality. That is still seen in the small lobster and fishing shacks that seem to grow out of the rocks and have changed little during the past 100 years, as well as in the new **Maine Maritime Museum** in Bath, I.M. Pei's **Portland Art Museum**, and perhaps the most famous home in Maine, the **Olson House** in Cushing, made so by artist Andrew Wyeth in his painting *Christina's World*.

For architecture buffs, there is a state inventory of Maine architecture on file at the architectural archives at **Colby College** in Waterville. **The Frances W. Peabody Research Library** at Greater Portland Landmarks (207-774-5561;165 State Street, Portland) is a good place to get a basic education in the region's architectural heritage. The organization offers an excellent walking tour map of the city's historical districts which include an impressive Victorian residential district with homes of the Italianate, Gothic Revival, Queen Anne, Colonial Revival, and Shingle styles. Walking tour maps are available for a nominal fee, and throughout the summer Landmarks offers a series of guided tours of historically and architecturally significant neighborhoods in Portland and the islands of Casco Bay. Guided walking tours detailing Kennebunk's architectural heritage leave from the **Brick Store Museum**. Call 207-985-4802 for information.

Several chambers of commerce, including Portland, Wiscasset, and Belfast offer maps for self-guided walking tours of local historic districts and buildings. Many of these annotated maps are available at state tourism offices (see *Information*, Chapter Eight). An excellent guide for those embarking on driving survey of coastal architecture is *Maine: A Guide 'Downeast'* published in 1970 by the Maine League of Historical Societies and Museums. Although the book is out of print, it is available in the Maine collections of most local libraries.

FILM

Film on the coast can mean everything from foreign and art films shown in funky old opera houses to full-blown Hollywood extravaganzas playing the screen at the neighborhood multiplex. The **Leavitt Theatre** in Ogunquit has shown first-run movies on their big screen since 1923. The **Movies at Exchange Street** in Portland also offers a steady repertoire of old classics, art, and foreign films for dedicated movieholics.

South Coast

Cinema Center (207-646-0500; Wells Plaza, Rte. 1, Wells).
Cines 8 (207-282-5995; 5 Points Shopping Center, Biddeford).
Leavitt Theatre (207-646-3123; Rte. 1, 40 Main St., Ogunquit). Seasonal.
Ogunquit Square Theatre (207-646-5151; Shore Rd., Ogunquit). Seasonal.
Saco Drive-In (207-283-0838; 969 Rte. 1, Saco).
Saco River Grange Hall (207-929-6472; Salmon Falls Rd., Bar Mills).
Sanford Cinema 4 (207-324-6134; 277A Maine St., Sanford).
York Beach Cinema (207-363-2074; 6 Beach St., York Beach).

Casco Bay

Cinema City (207-729-0116; Cooks Corner Shopping Center, Brunswick).
Evening Star Cinema (207-729-5486 or 888-304-5486; Tontine Mall, Brunswick).
Flagship Cinemas (207-781-5668; 206 U.S. Rte. 1, Falmouth).
Hoyts Brunswick Cinema 10 (207-798-3996; 19 Gurnet Rd., Brunswick).
Hoyts Cinema 8 (207-879-1511; Clarks Pond Pkwy., So. Portland).
Keystone Theater Cafe (207-772-0606; 504 Congress St., Portland). A new addition to the city of Portland, the Keystone is the latest in the wave of dinner cinema.
Maine Mall Cinema (207-774-1022; Maine Mall Rd., So. Portland).

Movies at Exchange Street (207-772-9600; 10 Exchange St., Portland).
Nickelodeon Cinema (207-772-9751; Temple & Middle Sts., Portland).

Midcoast

Bay View Street Cinema 9 (seasonal: 207-236-8722; Bay View St., Camden).
Belfast Maskers (207-338-9668; 43 Front St., Belfast).
The Colonial Twin Cinemas (207-338-1930; 121 High St., Belfast). If you want
to know what the movie's about and what the critics say, please press 6.
Harbor Light Cinema (207-633-3799; Harbor Village Shopping Center, Booth-
bay Harbor). Seasonal
Strand Twin Cinema (207-594-7266; 339 Main St. Rockland).

Down East / Acadia

Criterion Theatre (207-288-3441; 35 Cottage St., Bar Harbor). Seasonal.
The Grand (207-667-9500; Main St., Ellsworth).
Maine Coast Mall Cinemas (207-667-3251; Maine Coast Mall, Ellsworth).

East of Schoodic

The Milbridge Theater (207-546-2038; Main St., Milbridge).

GALLERIES

Painters and artists seem to flourish in Maine, so well that often it seems
there are as many galleries as lobster pounds. We have culled through the
many public, non-profit, and commercial galleries to offer a snapshot of the art
scene on the coast. Many of the galleries listed below specialize in the work of
Maine artists and that of artists who regularly summer on the coast.

South Coast

Mast Cove Gallery (207-967-3453; Main St., Kennebunkport). This gallery
offers what art critic Gail Glickman calls a "solid introduction to Maine Art."
Ogunquit Museum of American Art (207-646-4909; 183 Shore Rd., Ogunquit).
This gallery features works by Peggy Bacon, Thomas Hart Benton, and
many others. Open July 1– Sept. 30, Mon.–Sat. 10:30–5, and Sun. 2–5.

Casco Bay

Chocolate Church Gallery (207-442-8455; 804 Washington St., Bath). Part of
the lively, regional arts center housed in a grand old church, this gallery features the work of its members and other Maine artists.

Frost Gully Gallery (207-773-2555; 411 Congress St., Portland). Drawings, paintings, prints, and sculptures by contemporary Maine artists.

Icon Contemporary Art (207-725-8157; 19 Mason St., Brunswick). This gallery, featuring the work of contemporary Maine artists, is really two separate spaces where two shows are staged simultaneously.

Institute of Contemporary Art (207-775-5152; Maine College of Art, 522 Congress St., Portland). Work by the faculty of this growing art school, plus frequent shows of students' work. This is a good place to find out what's on the mind and in the eye of young artists everywhere. This new building has encompassed the prior Baxter Gallery.

Joan Whitney Payson Gallery of Art (207-797-7261; 716 Stevens Ave., Westbrook College, Portland). Remember the stir caused when a Japanese company bought Van Gogh's *Irises*? The painting had been part of this collection, and there are still several great works on display here, including those by Van Gogh, Picasso, Degas, and Winslow Homer. This is a gem of a gallery housed in handsome building.

June Fitzpatrick Gallery (207-772-1961; 112 High St., Portland) Tucked in an old house on a busy street, this tiny gallery often offers a fresh alternative to more "established" art hanging on the walls of the Portland Museum of Art (which is up the street and around the corner).

O'Farrell Gallery (207-729-8228; 46 Maine St., Brunswick). Works by local artists.

Nancy Margolis Gallery (207-775-3822; 367 Fore St., Portland). Nationally known artists. Features contemporary American crafts, especially textiles, ceramics, and jewelry.

Salt Gallery (207-761-0660; 17 Pine St., Portland). Operated by the Salt Center for Documentary Field Studies, this gallery features documentary photographic works by Salt students, alumni, and professional photographers.

Midcoast

Art Fellows (207-338-5776; 104B Main St., Belfast). A cooperative gallery run by Maine artists featuring monthly changing exhibits. Open early May–late November, Wed–Sat. 11–4 p.m. Closed Sun., Mon., and Tues.

Blue Heron Gallery (207-348-6051; Church St., Deer Isle). A barn full of contemporary crafts including works by faculty members of the nearby Haystack Mountain School with a focus on "functional clay." Open June through September.

Deer Isle Artists Association (second floor, Seamark Bldg., Rte. 15, Deer Isle). Revolving, two-week exhibitions of members' sculptures, paintings, photographs, and drawings. Open June through August.

Frick Gallery (207-338-3671; 139 High St., Belfast). Exhibits of work by local artists, most of it contemporary and applied art.

Gallery Sixty Eight (207-338-1558; 68 Main St., Belfast). Prints and paintings by Maine coast artists.

Leighton Gallery (207-374-5001; Parker Point Rd., Blue Hill). Local critics and those from away rave about this gallery, owned by outdoor sculptor Judith Leighton, which shows her work as well as that of other well-known sculptors and painters. The gallery is happy to be celebrating its 18th year, and opens its season in late May.

M.H. Jacobs Gallery (207-338-3324 or 888-338-3324; 44 Main St., Belfast). Sells traditional and representational watercolors and acrylics by artist Marvin Jacobs.

Maine Coast Artists (207-236-2875; Russell Ave., Rockport). Their annual juried art show is a good introduction to new and rising local talent. Open June through September.

Round Top Center for the Arts (207-563-1507; Business Rte. 1, Damariscotta). This young organization sponsors shows of area artists in its Main Gallery, including an annual exhibit of members' work. They also offer alternative looks at the arts with exhibits of quilting and other crafts. Each show is accompanied by a lecture open to the public.

Turtle Gallery (207-348-9977; Rte. 15, Deer Isle). Paintings, drawings, prints, sculptures, and contemporary crafts by Maine artists.

East of Schoodic

Eastport Gallery and the Center (207-853-4166 or 853-4133; 69 Water St., Eastport). Sculpture, painting, and other media by almost two dozen regional artists. The Arts Center has a series of concerts as well as a theater company. Open June through October.

GARDENS & GARDEN TOURS

Winters on the coast are long. The growing season is short, and the soil, although rocky, is rich. It is little wonder that summer and year-round residents who garden here take so much pride in what they are able to accomplish during the short spring and cool summer (which by the way is an ideal climate for roses). The "rusticators" who settled summer coastal communities were renowned for their green thumbs, and their gardens often stretched for acres to the sea. These days, the *fin de siecle* show gardens of Bar Harbor, some of which required as many as 40 full-time gardeners, are gone, yet a few living relics of that era survive.

The Thuya Gardens, a public paradise that is open to what historian and summer resident Samuel Eliot Morison calls the "habitues of the motel and the Acadia National Park camp and trailer grounds," will give you an idea of what those grand plots fashioned after the great gardens of England were like. *The*

The gate to Thuya Gardens, a quiet throwback to the great summer cottage gardens of the late 19th and early 20th centuries.

Herb Swanson

New York Times described Thuya Gardens as an "accidentally available private retreat left over from another time."

In addition to the public gardens listed below, there are several annual garden tours no self-respecting garden lover would miss. ***Greater Portland Landmarks*** sponsors an annual house and garden tour which in early summer gains the tourist entrance to a selection of the city's splendid private gardens (207-774-5561). Late in June, there is ***Rose Day*** at Royall River Roses, an organic nursery in North Yarmouth that features an impressive selection of old roses. Call 207-829-5830 or 800-820-5830 for more information.

Since 1947, the ***Camden Open House & Garden Tour*** has taken place during mid-July (call 207-236-4404 for information). For further information about regional garden tours, call the chamber of commerce for the area you plan to visit (see Chapter Eight, *Information*).

Azalea Gardens (Rte. 3 and 198, Northeast Harbor, Mount Desert Island). Twenty different varieties of azaleas. They bloom in June. The rest of the year, the garden features native plants and trees and a Japanese sand garden. Open 7 a.m.–9 p.m. daily.

The Black House (Surry Rd., $^1/_2$ mi. off Rte. 1, Ellsworth) The formal gardens to the rear of this historic mansion weren't planted until 1903, about 100 years after construction of the house. Following a period of disrepair, the grounds and gardens have been returned to their original state.

Hamilton House (Vaughan's Ln., S. Berwick). Overlooking the Pisquataqua River, these are some of the most beautiful grounds in Southern Maine. Open dawn to dusk from June to mid-Oct.

Merryspring (Conway Rd. off Rte. 1, on the Camden-Rockport town line). A 66-acre nature park with an herb garden, a lily garden, a 10-acre arboretum and more cultivated wonders. Guided tours are available. Open dawn to dusk year round.

Nickels-Sortwell House (207-882-6218; Main and Federal Sts., Wiscasset). The gardens are being restored to their original design (1926) by the Wiscasset Garden Club. The ships captain's house and gardens are well worth the visit. June–Sept. 30, noon–5 p.m.

St. Anthony Monastery and Shrines (28 Beach Ave., Kennebunkport). This tranquil retreat is a turn-of-the-century Tudor mansion purchased by the Lithuanian Franciscans in 1949. The gardens and lawns are beautiful. A wooded walkway follows the Kennebunk River and offers fine views of the well-manicured grounds and the ocean. Grounds are open to the public. (207-967-2011; guest accommodations are available, see Chapter 3, *Lodging*).

Thuya Gardens at Asticou Terraces (Rte. 3, Northeast Harbor on Mount Desert Island). A formal English garden filled with country flowers — zinnias, dahlias, plume poppies, goatsbeards, monkshood. The garden was founded by Joseph Henry Curtis, a Boston landscape architect who summered in Northeast Harbor from 1880 to 1928. 7–7 daily.

The Wild Gardens of Acadia (Rte. 3, Sieur de Monts Spring entrance, Mount Desert Island). Maintained by the Bar Harbor Garden Club, this is an exquisite collection of native plants. Open year round.

HISTORIC BUILDINGS & SITES

Andre the Seal, honorary Harbormaster of Rockport Harbor, is dead, but his stone image continues to watch over the harbor. Harry Goodridge found Andre when he was a young pup; he raised and trained the seal, who became a local celebrity. The entire state mourned when Andre died in 1986, and his statue is one of the coast's most unusual historic markers. Andre was the subject of the forgettable 1994 movie, *Andre the Seal*.

There are hundreds of historic homes and sites that date from Maine's earliest days as part of the Massachusetts Bay Colony and are open to the public. Many of them are the product of the boom times the maritime industry experienced in the late 18th and early 19th centuries. Below, we provide an abbreviated list of notable ones, as well as forts and other coastal history hot spots. Many of these charge a nominal fee for admission (between $1 and $5); others are open to the public free of charge. Be aware that seasons, hours, and admission policies frequently change. When possible we have provided phone numbers for your convenience.

If you are a serious history buff and want to do some additional research, check in with the *Maine Historical Society* (207-774-1822; 485 Congress St., Portland 04101); the *Maine Historic Preservation Commission* (207-287-2132; 55 Capital St., State House Station 65, Augusta 04333); or the *Society for the Preservation of New England Antiquities* (603-436-3205; 141 Cambridge St., Boston, MA 02114). The last will provide you with a free visitors' guide to their historic homes in Maine if you send a self-addressed, postage paid envelope (you'll need two first-class stamps).

South Coast

FORT McCLARY
207-693-6231 or
  207-384-5160.
Rte. 103 (Kittery Point Rd.),
  Kittery Pt.
Season: May 30–Oct. 1.

The granite fortification that dates back to 1715 saw strategic duty during the Revolutionary War, the War of 1812, the Civil War and the Spanish-American War. The fort was named for Andrew McClary, a local soldier who died at the Battle of Bunker Hill.

J. David Bohl

Overlooking the Pisquataqua River, the Hamilton House has beautiful grounds and gardens.

HAMILTON HOUSE
603-436-3205.
Vaughan's Ln., S. Berwick.
Season: June–mid-Oct.;
  hourly tours Wed.–Sun.,
  11–5 p.m.
Nominal admission
  charged; grounds open
  dawn till dusk year
  round.

First built for a wealthy merchant during the 18th century, then altered by Boston residents Emily Tyson and her daughter Elise in 1898 to use as a summer home. The two women, friends of author Sarah Orne Jewett, outfitted it in grand Colonial Revival style. Several of the younger Tyson's period photographs are on view, testament to the civilized coastal summer life they enjoyed. The gardens and grounds are lovely, and many visit just to picnic in warm weather or cross-country ski in winter.

OLD YORK HISTORICAL SOCIETY
207-363-4974.
Lindsay Rd. and Rte. 1A, Old York.
Season: Mid-June–Sept. 30.
Nominal admission.

A "living history" museum that includes six period village buildings including: the *Old Gaol* (1720), the oldest public building still in use; the *Emerson-Wilcox House* (1740); the *Elizabeth Perkins House* (1731); the *Jefferds Tavern* (1750); the *Old Schoolhouse*; and the *John Hancock Wharf and Warehouse*. A good representation of the life and commerce of an 18th-century seaside town. Demonstrations of cooking and maritime crafts; displays of period furniture, china and glass, and the only complete set of the American crewel work in existence (at the Emerson-Wilcox House).

NOTT HOUSE
207-967-2751
Maine St., Kennebunkport.
Season: Open mid-June through mid-Oct., Wed.–Fri. 1–4.

Also known as "White Columns," this beautiful Greek Revival home dates to 1853. It still retains many of its original features and furnishings including wallpapers, carpets and furniture.

LADY PEPPERELL HOUSE
Kittery Pt.
Season: Summer: 1–4.
Admission charged.

The 1760 Georgian home of Sir William Pepperell's widow (Sir William led colonial forces at the definitive battle at Louisburg on Cape Breton and was given a baronet for his success). The house contains period furnishings and several family portraits — including a portrait of Jane Pepperell, the first painting to be associated with Maine — as well as a good collection of fans and dishes.

SAYWARD-WHEELER HOUSE
603-436-3205.
79 Barrell Ln. Extension, York Harbor.
Season: June–mid-Oct., Sat., Sun. 11–5; hourly tours.
Admission charged.

This mansion was built in 1718 and later enlarged and remodeled for civic leader Jonathan Sayward who was well known during the Revolution for his Tory sympathies. The owner was wealthy but frugal, and with its small, modest rooms and good, locally made woodwork and furniture, this well-preserved home provides a realistic view of a typical Mainer's lifestyle during the 18th century. The house also has a good collection of Chippendale and Queen Anne furniture, family portraits and china brought back as booty from the successful skirmish with the French at Louisburg in 1745. Maintained by the Society for the Preservation of New England Antiquities.

SARAH ORNE JEWETT HOUSE
603-436-3205.

This is the home in which Ms. Jewett spent much of her life, and her room remains today as it was when she lived here. Beyond the literary con-

Writer Sarah Orne Jewett's home in South Berwick. Jewett is the author of The Country of the Pointed Firs, *an entertaining chronicle of life on the coast during the late 1800s.*

Maine Historic Preservation Commission

5 Portland St., S. Berwick.
Season: June 1–Oct. 15,
  Wed.–Sun., 11–5; tours
  on the hour.
Nominal admission.

nections, the house itself is an attractive mid-Georgian structure that has been restored to reflect the sophisticated mix of family heirlooms and arts and crafts pieces that Jewett and her sister used in their decoration. Maintained by the Society for the Preservation of New England Antiquities.

Casco Bay

**JOSHUA L. CHAMBER-
  LAIN HOUSE**
207-729-6606.
226 Main St., Brunswick.
Season: June–Aug.,
  Tues.–Sat. 1–4; by
  appointment during the
  rest of the year.
Admission charged.

Joshua Chamberlain led a large life. He won a Congressional Medal of Honor for his defense of "Little Round Top" in the battle of Gettysburg. He accepted the Confederate Army's surrender at the close of the Civil War. He went on to become governor of Maine (1866-1870) and president of nearby Bowdoin College (1871-1883). He occupied this house (built in 1825) while serving Bowdoin. Several rooms have been restored and are on view, as well as a collection of Chamberlain's Civil War memorabilia.

FIRST MEETINGHOUSE
207-833-6336 or
  207-833-6322.
Rt. 123, Harpswell Center.
Open by request only.
No charge.

Constructed in 1757, this is Maine's oldest meetinghouse, and its earliest congregations included what residents called "praying Indians." The building is still in general use as a town office and is an excellent example of early church architecture.

NEAL DOW MEMORIAL
714 Congress St., Portland.
Open year round,
 Mon.– Fri., 11–4.
No charge.

Neal Dow was a Quaker who was a leader in social reform during the 19th century. The memorial is the home he and his wife, Maria Cornelia Durant Maynard, built in 1829. Dow was an outspoken advocate for temperance, an abolitionist, Civil War general, two-time mayor of Portland and candidate for the U.S. presidency on the Prohibition Party ticket. His home, now managed by the Maine Women's Christian Temperance Union, is on the National Register of Historical Places and is a Colonial Revival gem.

**ADMIRAL ROBERT E.
 PEARY HOME**
207-624-6080.
Eagle Island, Casco Bay.
Season: June–Labor Day;
 accessible by boat.
Admission charged.

Construction of this handsome summer home began five years before Peary discovered the North Pole. The restored home features many striking design elements, including three quartz and fieldstone fireplaces. There are nature trails and a public pier where ferries, tour boats and visiting sailors can tie up.

**PORTLAND
 OBSERVATORY**
207-774-5561.
138 Congress St., Portland.
Season: Memorial Day to
 Labor Day.
Nominal fee.

Built in 1807, this is the last remaining signal tower on the eastern seaboard. The architecture is striking with heavy timbers forming a hexagonal shingled tower that narrows at the top. The views of Greater Portland and the Casco Bay provide a good orientation for the traveler who has just arrived in town. The building is maintained by Greater Portland Landmarks. The observatory will be closed a short time for reconstruction. Call for more information.

**SKOLFIELD-WHITTIER
 HOUSE**
207-729-6606.
161 Park Row, Brunswick.
Season: June–Sept., Tues.–
 Fri. 10–4; Sat. 1–4.

Three generations of prominent Brunswickians resided in this handsome 17-room home. They were doctors, mariners, and educators, and the house remains pretty much as it was when the family last lived here in 1925. Maintained by the Brunswick Historical Society.

VICTORIA MANSION
207-772-4841.
109 Danforth St., Portland.
Season: May–Oct., Tues.–
 Sat. 10–4; Sun. 1–5. Open
 by appointment the rest
 of the year.
Admission charged.

Also known as the Morse-Libby House, the imposing brownstone Italianate villa built for Ruggles Sylvester Morse looks as if it were a set for an episode of *The Addams Family*. Morse was a hotelier between 1858 and 1860, and much of this small mansion is packed with lavish, hotel-sized Victorian details. The house is still in the process of being restored, but is well worth visiting for its seven hand-carved Italian marble fireplaces and mantels alone. Our favorites are the "Turkish" room, where the gentlemen gathered to smoke, and the collection of Confederacy memorabilia.

**WADSWORTH-
   LONGFELLOW HOUSE**
207-879-0427.
489 Congress St., Portland.
Season: June–mid-Oct.,
   Tues.–Sun. 10–4; tours
   every half hour.
Nominal fee.

This is the boyhood home of poet Henry Wadsworth Longfellow. Built in 1785 by Henry's grandfather, Gen. Peleg Wadsworth, it is the oldest brick house in Portland, and today contains family artifacts and furnishings dating from 1750 to 1900. This is reported to be the most visited historic home in the state, but don't worry about lines. During warm weather the shaded garden is a wonderful place for a picnic.

Midcoast

**BOOTHBAY REGION
   HISTORICAL SOCIETY**
207-633-0820.
Elizabeth Reed House.
70 Oak St., Boothbay
   Harbor.
Season: July–Labor Day,
   Wed., Fri., Sat. 10–4; rest
   of the year Sat. 10–2.

An excellent collection of period photographs depicting the region's daily activities, including fishing, ice cutting, lumbering, farming, shipping, and shipbuilding. Plus early fishing gear, shipwrights' tools and navigation instruments.

CASTLE TUCKER
207-882-7364.
Lee and High Sts.,
   Wiscasset.
Season: July–Aug.,
   Thurs.–Sat. 12–4; June
   15–30, Sept. by
   appointment.
Hourly tours.
Admission charged.

The coast is rich with boom-and-bust stories, and Castle Tucker is a perfect example. In 1807 Judge Silas Lee decided to build himself a "great house" on the hill overlooking Wiscasset Harbor, and nothing stopped him, not even his bank account. By the time of his death seven years later he had so heavily mortgaged the house that it became the property of his three neighbors. It was bought in 1858 by Capt. Richard Tucker, a third-generation mariner. Today the house is still owned by the Tucker family. It has original Victorian furniture, kitchen and wallpapers, and a handsome elliptical staircase.

**COLONEL BLACK
   MANSION**
Rte. 172 (Surry Rd.), one
   quarter mi. off Rte. 1,
   Ellsworth.
Season: June–mid-Oct.,
   Mon.–Sat. 10–5.

John Black's father-in-law and employer was a member of George Washington's staff during the Revolutionary War, and his stately brick Gregorian mansion dates to 1802. Inside there is an intriguing mix of (among others) Jacobean, Queen Anne, and Chippendale furniture, as well as Waterford and

The 1802 Georgian facade of the Black Mansion near Ellsworth. The house is a museum open to the public, and the grounds, laid out in 1902, are a lovely example of a Maine summer garden.

Maine Historic Preservation Commission

Sandwich glass, all used by Black and his descendants. The mansion has a new gift shop offering Maine-made pottery, glassware, and antique reproductions. On Wednesdays, an afternoon tea is offered from 2–4 p.m.

PARSON FISHER HOUSE
207-374-2459.
Rte. 15, approx.1 mi. from center of Blue Hill .
Season: Early June–mid-Sept.; Mon.–Sat. 2–5; other times by appointment.
Admission charged.

This house was built in 1814 by Jonathan Fisher, the town's first settled minister. Fisher was a man of many avocations — farmer, missionary, scientist, mathematician, portrait and landscape painter, and poet, among others. His house is full of the fruits of his labors, including his paintings, furniture, manuscripts, and other unusual memorabilia. Tours are available.

FORT EDGECOMB
Right off Rte. 1 just past Wiscasset Bridge, Edgecomb.
Free.

The restored fort with an octagonal, two-story blockhouse was first built in 1808 to protect the port of Wiscasset from its vantage point overlooking the Sheepscot River. Great place for a picnic.

FORT KNOX
207-469-7719.
Rte. 174 off Rte. 1 just east of Stockton Springs.
Season: May–Nov.; daily, 9–sunset.
Admission charged.

Looking west across the Penobscot River from Bucksport, this great granite fort looks like a medieval castle. It was built in 1844 as a defense against the British during the Aroostook War. In 1842, U.S. troops based here tromped north to meet British troops in New Brunswick; the "war" reached a negotiated settlement after some tense posturing on both sides. Today, the fort is the state's most complete historical military structure.

A historical re-enactment at Fort Knox near Stockton Springs. The fort was built in 1842 to defend the coast from a threatened invasion by the British.

Tom Hindman

It was constructed of granite mined from nearby Mount Waldo and named for the first U.S. Secretary of War, who was from the territory that eventually became the state of Maine.

FORT WILLIAM HENRY
Pemaquid Peninsula.
Admission charged.
Season: May–Sept.
  Grounds open year
  round.
Admission charged.

The fort was a hot spot before and during the French and Indian Wars and changed hands — and names — several times. Fort Pemaquid (1632) was looted by pirates; as Fort Charles, it was captured by the French in 1689; Fort William Henry, believed to be New England's first stone fortification, was captured by the Baron de Castine; Fort Frederic was built from the ruins of Fort William Henry in 1729. What you see today is an impressive replica of the fort in addition to the authentic Old Fort House built in 1729. The *Old Burial Ground*, just down the road from here, has graves dating to 1695. Also nearby is an archaeological excavation of the Pemaquid settlement established in the 1620s. A museum with artifacts from the dig is nearby. Many consider this to be one of the prettiest — and most significant — historical spots in Maine.

MONTPELIER
207-354-8062.
Rtes. 1 and 131, Thomaston.
Season: May 30–mid Oct.;
Tues.–Sat. 10–4 , Sun.
1–4.

A replica of the 1795 house built by Gen. Henry Knox and his wife, Lucy Flucker. Knox served in President Washington's cabinet as Secretary of War (see Fort Knox, above). In addition to guided tours of the reconstructed mansion, Montpelier offers programs throughout the summer featuring guides in authentic Colonial costumes, an antique fashion show, and an Independence Day celebration with "Henry Knox," and a silver high tea.

NICKELS-SORTWELL HOUSE
207-882-6218.
Main and Federal sts.
(Rte. 1), Wiscasset.
Season: June 1–Sept. 30,
Wed.–Sun.; tours at
noon, 1, 2, 3, 4.
Admission charged.

Built in 1807 for Capt. William Nickels, a shipmaster in the lumber trade, this elegant Federal mansion also did service as a hotel. The furnishings are Colonial Revival style. Don't miss the beautiful elliptical stairway, and the wooden inlay work on the facade of the house. The gardens are currently being restored to their original 1926 design.

OLD CONWAY HOUSE
207-236-2257.
Conway Rd., Camden.
Season: July 1–late Aug.;
Tues.–Fri. 10–4.
Admission: $3 adults; $2
seniors; $1 students 6–18;
children under 6 free.

The Camden-Rockport Historical Society has restored this old farmhouse, which offers an authentic picture of Maine farm life during the 1700s. There is a blacksmith shop on the premises and a small historical museum.

OLD GERMAN MEETING HOUSE
Rte. 32, Waldoboro.
Season: June–Aug., daily
1–4.
Free.

This meetinghouse, which has a spectacular wineglass pulpit and striking, unpainted square-benched pews, was built in 1772 by the German families that settled the town 24 years earlier. The church was built on the eastern bank of the Medomak River, but later was moved to its current location.

ST. PATRICK'S CHURCH
207-563-3240.
Academy Hill Rd., just off
Rte. 1, Newcastle.

The oldest surviving Catholic church in New England, St. Patrick's was dedicated in 1808 and served a small group of Catholics who had emigrated from Ireland. The early Federal-style

Open year round 9 a.m.–
sundown.

church was designed by architect Nicholas Codd and built from locally fired bricks. The pews and colored glass window date from 1896, but mass has been served continually from the altar since 1808. Be sure to check out the Paul Revere church bell.

**WALDOBOROUGH
HISTORICAL SOCIETY**
Rte. 220, just south of
Rte. 1, Waldoboro.
Season: July & Aug.,
daily 1–4:30.
Admission free.

This is three buildings — a schoolhouse, a barn, and a small museum — in addition to an 1819 pound where stray livestock were impounded. The barn houses displays of old toys, period clothing, china, and glass, as well as a library and a reconstructed 19th-century kitchen and Victorian-style bedroom.

Down East / Acadia

THE WILSON MUSEUM
Perkins St., Castine.
Season: Late May–Sept.,
Tues.–Sun. 2–6.
Admission free.

This is really a series of several historic houses and commercial buildings, including a working blacksmith shop, the *Hearse House* (with 100-year-old summer and winter hearses) and the pre-Revolutionary *John Perkins House* (admission is charged here). The Wilson is home to a collection of prehistoric artifacts from North and South America, Europe, and Africa that stress man's development of tools from the Paleolithic to the Bronze and Iron ages. It also has a collection of ship models, rocks and minerals, and an 1805 kitchen exhibit.

**FORT GEORGE & FORT
MADISON**
Castine.
Season: Open year round.

Castine played a major role in the military history of the region, trading hands between the colonists and British during the Revolutionary War and after. Much of that military history can be told by these two forts located at opposite ends of the Castine peninsula. The Brits built Fort George in 1779 and only gave it up to the colonists at the close of the war. Excavation has exposed remnants of the old fort making this a great place to scramble over the ramparts.

When the British tried to reassume sovereignty over their former colonies during the War of 1812, this small community was one of their staging grounds. Fort Madison, on the other side of this small town from Fort George, was built in 1811 by the U.S. The British captured it in 1814, renamed it Fort Castine, and held the fort and the town until the close of the war one year later. This town owned park is a good staging ground for a picnic.

East of Schoodic

BURNHAM TAVERN
207-255-4432.
Main St., Machias.
Season:Summer,
  Mon.–Fri. 9–5; winter
  by appointment.
Admission: $2 adults;
  25¢ kids.

Revolutionary War afficionados will appreciate the importance of this 1770 gambrel-roofed tavern, the oldest building in the U.S. east of the Penobscot River. This was where local leaders met and planned the first naval battle of the war in which Machias patriots aboard the schooner *Unity* captured the British schooner *Margaretta*. The building also served as a hospital during the war and a meeting place for local Masons.

RUGGLES HOUSE
207-483-4637.
Just off Main St. (Rte. 1),
  Columbia Falls.
Season: June–mid-Oct.,
  weekdays 9:30–4:30;
  Sun. 11–4:30.

Judge Thomas Ruggles did it all; he was a lumber dealer, a store owner, the local postmaster, captain of the local militia, and a judge of the Court of Sessions. His house, designed by Massachusetts architect Aaron Sherman and built in 1818, befits a man of his many talents and high standing in society. The "flying" staircase is a marvel. So is the hand-carved woodwork, which took an English woodworker three years to complete.

LIBRARIES

South Coast

Dyer Library (207-283-3861; 371 Main St., Saco). Part of the York Institute Museum since 1976, the Dyer is home to genealogical materials, city records, and manuscripts of local interest.

Historical Society of Wells & Ogunquit (207-646-4775; Rte. 1, Wells). A collection of manuscripts and genealogies pertaining to the two towns and their early residents.

Ogunquit Memorial Library (207-646-9024; 74 Shore Rd., Ogunquit). Nannie Connarroe built the library in 1897 as a memorial to her late husband George M. Connarroe. It is on the National Register of Historical Places.

Rice Public Library (207-439-1553; 8 Wentworth St., Kittery). Housed in its original 1888 building, the Rice has an extensive collection of Maine books and historical materials on Kittery.

Casco Bay

Maine Historical Society Library (207-774-1822; 485 Congress St., Portland). More than 60,000 monographs and serials published after 1497, including the state's most comprehensive collection of historical documents and printed materials. Open Tues.–Fri. 10–4, and the second and fourth Sat. of every month 10–4.

Portland Public Library (207-871-1700 or 800-649-7697; 5 Monument Sq., Portland). One of the largest libraries in the state. The Portland Room houses an excellent Maine collection, including old children's books. Mon., Wed., Fri. 9–6; Tues., Thurs. noon–9; Sat. 9–5.

Salt Documentary Archive (207-761-0660; 19 Pine St., Portland). Collection of photographs and tape-recorded interviews detailing the way of life of people in Maine. Home of *Salt* magazine.

Midcoast

Bagaduce Music Lending Library (207-374-5454; Rte. 172, Greene's Hill, Blue Hill). A music resource with a collection of more than 500,000 items. Open year round: Tues. 10–6; Wed. & Fri. 10–3, or by appointment.

Farnsworth Art Museum Library (207-596-6457; 352 Main St., Rockland). A collection of art reference materials, including books, magazines, and videotapes in a handsome Greek Revival setting. Call for library hours.

Maine Crafts Association (207-348-9943; 6 Dow Rd., Deer Isle). The group has put together an impressive collection of books and periodicals for craftspersons. Members' portfolios are also on file. Open Mon.–Fri. 9–4; also Sat. 10–5 and Sun. 12–5 during the summer months.

Southport Memorial Library (207-633-2741; Cape Newagen). Home of one of the largest butterfly collections in the country. July–Aug., Tues. Thurs., and Sat. 1–4 and Tues. & Thurs. evenings 7–9.

Stephen Phillips Memorial Library (207-548-2529; Church Street, Searsport). Part of the Penobscot Marine Museum. Open April–Nov., Mon.–Fri. 9–4; Nov.–March, Tues.–Fri. 9:30–3:30.

Down East / Acadia

Jesup Memorial Library (207-288-4245; 34 Mount Desert St., Bar Harbor). An interesting collection of historical records of the island's past, including old hotel registers and scrapbooks, some with photos of the island before the 1947 fire. The library is open mid-June through Oct., Mon.–Sat. 1–4 and Wed. 7–9, and by appointment during the winter. Closed holidays.

LIGHTHOUSES

L ighthouse keepers are no more. Most of the lighthouses in the country have been automated. The historic, whitewashed lighthouse at *Goat Island,* near George Bush's Kennebunkport summer home, was automated in 1990 as a cost-saving measure by the government. With the lightkeeper retired, during the former president's term the island served as an air-sea command center that could warn the Secret Service if a plane was headed toward Walkers Point — that's the huge, black, constantly whirling radar beacon that stands next to the old lighthouse.

All told, there are 60 lighthouses along the coast of Maine (we've listed some of the more prominent ones below). Each has its own legends of shipwrecks, ghosts, drownings, and rescues. Some now serve as museums, private homes, or bed and breakfasts.

Today, there are societies dedicated to the restoration and preservation of these symbols of our maritime heritage: the **Lighthouse Preservation Society** (508-281-6336, Rockport, MA 01966) and the **United States Lighthouse Society** (415-362-7255; 244 Kearny St., Fifth Floor, San Francisco, CA 94108).

If you'd like to get a bird's eye view of midcoast lighthouses, **Acadia Air** out of Bar Harbor Airport offers a lighthouse flight. The 45-minute flight provides panoramic views and commentary on six historic lighthouses and the surrounding coast. For information call the airline (207-667-5534). To view inaccessible lighthouses way Down East and catch sight of a local colony of puffins or seals, you can sign up for a lighthouse cruise with **Capts. Barna and John Norton** (207-497-5933; Rte. 187, West Jonesport 04649-9704). If you'd like to spend the night in a lighthouse, try the **Keeper's House** on the tranquil island of Isle au Haut (see Chapter Three, *Lodging*). If you'd like to learn more about lighthouses, visit the **Museum at Portland Head Light** in Cape Elizabeth or the **Shore Village Museum** in Rockland (see "Museums," below). It has one of the largest collections of lighthouse material in the country.

South Coast

You can check out **Cape Neddick Light** from Sohier Park (follow the signs leading off Rte 1A in York). Stay for a picnic. This is a lovely park with interesting rock formations and good vantages for birdwatching. The lighthouse was built in 1879.

Casco Bay

Portland Head Light (207-799-2661; Shore Rd., Cape Elizabeth), constructed in 1791 at the order of President George Washington, is the oldest on the East Coast. The lighthouse and quarters were renovated in 1992 and now are home to the Museum at Portland Head Light. The lighthouse and museum adjoin Fort Williams Park, a pretty seaside park complete with ruins of an old fort built in the late 1800s, tennis courts, and a baseball diamond. The town park is open year round. The museum is open on weekends off season and daily during the summer.

Contrary to its name, the **Cape Elizabeth Light at Two Lights State Park**

*The Pumpkin Island Light
in Penobscot Bay is near
Deer Isle. Built in 1854, it
is visible from the air but
hard to see from land.*

Tom Hindman

(Two Lights Rd. off Rte. 77, Cape Elizabeth) is only one working lighthouse. In 1824, two lights were built to mark the spot. In 1874, the lighthouses were rebuilt and only one remains active today. This park is a favorite summer evening cool spot for local residents.

Midcoast

As far as Maine lighthouses go, ***Grindle Point Light***, built in 1935, is young. Today the building on Isleboro houses the ***Sailor's Memorial Museum***. It is open mid-June through Labor Day. Call the Islesboro Town Hall for more information (207-734-2253).

Marshall Point Light (1895) in Port Clyde is home to a collection of light-house memorabilia. It is open weekend afternoons in May, September, and October, and Tuesday through Sunday afternoons in June, July, and August (207-372-6450).

A ferry ride away, the keeper's house at ***Monhegan Island Light*** (1824) is worth a visit because it now serves as a museum that contains exhibits of the island's native plants, wildlife, and Native American artifacts.

Owls Head Light sits on a park called the U.S. Lighthouse Reservation (near Thomaston). The light was built in 1826 and is located at the head of the Saint George Peninsula on West Penobscot Bay. Although Owls Head Light is only 26 ft. high, it can be seen from 16 miles at sea.

Pemaquid Lighthouse Park (Lighthouse Rd. off Rte. 130, Pemaquid Point) is a good place to relax for a picnic. The lighthouse was built in 1827, and the keeper's house has been converted to an art gallery and museum featuring exhibits about saltwater fishing.

You can walk on the breakwater $^7/_8$ mi. to the ***Rockland Lighthouse*** (take

Rte. 1 north to Waldo Ave. and Samoset Rd.). A favorite fishing spot is at the end of the breakwater under the lighthouse.

East of Schoodic

The boldly striped light at **West Quoddy Head** in Lubec sits at the easternmost point in the U.S. It was built in 1807 and was featured on a 1990 U.S. Postal Service stamp commemorating the 100th anniversary of the Coast Guard.

MUSEUMS

There are more than 115 registered museums in Maine, and it is estimated there would be more than 300 if you count all the small private collections of painting, sculpture, memorabilia, ephemera, and historical bric-a-brac that are put on display here. Here is a list of a few museums on the coast.

South Coast

AUTO MUSEUM AT WELLS
207-646-9064.
1181 Post Rd., Wells.
Season: Mid-June–mid-Sept.: daily 10–5 p.m.; Memorial Day–Columbus Day, weekends 10–5 p.m.
Admission: $4 adults; $2 children 6–12; under 6 free.

Once a private collection, now a nonprofit car-lovers' organization, this museum has a collection of more than 70 gas-, steam-, and electric-powered automobiles that have been restored. Stanley Steamers, Rolls Royces, Fords, and motorcycles, license plates, bicycles, antique toys, and nickelodeons, this is an entertaining look at our motoring past among other things. Particularly fun are rides in one of the museum's Model T's.

BRICK STORE MUSEUM
207-985-4802.
117 Main St., Kennebunk.
Open year round except Dec. 15–Jan. 1: Mon.–Sat. 10–4:30. Mid-Dec.–mid-April: Tues.–Sat. 10–4:30.
Free.

This museum that tells the story of Kennebunk began as a small collection of artifacts on display in the town's old general store. These days it encompasses an entire block and runs changing exhibits that tell about the region's maritime and social history. From June to September, the museum offers guided walking tours pointing out the town's architectural highlights.

KITTERY HISTORICAL AND NAVAL MUSEUM
207-439-3080.
Located near the intersection of Rte. 1 and Rte. 236, next to the Town

Kittery is Maine's oldest town, and this relatively young museum (1976) commemorates the port's history as a shipbuilding town. There is a 12-foot model of the *Ranger*, John Paul Jones' ship that had its keel laid here. There are other exhibits

Office on the Rogers Rd. Extension.
Season: June–late Oct.: weekdays 10–4, or by appointment.
Admission: $3 adults; $1.50 kids 7–15; those under 7 free; families of 3 or more, $6 max.

MAINE AQUARIUM
207-284-4511 (recorded message).
Rte. 1 (2 mi. north of exit 2B on Maine Turnpike), Saco.
Season: Open year round: daily 9-5.
Admission: $6.50 adults; $5.50 seniors; $4.50 children 5 to 12 years; $2.50 children 2 to 4 years.

OGUNQUIT MUSEUM OF AMERICAN ART
207-646-4909.
183 Shore Rd., Ogunquit.
Season: July 1–September 1: daily, 10:30–5. Sun., 2–5.
Admission: $3 adults; $2 seniors and students; those under 12 free.

SEASHORE TROLLEY MUSEUM
207-967-2800.
195 Log Cabin Rd., Kennebunkport.
Season: Early May–Oct., daily; winter by appointment.
Donations.

about the accomplishments of the naval yard, the first U.S. shipyard and the one responsible for the building of several Civil War ships, as well as the country's first submarine.

Sharks! Penguins! Seals! Live sea animals from the world over are on display in this zoo of underwater creatures. Aquatic animals from the Gulf of Maine and a "touchable" tidepool full of seashore plants and animals for the young ones (summer only). The aquarium also features a unique blue lobster that has been described as "one in a million"!

Built by the painter Henry Strater, the museum houses a good collection of 20th-century American artists who came here to scramble over the rocks, soak up the summer sun and, of course, paint and sculpt. A late director of the Metropolitan Museum of Art described this as a gem, "the most beautiful small museum in the world." A new wing has been added to house special summer shows and selections from the permanent collection. Works on view are by Walt Kuhn, Marsden Hartley, Rockwell Kent, and others.

Back when mass transportation was fashionable, handsome trolleys like the ones on display here carried passengers almost everywhere. If you made your connections right, you could trolley all the way from Washington, D. C. to Portland. This museum has the world's largest and oldest collection — more than 100 vintage cars from Biddeford, Saco, San Francisco, Nagasaki, and Rome. It also operates a two-mile stretch of track for sunset trolley rides and a streetcar workshop where visitors can see a trolley restoration in process. Call or write them for a list of special streetcar events sponsored by the museum throughout the year.

YORK INSTITUTE MUSEUM
207-283-0958 or 207-283-0684.
371 Main St., Saco.
Season: Year round, Tues., Wed., Fri., Sun. 12–4.; Thurs., 12–8.
Admission: $4 adults; $3 seniors; $1 students; $10 family.

This regional history and art museum has been a growing concern since 1866. Exhibits of paintings, textiles, household items, and furnishings from several periods in American history, including Colonial, Federal, and Colonial Revival. The adjoining gallery hosts changing art exhibits, and the library has an excellent Maine history collection.

Casco Bay

CHILDREN'S MUSEUM OF MAINE
207-828-1234
142 Free Street, Portland.
Open year round: Mon.-Sat. 10-5; Fri. 10-8; Sun. 12-5.
Admission: $4 children and adults; children under one free.

The museum moved to its spiffy new quarters next door to the Portland Museum of Art in 1993 and was an instant hit with kids and parents. Not only are there many "hands-on" exhibits covering the science bases, but the museum also pays homage to commerce and business. Among other entertaining experiences are exhibits that show how a bank, a supermarket, a jet, and a farm work. Check out the Camera Obscura at the top, which on clear days offers a bird's eye view of Portland and the islands of Casco Bay.

DESERT OF MAINE
207-865-6962.
95 Desert Rd. (just off Rte. 1 and I-95), Freeport.
Season: Early May–mid-Oct., daily 9–6.
Admission: $6.50 adults; $4.50 ages 14–16; $2.50 ages 6–12; children 5 and under free.

The first chapter in the history of this geologic oddity occurred during the Ice Age, when glaciers deposited sand and minerals. During the late 1700s and early 1800s a family of farmers came, clearcut the land, grew crops, grazed their animals, and failed to use good farming techniques to prevent erosion of the thin layer of topsoil. What remains is a genuine sand desert smack in the middle of coastal Maine, a favorite local tourist attraction since the mid-1930s. Walking and coach tours available. Gift shop, picnic grounds and campground on the premises.

PEARY-MacMILLAN ARCTIC MUSEUM
207-725-3304.
Hubbard Hall, Bowdoin College, Brunswick.
Open year round: Tues.–Sat. 10–5; Sun. 2–5.

Admirals Robert E. Peary and Donald B. MacMillan were both graduates of Bowdoin College, and this museum commemorates their joint explorations. Peary was the first man to reach the North Pole on April 6, 1909; MacMillan was Peary's chief assistant on that expedition.

Guided tours available during the academic year; call to schedule.

Exhibits include the log and a sledge from the 1909 expedition, as well as displays of Inuit art and artifacts from Labrador and Greenland that MacMillan gathered on subsequent expeditions to the north.

The Portland Museum of Art.

Herb Swanson

PORTLAND MUSEUM OF ART
207-773-2787.
7 Congress Sq., Portland.
Open year round: Mon., Tues., Wed., & Sat. 10–5; Thurs., Fri. 10–9; Sun. 12–5.
Admission: $6 adults; $ 5 seniors and students; $1 youths 6–12; children under six free.

Maine's oldest public museum resides in an impressive granite and brick structure designed by I. M. Pei. Inside exhibit space is open and airy, much like space Pei designed for the East Wing of the National Gallery of Art in Washington, D. C. The permanent collection includes a worthwhile selection of American and European art, including paintings by Van Gogh, Picasso, Degas, and many by Winslow Homer (he painted and lived part of the year at Prouts Neck, about 15 minutes from the museum) and a significant holding of Colonial and Federal portraits. The museum also is temporary home to visiting exhibitions. On Fridays after 5 p.m. the doors are opened free of charge.

WALKER ART MUSEUM
207-725-3275.
Bowdoin College, Brunswick.
Open year round. Tues.– Sat. 10–5; Sun. 2–5.

A beautiful Greek Revival building houses the museum's permanent collections including ancient Mediterranean art and European and American paintings, sculpture, drawings, prints, and photos. Of special interest are the selection of

Closed Mondays and
national holidays.
Free.

Midcoast

**BOOTHBAY RAILWAY
VILLAGE**
207-633-4727.
Rte. 27, Boothbay.
Season: Mid-June to
Columbus Day, daily
9:30–5.

**BULL MOOSE
RAILROAD**
207-338-2931.
11 Water St. off City
Landing, Belfast.
Season: June–mid-Oct.,
several one-hour runs a
day. Call for schedule.
Admission charged.

FARNSWORTH MUSEUM
207-596-6457.
352 Main St. (off Rte. 1),
Rockland.
Season: Memorial
Day–Columbus Day;
Mon.–Sat. 9–5, Sun. 12–5.
Closed Mon. during
winter months.
Admission: $5 adults; $4
seniors; $3 ages 8–18;
children under 8 free.

Colonial and Federal portraits and paintings by
Winslow Homer, John Sloan, and Rockwell Kent.
The museum also regularly features changing art
exhibits.

They have recreated a quaint New England village and its transportation system on eight acres
here. There are more than 24 buildings of historical
exhibits and 60 vehicles on display, including a
steam locomotive, which for 15 minutes carries you
back to a simpler time on 1.5 miles of narrow-gauge
track. A doll museum is on the premises.

The Belfast & Moosehead Lake Railroad (nick
named "Bull Moose") was founded in 1867 to
carry lumber from inland Maine to the coast. That
plan was short-circuited only a few years later
when B&ML RR decided to hook up with the
Maine Central Railroad just 33 miles inland. These
days, the line is operated by the City of Belfast,
and its mixed freight and passenger runs are
shorter. Visitors are invited to ride the rails for a
one-hour excursion along the coast several times a
day.

One of our favorite museums, the story behind
the Farnsworth is nearly as fascinating as its
collection. The citizens of Rockland were stunned
in 1935 when their neighbor Lucy Copeland
Farnsworth left $1.3 million and instructions that
the money be used to build a library and one-room
art museum. The mystery? During her lifetime,
Ms. Farnsworth had never been known to be an
art lover. With a little finagling, the Farnsworth
legacy became one of the best regional collections
in the country. The home of this collection is a well
kept complex with the museum, an excellent art
library, and the Farnsworth Homestead (1850), a gorgeous Greek Revival
home with original high-Victorian furnishing and decor. The focus of the
museum's permanent collection is on American art and includes work by the
Wyeths, Winslow Homer, John Marin, Fitz Hugh Lane, Edward Hopper, Neil
Welliver, and sculptor Louise Nevelson. The Farnsworth will be undergoing a

capital campaign for the construction of a 2-part Farnsworth Center for the Wyeth Family in Maine. The addition will include a renovated Pratt Memorial Church featuring works by Jamie and N.C. Wyeth, and a new wing showing pieces by artist Andrew Wyeth.

FRIENDSHIP MUSEUM
Call the town office for
   more information:
   207-832-7644.
Rte. 220 and Martin's Pond
   Rd., Friendship.
Open Mon.–Sat. noon–5.
Donations welcome.

A one-room brick schoolhouse dedicated to the history of the Friendship sloop.

**OLD LINCOLN COUNTY
   JAIL & MUSEUM**
207-882-6817.
Rte. 218, Federal St.,
   Wiscasset.
Season: July–Aug.,
   Tues.–Sat. 11–4.
Admission: $2 adults; $1
   children.

An unusual view of life in the 19th century. Visitors can peruse prisoners' cells with original graffiti. The jail was built in 1811, has granite walls 41 inches thick, and saw service as recently as 1953. Inside the jailer's house there is a display of early American tools, costumes, artifacts, and changing exhibits about local history.

**MAINE MARITIME
   MUSEUM**
207-443-1316.
243 Washington St., Bath.
Open year round 9:30–5
   except Thanksgiving,
   Christmas and New
   Year's Day.
Admission: $7.75 adults; $5
   children 6 to 17; $20 per
   family.

With an abundance of interpretive and hands-on exhibits, ships you can climb aboard, and a museum-sponsored narrated cruise along the waterfront, this is a great museum for visitors of every age. The core of the museum is the Percy & Small Shipyard (open late spring through late fall), the only surviving shipyard in the country where large wooden sailing ships were built at the turn of the century. It is also home to the *Sherman Zwicker*, a Grand Banks fishing schooner, visiting historic boats that stop in during the warm months.

**MUSICAL WONDER-
   HOUSE**
207-882-7163.
18 High St., Wiscasset.
Season: Late May–late Oct.,
   daily 10–5.
Admission: $1 general
   admittance fee. One-hour
   guided presentations: $10
   adults; $7.50 seniors and
   children under 12. Three-
   hour guided presentations

For more than 30 years, travelers and music lovers from around the world have made their way to view Danilo Konvalinka's marvelous collection of restored music boxes and musical instruments on display in a handsome Greek Revival ship captain's home. Many are works of art and are capable of playing complicated songs with a wide range of notes. Some date from 1750. There are pocket boxes and floor models. He also keeps player pianos and other mechanical musical available by appointment only: $30 per person, $50 per couple.

OWLS HEAD TRANSPORTATION MUSEUM
207-594-4418.
Rte. 73, Owls Head.
Season: May–Oct.,
Mon.–Sat. 10–5;
Nov.–April 10–4.
Admission: $6 adults; $4 children under 12; under 6 free. Special events: $7 adults; $5 children under 12. Members: free.

treasures. Konvalinka also buys, sells, and repairs music boxes. Ask about the candlelight concerts.

An interesting collection of pioneer aircraft, automobiles, engines, motorcycles, bicycles, and carriages — almost anything that moves. The museum has guided tours of these conveyances, all of which are run from time to time. Some planes and vehicles operated on weekends.

The Penobscot Marine Museum

The Penobscot Marine Museum is housed in several period buildings in Searsport, which during the 1800s was a lively port and home to hundreds of ships' captains. The museum has one of the largest collections of marine paintings in the world.

PENOBSCOT MARINE MUSEUM
207-548-2529.
Church St., Searsport.
Season: Memorial
Day–mid-Oct.: Mon.–Sat.
10–5; Sun. 12–5.
Admission: $5 adults; $4 senior citizens; $2 children 7–15; under 6 free.

At the height of the shipping industry in Maine during the 19th century, 10 percent of America's deep water shipmasters lived in Searsport. They brought mementos of the world back to this pretty little town. This museum, consisting of nine buildings restored or converted to individually themed galleries, is a terrific place to spend the day. It is home to one of the largest collections of marine paintings in the state, including ship portraits commissioned and painted in the ports of Europe and China. The Old Town Hall is devoted to the description of the great Down Easters, the square-rigged vessels built in Maine during the late 1800s. The museum sponsors annual events, concerts, lectures, and readings by Maine authors.

SHORE VILLAGE MUSEUM
207-594-0311.
104 Limerock St., Rockland.
Season: June–mid-Oct., daily 10–4; by appointment the rest of the year.
Donations.

This small, lively museum situated on an old Rockland street is crammed to the rafters with an odd and ever growing assortment of historical materials: the world's largest selection of lighthouse paraphernalia from old candle-powered lights to the latest solar-powered lenses; Coast Guard memorabilia; uniforms, weapons, and papers concerning the Maine soldiers who fought in the Civil War; and the Llewella Mills collection of 34 dolls dressed in period costumes from the Middle Ages to the Gay '90s (she was a sea captain's daughter).

Down East/Acadia

ROBERT ABBE MUSEUM OF STONE AGE ANTIQUITIES
207-288-2179.
Rte. 3 near Sieur de Monts Spring, Acadia National Park.
Season: Spring and fall, 10–4; summer, 9–5.
Admission: $2 adults; 50¢ children 12 and under.

This impressive small museum houses a record of Maine's native inhabitants of 11,000 years ago to now. Stone tools, baskets, musical instruments, and ornaments — some as old as 5,000 years — and a canoe made from a single piece of birch bark are among the items that have been brought together from the Frenchman Bay and Mount Desert Island area. During the summer weekends members of the Micmac, Maleseet, Passamaquoddy, and Penobscot tribes demonstrate Native American art such as basket and jewelry making.

WENDELL GILLEY MUSEUM OF BIRD CARVING
207-244-7555.
Herrick Rd. and Main St. (Rte. 102), Southwest Harbor.
Season: Closed at the end of January for the winter.
Call for museum hours.
Admission: $3 adults; $1 children; free to members.

Wendell Gilley was a plumber until he decided to turn in the wrench and devote himself to his hobby full time. He carved birds, more than 10,000 of them. Beautiful specimens of airborne nature — wooden eagles, chickadees, ducks, owls, and tiny lyrical songbirds. His birds are in full feather and on view here.

JACKSON LABORATORY
207-288-3371.

The Jackson Laboratory was founded in 1929, and since that time has made a name for itself in the

600 Main St., Bar Harbor.
Season: Mid-June–Aug.,
    Call for hours and dates.
No

world of mammalian genetic research. Currently the laboratory performs research on such varied human maladies as obesity, cancer, AIDS, allergies, diabetes, reproductive disorders, aging, and transplantation rejection. It also raises more than 1,300 genetically unique laboratory mice and sells them to research scientists around the world. They offer a one-hour lecture and multimedia presentation describing the lab's mission and ongoing research every Tuesday and Thursday at 2 p.m.

**M.D.I. BIOLOGICAL
LABORATORY**
207-288-3606.
Old Bar Harbor Rd., Rte. 3
    (northwest of Bar Harbor), Salisbury Cove.
Season: July–Aug., Wed.
    only, 1:30.
No charge.

M.D.I. is a laboratory that conducts research in marine organisms. While most of its work is confined to animals that live in the sea, it has many implications for human health and the environment. Once a week the lab provides the public an opportunity to see what goes on here during a lecture, tour, and video presentation.

**MOUNT DESERT
ISLAND HISTORICAL
SOCIETY**
207-244-5043.
Rte. 102, Somesville, Mount
    Desert Island.
Season: June–Oct.,
    Tues.–Sat. 10–5.
Admission: $1.

Bric-a-brac and other interesting stuff from Mount Desert's past including period clothing, furniture, early household items, sleigh bells, guns from the Revolutionary War days, and old pewter. Tools from the wool, grist, saw, tannery, and barrel stave mills that were operated nearby. Kids will want to see Dr. Nehemiah Kittredge's tooth extractor. It will make them cringe.

**MOUNT DESERT
OCEANARIUM**
207-288-5005.
Two locations: Rte. 3,
    Thomas Bay, Bar Harbor;
    Clark Point Rd.,
    Southwest Harbor.
Season: Both mid-May–Oct.
    9–5.
Nominal admission.

The two museums are fun stops for any aquatic-minded tourist, particularly the younger ones. The Thomas Bay branch is home to some happy harbor seals, and, at the Maine Lobster Museum, a licensed lobster fisherman will take you aboard a real lobster boat and answer your questions about crustaceans (the organization also offers a guided walk through Thomas Bay Marsh). There is a working lobster hatchery on the grounds where you can see between 5,000 and 10,000 tiny lobsters being raised for future release in the Gulf of Maine. The Southwest Harbor Oceanarium, located right next to the Coast Guard base, has 20 tanks filled with resident Maine sea life, a touch tank, and an audio-visual exhibit where you can hear whale songs.

COLLEGE OF THE ATLANTIC NATURAL HISTORY MUSEUM
207-288-5015.
College of the Atlantic, 105 Eden St., just north of Bar Harbor.
Season: Memorial Day–Labor Day, daily 9–5. Labor Day–Columbus Day, daily 10–4.
Admission: $2.50 adults; $1.50 seniors and teens (13–18); $1 children ages 3–12.

In earlier times this lovely granite summer cottage was known as the Turrets. Today it is a museum that offers an environmental perspective on Mount Desert Island. On display are interpretive exhibits about more than 50 species of island animals, plants, and trees. Every day at 11 a.m., there is a free program open to all visitors; and the museum hosts weekly evening lectures on topics regarding the native populations of the island from Native Americans to seabirds and coyotes. Call for a schedule of events.

STATE OF MAINE
207-326-2255.
Maine Maritime Academy, Castine.
Season: mid-July–late April.
Free.

This is the training ship for students at nearby Maine Maritime Academy. When it is in port, you can go aboard for a free tour and check it out. Call for scheduled times.

East of Schoodic

WAPONAHKI MUSEUM AND RESOURCE CENTER
207-853-4001.
Pleasant Point Indian Reservation, Perry.
Season: Mon.–Fri., 9–11, 1–3.
Donations.

The Passamaquoddy Indians were among the tribes that once inhabited Maine shores during the summer. After Europeans settled the coast, their numbers diminished. In 1822 there were 379 Passamaquoddy. Today there are more than 2,000. This museum offers a glimpse of their rich culture through the implements they fashioned from nature — graceful birch bark canoes, handsome ash baskets, snowshoes, clothing, and arrowheads. Also on exhibit are photographs that document life on the reservation in the past and present. The museum is a repository for a growing collection of books, tapes, dictionaries, and reference books, all of which serve to preserve the Passamaquoddy language. Classes in the tribe's new written language are taught here.

Near the Coast

Both of these museums are near enough to the coast and worthwhile enough for a half-day excursion.

ROOSEVELT CAMPOBELLO PARK

Just a stone's throw from Lubec sits the island summer home of former U.S. President Franklin

Herb Swanson

The lighthouse on Campobello Island, where FDR summered.

Campobello Island, New
 Brunswick.
Free.

D. Roosevelt. Although on Canadian soil, the historic site is maintained jointly by the U.S. and Canada and the only auto route to the island is via the international bridge at Lubec (a ferry provides access on the Canadian side). The house recently has been restored and contains many of the Roosevelt family's original furnishings.

SHAKER MUSEUM
Sabbathday Lake, Rte. 26,
 Poland Spring.
Season: Memorial
 Day–Columbus Day,
 10– 4:30. Closed Sundays.
Nominal admission.

A small community of Shakers still lives and works here today, tending their gardens, drying herbs, and preserving the Shaker heritage. The view from this historic hillside religious community is breathtaking. Once inside the small, spare buildings on the compound, you begin to understand why the Shakers' simple, elegant style of dress and furniture is so popular even today. Shaker furniture, tools, textiles, tin, woodenware, and folk art are on display, and if you like, you can sign up for a guided walking tour of the village.

MUSIC

Music is a passion on the coast. Small chamber groups like the *Portland String Quartet* and amateur opera companies such as the *Surry Opera Company* in Surry, make sure there's a program of good music year round.

During the past century and a half the coast has been home to many musicians as well. American composer and Harvard professor Walter Piston

Band concert in Boothbay Harbor.

Herb Swanson

(1894–1976) was born in Rockland. French-born conductor Pierre Monteux (1875–1964) once made his home in Hancock, a small hamlet outside of Bar Harbor. Although he led world-class orchestras in Boston, Paris, and San Francisco, he took great pride in being named chief of Hancock's Volunteer Fire Department. Today Hancock hosts a music festival named for him, and the school he founded for conductors still convenes every summer. Portland is home to the famed Kotzschmar Memorial Organ at the Merrill Auditorium. Citizens are working to have the organ, which is dusted off for periodic recitals, fully restored to its former glory.

Harps, dulcimers, brass quintets, jazz quartets — the coast is home to dozens of musical groups and festivals every year. Below we've listed some of the larger and better-known musical organizations on the coast. But be warned, there are many more. For a comprehensive schedule of musical events for the area you plan to visit, contact the local chamber of commerce (see *Information*, Chapter Eight).

Casco Bay

CUMBERLAND COUNTY CIVIC CENTER
207-775-3458.
1 Civic Center Sq. (at the corner of Spring and Center Sts.), Portland.
Open year round.
Tickets: $6–$35, depending on event.

The acoustics aren't great, but that doesn't daunt folks who travel from way Down East and the far northern reaches of the state to hear good music. Folk, rock, heavy metal plus the occasional circus, ice show or traveling Broadway hit play here.

PCA GREAT PERFORMANCES
207-773-3150.

Every year this group books a range of traveling talent from perennial favorites like the Canadian Brass Ensemble or the Flying Karamazov

477 Congress St., Portland.
Season: Oct.–June.
Tickets: $10–$50.

Brothers to world class performers like Isaac Stern and the New York City Opera Company. Concerts are held at the Merrill Auditorium.

Music Director and Conductor Toshiyuki Shimada conducts the 81-member Portland Symphony Orchestra at Merrill Auditorium.

Courtesy Portland Symphony Orchestra

PORTLAND STRING QUARTET
207-761-1522.
22 Monument Sq., Portland.
P.O. Box 11, Portland 04112.
Season: Oct.–April.
Tickets: $22 single concert;
$77 season's pass (4 concerts).

This is one of the few classical quartets to endure a quarter of a century rehearsing, touring, and performing together without a single change in personnel. The result is a mature sound that can take on the most difficult work and play it beautifully. The group's music is an impeccably performed mix of classic and new chamber works commissioned for the group. When this talented quartet isn't on the road, they perform at an auditorium at Maine Medical Center.

PORTLAND SYMPHONY ORCHESTRA
207-773-8191 or
800-639-2309.
30 Myrtle St. off Congress,
Portland.
Concerts throughout the year.

Portland is the smallest city in the U.S. to have a full-time symphony orchestra, and local audiences are extremely appreciative. The symphony, under conductor and music director Toshiyuki Shimada, performs the classics and pops most of the year in the Portland City Hall Auditorium just down the street from their offices. During the summer, they take to the outdoors with a series of concerts at beautiful Fort Williams Park in Cape Elizabeth.

Midcoast

BAY CHAMBER CONCERTS
207-236-2823 or
888-707-2770.

This group has brought music to mid-coast-Maine for nearly 40 years. The summer season runs from mid-July through August, and includes

P.O. Box 191, Camden
   04843.
Season: Winter series:
   Oct.–June; summer series
   July & Aug.
Tickets: Winter $5–$12;
   Summer $7–$17.

twice weekly lectures and concerts with the Vermeer Quartet and guest artists. The organization also promotes the music of young performers with five prizes to Maine musicians and its Next Generation program in August. During the winter the group sponsors monthly classical and jazz concerts by world-renowned artists. All concerts take place at the renovated Rockport Opera House.

**ROUND TOP CENTER
   FOR THE ARTS**
207-563-1507.
Bus. Rte. 1, Damariscotta.
Open year round.
Tickets: $8–$14 for music
   and theater events; $2
   and up for craft and art
   shows.

The Round Top was a dairy farm in a former life. The cows are long gone, but you can still enjoy 30 flavors of the ice cream made here. Now the farm's main product is music, theater, arts, and crafts, taught and put on display. Business has been so good they can hardly restore and convert the old farm's buildings fast enough to accommodate the growth. During the warm weather many of their concerts, children's and adults' plays, art and crafts shows, lectures and workshops are staged outside. Come winter, activities move indoors. One of their most anticipated events is the annual Festival Day and Concert on the Lawn. This event is fun for everyone, with children's activities and crafts in the morning and orchestra or brass quintet music in the evening. People sprawl out on the lawn with blankets and picnic baskets for a jam-packed day of fun and enjoyment.

Down East/Acadia

**MOUNT DESERT
   FESTIVAL OF
   CHAMBER MUSIC**
207-276-3988.
Mount Desert Island.
Tuesday concerts from
   mid-July–Aug.

Since the late '60s the Composers String Quartet, a resident ensemble, has celebrated the works of Hadyn, Schumann, Brahms, and Bartók as well as other classical and contemporary composers.

**SURRY OPERA
   COMPANY**
207-667-9551.
Surry 04684.
Season: Call for schedule.

Walter Nowick founded this small, amateur opera company in 1984 with high aims — "to promote beautiful music and work toward peace through people-to-people experiences." During the summer of 1991 the group hosted a festival of Russian opera with the Leningrad Amateur Opera Company.

East of Schoodic

**MACHIAS BAY CHAM-
   BER CONCERTS**

This group has brought classical chamber music to Machias for almost a quarter of a century.

207-483-6631.
P.O. Box 332, Machias 04654
Season: July–early Aug.
Tickets: $8 adults; $5 students; under 12 free.

Many of the same instrumental groups that play in Rockport's Bay Chamber series play here in the Machias Congregational Church, which is known for its excellent acoustics. The series of six concerts begins on the first Tuesday evening after July 4.

STAGE FRONT: THE ARTS DOWNEAST
207-255-1200.
9 O'Brien Ave., Machias.
Season: early Sept.–April.
Tickets: $5–$9.

Folk music from Bolivia, gospel, jazz, classical, and country music. For 13 years Stage Front has been bringing a broad spectrum of music to the Performing Arts Center at the University of Maine, Machias. The group also sponsors theater and dance performances.

The Hallowell Community Band performs on the green in Boothbay Harbor.

Herb Swanson

Seasonal Music Events

Annual Bar Harbor Music Festival (212-222-1026; 207-288-5744 after July 1; locations throughout Bar Harbor). This series of classical, jazz, and pops concerts, with an emphasis on young and upcoming talent, celebrated its 30th year in 1996. The Festival has a series of 9 or 10 concerts, three of which offer a buffet dinner. Admission is $15 adults; $10 seniors and students; $18 dinner and music. Season: Mid-July–mid-August. Call box office for scheduled times and events.

Annual Bluegrass Festival (207-725-6009; Thomas Point Beach, Brunswick). This Bluegrass music fest is the finale to a long season of camping, music, and fun. Take in just a day of this country music with a twang or stay for the whole weekend. Date: Labor Day weekend. Admission: $15–$30, day; $65–$80, weekend (music and accommodations); children under 12 free.

Annual Downeast Jazz Festival (207-594-1837; Rockport). Jazz greats gather every summer for this day of music. A jazz luncheon is offered in the afternoon, with three hours of food and music, while night time concerts take place separately later in the evening. Admission: $15, afternoon luncheon; $10–$12, evening. Call for more information.

Annual Rockport Folk Festival (207-594-1041; Rockport Opera House). For more than two decades top folk singers have collected here in mid-July.

The Arcady Music Festival (207-288-3151; Mount Desert Island High School). Guest artists perform every Mon., Tues., and Thurs. for seven weeks throughout the summer. The season commences in mid-July. Call for locations.

Downeast Dulcimer & Harp Festival (207-288-5653; Agamont Park & Congregational Church, Bar Harbor). Song sharing, workshops, and concerts featuring these traditional American instruments. Early July.

Lincoln Arts Festival (888-337-2710). An annual festival of choral and classical music performances by American musicians held in various locations in the Boothbay area. There are more than a dozen performances throughout the summer, including a jazz weekend. Season: mid-June–Sept. Admission: prices vary with each performance.

NIGHTLIFE

South Coast

The Brunswick (207-934-4873; 39 West Grand Ave., Old Orchard Beach).

The Club (207-646-6655 or 207-646-2345; 13 Main St., Ogunquit). This is the place to dance on the south coast.

Federal Jack's Brew Pub (207-967-4322; 8 Western Ave., Kennebunk). Live music on the weekend, and the neighborhood brew on tap.

The Front Porch Cafe (207-646-3976; Ogunquit Square, Ogunquit). Listen to the strains of the piano until the wee hours in this piano bar. There is also a restaurant here.

Marvin's Brick Oven Tavern (207-967-3358 or 207-967-8373; Ocean Ave., Kennebunkport). Catch a bite to eat while watching the brick oven pizza being made or listening to the sounds of an acoustic guitar. An accordion player also roams the tavern on occasion.

Norton's Sports Bar and Music Club (207-439-7892; 518 Rte. 1, Kittery).

One Soho Square (207-934-4524; 43 West Grand Ave. (the Oceanic Inn), Old Orchard Beach). This subterranean British pub features over 40 different brews, the occasional live band, and a deli.

Pockets II (207-284-9283; 23 Lincoln St., Biddeford). Pool, darts, live bands, burgers, and club sandwiches.

Port Gardens Pub (207-967-3358; Ocean Ave., Kennebunkport). A place for Bush watchers to relax.

Shelley's (207-284-9283; 12 Lincoln St., Biddeford). Karaoke, pool, darts, and proper dress.

Casco Bay

The Asylum (207-772-8274; 121 Center St., Portland). People are becoming 'totally committed' to the Asylum with its dance club, sports bar, and restaurant. The club features both live bands and DJs playing Disco, House & Hip Hop, Latino, modern rock, and R&B. Open for lunch and dinner, 11 am to 1 am.

Bad Habits Live & Zootz (207-773-8187; 31 Forest Ave., Portland). Club where there's more dancing than listening to regional and touring acts. DJ plays eclectic selection. This is Portland's best place to dance.

The Big Easy (207-780-1207; 416 Fore St., Portland). Somehow they pack a band and an audience into this tiny blues bar.

The Comedy Connection (207-774-5554; 6 Custom House Wharf, Portland). A barrelful of laughs at Maine's only full-time professional stand-up comedy club. The Connection has had many of their comedians receive nationwide recognition from "the Tonight Show" and "Saturday Night Live," among others. A light fare menu and wait service is available before, during, or after the show at the Waterfront Cafe. Reservations welcomed.

Granny Killam's Industrial Drink House (207-761-5865; 164 Middle St., Portland). A basement dance club. Granny's has a full bar and offers the occasional all ages dance night.

The Industry (207-879-0865; 50 Wharf St., Portland). A hopping dance club for those 18 and older. Serves alcohol and is open Friday and Saturday nights.

Morganfield's (207-774-JUKE; 121 Center St.) A full diet of the blues and 77 microbrews.

The Night Crawler (207-874-6484; 51 Oak St., Portland). A perfect stop for those who wish to be out at night, but don't want to go to a bar. The Night Crawler has a light but interesting menu, just right for a little something after a movie or a show. Music, B.Y.O.B.

Raoul's Roadside Attraction (207-773-6886; 865 Forest Ave., 1.5 mi. from exit 6B,I-295, Portland). Bands play rock, country, pop. More listening than dancing. We like this place because of the interesting mix of performers, the wholesome and plentiful Mexican food, and the air filtration system which means we can enjoy a night out without suffering from smoke inhalation.

Stone Coast Brewing Company (207-773-2337; 14 York St., Portland). Restaurant, nightclub, brewery: go from casual dining and pub-fare downstairs to live entertainment and a DJ upstairs. The music varies from night to night with live bands and a DJ playing retro dance music. It's been called the "Best live music venue" around by a local newspaper.

Midcoast

The Blue Goose (207-338-3003; Rte 1, Northport).

Gilbert's Publick House (207-236-4302; Bay View Landing, Camden). Live music and dancing Thurs., Fri., & Sat. nights with pub-styled food and reasonable prices.

Gray's Wharf (207-633-5629; Pier One, Boothbay Harbor). Seafood dining offering the "best lobster roll around." Open year round with entertainment five nights a week throughout the summer and on weekends in winter months.

Downeast/Acadia

Left Bank Bakery and Cafe (207-374-2201; Rte. 172, Blue Hill). In addition to serving a great meal (breakfast, lunch, and dinner), these guys serve up good music: Mose Allison, Odetta, Bill Staines, Bill Morrisey, The Persuasions, Greg Brown, and local Noel Paul Stookey of *Peter, Paul and Mary* fame. Music starts at 8:30 p.m.

SCHOOLS

What is culture, anyhow? We raise the question because maybe this section on schools suggests an answer. Here you will find schools not only for painters and musicians but also schools for fly fishermen and ocean navigators.

L. L. Bean Outdoor Discovery Program (207-865-3111 Ext. 6666; Casco St., Freeport). An interesting series of low-cost lessons that cover everything from cross-country skiing (on weekends beginning in January) and fly fishing to orienteering and emergency wilderness medicine. The program also offers free evening lectures on topics ranging from survival in the Maine woods to making soap, tanning hides, paddling sea kayaks, building fly rods, and cooking small game.

Haystack Mountain School of Crafts (207-348-2306; P.O. Box 518, Deer Isle 04627). One of the foremost craft schools in the country, Haystack offers two- and three-week sessions for artists and craftspersons working in a variety of media. Evening lectures by faculty and visiting artists are open to the public. Public tours are offered Wednesdays at 1 from June to August.

Hurricane Island Outward Bound School (207-594-5548 or 800-341-1744 out-of-state; Mechanic St., Rockland). Courses lasting 5 to 26 days are offered, as well as semester courses lasting 72 days in Penobsot Bay, Greenville, and Newry. There are sessions year-round for every age and both sexes; they focus on sailing, rock climbing, dog-sledding, and outdoor problem-solving. Prices are a bit steep. An international program begun in Wales, O.B. chal-

Learning how to pull together on one of Outward Bound's pulling boats.

Courtesy of Outward Bound

lenges participants to do things they never thought they could do and then pushes them just a little further. For details, write Box 429, Rockland 04841.

Kneisel Hall School for String and Ensemble Music (207-374-2811; Blue Hill). Summer school for chamber musicians. Kneisel Hall also provides a summer concert festival to the public, featuring student and faculty artists.

Landing School of Boat Building and Design (207-985-7976; River Rd., Arun-

The Maine Photographic Workshops

Students at The Maine Photographic Workshops take a break on a field trip to Monhegan Island.

del). Learn how to build your own sailing craft in their program that runs the months from September to June.

Maine Coast Art Workshops (207-372-8200; P.O. Box 236, Port Clyde 04855). Throughout the summer, five-day workshops with recognized artists are held here on the St. George peninsula, taking advantage of the surrounding natural setting. Sixteen workshops to choose from; tuition is about $350.

Maine Photographic Workshops (207-236-8581; Two Central St., Rockport). Photography, cinematography, television production, acting, and other related courses for the aspiring and experienced visual artist. All are taught by established professionals from around the country and the world. The workshop also operates an excellent gallery on the premises and a good retail store with photographic equipment and accessories.

At WoodenBoat School in Brooklin, students learn to build traditional wooden craft including canoes, Friendship sloops and other small boats that have been made in Maine for centuries.

WoodenBoat

National Audubon Ecology Camp at Hogg Island (203-869-2017; or write National Audubon Society Ecology Camps and Workshops, 613 Riversville Rd., Greenwich, CT 06831). For more than 50 years campers have studied wildlife on the island, an Audubon reserve well known for its bird life. They learn from well-educated and noted naturalists. About 50 adults are chosen for each one-week session. Rustic accommodations are provided.

Penobscot School (207-594-1084; 28 Gay St, Rockland 04841). Founded in 1986, this non-profit school began as one woman teaching French to area children. Today the school offers 10-12 week classes in conversational Arabic, Japanese, Spanish, French, Italian, and German and occasional intensive French, Spanish, Chinese, and German courses — most taught by native speakers. During the summer they teach English as a second language and provide informal cultural seminars.

Pierre Monteux School for Conductors and Orchestra Players (207-422-3931; Monteux Hall, off Rte. 1, Hancock). Named for the conductor who made his home here, this is where one goes to learn to lead in the musical sense. About 20 gifted musicians take part in this two-week summer program. Six concerts are performed.

Shelter Institute (207-442-7938; 38 Center St., Bath 04530). As featured on *Good Morning America*, the Shelter Institute teaches its international student body how to make their houses energy efficient from the ground up. The Institute offers prospective home builders daily in-depth classes that last one, two, or three weeks at a time from Feb.–Nov. Locals usually opt for the intensive weekend workshops offered Jan.–April. They sell all energy related products and house an incredible home builder's library.

Watershed Center for the Ceramic Arts (207-882-6075; 19 Brick Hill Rd., Newcastle). This is a Yaddo for the clay set. Big time and up-and-coming potters come here to get away from it all and devote themselves to their craft. They also teach the general public the secrets of handbuilding, wheel throwing, glazing, and firing.

WoodenBoat School (207-359-4651; P.O. Box 78, Naskeag Point Rd., Brooklin 04616). Founded by the management at *WoodenBoat* magazine, this is where readers and armchair seafarers come to live out their dreams. The school offers more than 75 courses on topics like navigation, boat building, and sailing for around 700 students every summer.

SEASONAL EVENTS

South Coast

July 4th Weekend Celebration (207-967-0857; Kennebunk and Kennebunkport). Concerts, picnic, silent auction, and probably a former president.

Conductor Bob, in front of his train. Maine Coast Railway at Wiscasset.

Herb Swanson

Harvestfest (207-363-4422; York). An old-fashioned New England harvest festival with old-time entertainment including oxcart races, apple bobbing, and a big-time tug of war. Mid-October.

Laudholm Trust Nature Crafts Festival (207-646-1555; Wells Reserve at Laudholm Farm, Wells). Juried crafts show by artists and craftspeople. Early September.

La Kermesse-Franco Americaine Festival (207-283-2826; Biddeford). Food, entertainment, parade, cultural displays documenting the French-American heritage in Southern Maine. Mid- to late June.

Sandbuilding Contest (207-646-2939; Ogunquit). Late July.

Casco Bay

Cumberland County Fair (207-829-4182; Cumberland Fairgrounds, Cumberland). Livestock, rides, agricultural and cooking competitions. Mid- to late September.

Maine Festival (207-772-9012; Thomas Point Beach, Brunswick). More than 600 artists and craftsmen on site. Folk Arts Village highlighting music and crafts traditional to Maine, plus bands and performers from other parts of the country. Early August.

Maine Highland Games (207-364-3063; Thomas Point Beach, Brunswick). People of Scottish ancestry show their colors. Bagpipe bands, highland dancing, food, border-collie demonstrations, and clan exhibits. Mid-August.

Yarmouth Clam Festival (207-846-3984; Main St., Yarmouth). Entertainment, crafts, bike race, midway and, of course, clams. Mid-July.

Relaxing at the Blue Hill Fair, which has been held every year at summer's end for almost a century, and was the inspiration for Charlotte's Web.

Tom Hindman

Midcoast

Arts & Crafts Festival (207-236-4404; Public Library, Bok Amphitheater, Camden). Crafters from all over show and sell their work. Mid-July.

Fall Foliage Festival (207-633-4727; Boothbay Railway Village, Boothbay Harbor). Leaves, music, crafts, food, and fun for the family. Mid-October.

Fishermen's Festival (207-633-2353; Boothbay Harbor). Miss Shrimp Contest, lobster boat races, chowder contest, and other great fisherman things, all to benefit the Fishermen's Memorial Fund. Late April.

Military Aviation Airshow (207-594-4418; Transportation Museum, Owls Head). Fly-bys and demonstrations of armed forces aircraft. Late June.

Rockland Maine Lobster Festival (207-596-0376; Public Landing, Rockland). Just about everything to do with lobster, including lots to eat. Early August.

A ceremonial dance at the annual celebration in Perry; a chance for visitors to experience a mix of old and new customs of the Pasamaquoddy tribe.

Tom Hindman

Windjammer Days (207-633-2353; Boothbay Harbor). For more than thirty years this windjammer parade has attracted an international crowd. Also antique boat parade, concerts, and exhibitions. Late June.

Down East/Acadia

Blue Hill Fair (207-374-9976; East Blue Hill). This fair was the inspiration for E.B. White's children's classic *Charlotte's Web*. Late August to early September.

East of Schoodic

Blueberry Festival (207-255-6665; Centre & Main Sts., Machias). Fish fry, parade, 5-mile blueberry run — all to celebrate the wild blueberry harvest. Going on for more than two decades. Mid-August.

The Gathering, Passamaquoddy Tribe (207-853-4001; Pleasant Point Reservation, Rte. 190, Perry). Traditional dances, crafts, lighting the sacred fire. Mid-August.

July 4 and Old Home Days (207-853-4644; Eastport). Every year this small fishing town of 2,000 quadruples in size when everyone who has ever lived here comes to celebrate the easternmost 4th in the country. Great parade. Make sure to make your lodging reservations early. July 1–4.

Salmon Festival (207-853-4644; Eastport). All you can eat, tours of the salmon pens from the water and codfish relays. Early September.

THEATER

*The arts continue to thrive Down East. A new theater is being established in Machias on the top floor of the Howard's Men's Shop. According to store owner Wayne Mallar, the new theater, to be called **The Rubicon,** will focus on community productions. The inaugural offering will be a mystery entitled* Catch Me If You Can.

The Downeast Coastal Press, Oct. 1, 1991

Theater in coastal Maine is generally an unpretentious experience. Patrons often arrive in jeans and Bean boots to enjoy Shakespeare, Fugard, Mamet or Pinter. The play is the thing. Here are some of the more established companies on the coast. Call to find out their season schedules, times, and ticket prices.

South Coast

City Theater (207-282-0849; 205 Main St., Biddeford).

Ogunquit Playhouse (207-646-5511; Rte. 1, Ogunquit). For more than 65 summers they have presented musicals and comedies with big-name performers.

Vintage Repertory Company (207-774-1376; 35 Brackett St., Portland 04102). This professional touring company, based in Portland, performs classics and

European comedies at the Oak Street Theater and in other venues. The company is available for private functions and schools as well.

Casco Bay

Freeport Community Players (207-865-6041; Freeport High School, Freeport). Young community theater group that presents three shows annually — in the spring, summer, and winter. Visiting performers welcome to audition.

Mad Horse Theater (207-797-3338; 955 Forest Ave., Portland). Musical comedies, dramas in the round.

Maine State Music Theatre (207-725-8769; Pickard Theater, Bowdoin College, Brunswick). Topnotch musicals with resident professional talent who for nearly 40 years have belted out great show tunes.

Oak Street Productions (207-775-5103; 92 Oak St., Portland). A young and energetic company that performs a variety of modern and classic works.

Portland Stage Company (207-774-0465; 25A Forest Ave. Portland). Solid local company that often brings actors up from Boston and New York for bigger roles.

The Theater Project/Young People's Theater (207-729-8584; 14 School St., Brunswick). This theater company puts on more than seven productions a year featuring dramas, contemporaries, and musicals. The Young People's Theater has classes for school aged children and productions involving both kids and adults from the community. Tickets: $12 adults; $6 kids.

Midcoast

Belfast Railroad Maskers (207-338-9668; Maskers Railroad Theatre, Belfast). Wide assortment of comedies and dramas.

Camden Civic Theatre (207-236-2281; Camden Opera House, Rte. 1, Camden). Musicals.

Iron Horse Dinner Theater (207-338-2931; 11 Water St. off City Landing, Belfast). Actually, it's dinner, theater, and a train ride.

Outlore Theatre Co. (207-594-2522; 275 Main St., Rockland). Rockland's dinner theater overlooking the harbor. A variety of performances throughout the year by a professional theater troupe.

Studio Theater (207-442-8455; Center for the Arts at the Chocolate Church, 804 Washington St., Bath).

Down East/Acadia

Acadia Repertory Theater (207-244-7260; Masonic Hall, Rte. 102, Somesville, Mount Desert Island). Modern comedies and dramas every summer for more than 25 years.

Cold Comfort Summer Theater (207-326-4311 or 469-3131; several locations throughout Castine). Comedies, dramas, and other summertime fare. During the summer of 1997, this fun summer theater company took a brief hiatus. We hope it's not a permanent break! Call for more information.

East of Schoodic

Down River Theater Company (207-255-4244; Old Catholic Church, Rte. 1A, Whitneyville). Musical theater from South Pacific to Chicago. Summer.

Eastport Arts Center (207-853-4133; Dana and Water Sts., Eastport). The Center is comprised of three groups: Stage East, a theater company producing three shows a year ranging from Neil Simon's *Rumors* to Charles Dickens's *A Christmas Carol*; the Eastport Gallery featuring art work in a variety of media; and the Concert Series with at least 5 concerts a summer.

CHAPTER FIVE
Shore Food
RESTAURANTS & FOOD PURVEYORS

Mainers love to cook, and they love to eat. They always have. Coastal Native Americans introduced settlers to lobsters, clambakes, oysters, smoked salmon, maple syrup and baked beans, fiddleheads, popcorn, potato chips, vanilla, cornflakes, and what we call Indian pudding (the best on the coast can be had, and should be had, at The Seaman's Club in Portland's Old Port). If that's not enough, ice cream was invented in Maine by ice dealer David Robinson as a treat for the Marquis de Lafayette on his visit to Portland in 1825. That may explain why Mainers are reported to eat more ice cream than people from other states. Of course, ice cream also goes well with pie, another food many Maine cooks are expert at making.

Herb Swanson

Maine shrimp, a local delicacy, are in season from November through March, and are kept frozen to enjoy in summer.

There are thousands of restaurants along the coast. Except for San Francisco there are more restaurants per capita in Portland than any other city in the country. The competition has produced enough good places to eat and the promise that the quality of food will remain high. If the homegrown cooks weren't good enough already, the coast has attracted highly skilled chefs "from away." Usually these fine cooks are drawn to the quality of life here, and their happiness is well reflected in their cooking. We all benefit as a result.

When we first moved to the Maine coast nearly a decade ago, we were amazed by the quantity and variety of good food that could be found here. That has not changed, and we continue to discover many fine places to eat — as this chapter will prove.

Microbrews are even bigger and better here than they were four years ago. We also are happy to report the coffee craze has finally reached the coast and you can find a good French roast, latté, or cappuccino in almost any Maine population center. For that reason we have removed the Coffee section from this chapter.

On a sadder note, Alberta's and the Good Egg in Portland are no longer, casualties of changing economic times and fire. They were two of our favorite places, and we know travelers familiar with our home town will miss them, too.

Here then is a select list of restaurants, some coastal legends, a few new finds, places we found out about by badgering reluctant residents and neighbors, places we liked and places we didn't but were out-voted, plus places written up and sent in by friends, all experienced or professional eaters. It's a list long enough to get you up or down the coast and back next summer.

We've noted the restaurants' serving times and seasons as they were when we made the final survey for this guide. As with all things, times, phone numbers, and sometimes addresses are subject to change according to the changing seasons and demands of the economy. Call first. If you can, make reservations. Things can get pretty busy at the great places, especially during July and August. Many restaurants, even white tablecloth ones, don't take reservations, though. So if you're really hungry, plan to arrive early enough to stake a good place in line.

The price range we list is meant to reflect the cost of a single meal, usually dinner, unless the review talks about breakfast or lunch. What we've tried to represent as a typical meal is an appetizer, entree, dessert, and coffee, although several of the places we review are not appetizer places. We do not include the price of alcohol or other drinks in the estimated cost.

Dining Price Code:	Inexpensive	Up to $10
	Moderate	$10–20
	Expensive	$20–30
	Very Expensive	$30 or more

Credit Cards:	AE	American Express
	DC	Diner's Club
	CB	Carte Blanche
	MC	MasterCard
	D	Discover Card
	V	Visa

We have included a list of food purveyors for each region on the coast. Some are delicatessens that will sell almost anything to go, others are bakeries or gourmet, ethnic food and beer and wine stores. Visitors will want to note that wine and beer are available broadly, but hard liquor can be harder to find. Maine recently sold its state liquor store franchises, and liquor stores are not plentiful.

RESTAURANTS — SOUTH COAST

Fiddleheads, the young tips of ferns that are harvested in Maine during the spring, are a great regional specialty that can be found on the menu at the coast's best restaurants.

Tom Hindman

ALISSON'S
207-967-4841 or
  800-667-2896.
5 Dock Square,
  Kennebunkport.
Open daily.
Price: Moderate.
Cuisine: American.
Serving: L, D.
Credit Cards: AE, D, DC,
  MC, V.
Handicap Access: Yes.
Smoking section.

Alisson's is a neighborhood breakfast establishment and later-day burger joint. Because the neighborhood happens to be Kennebunkport, that means that this place is going to be jammed in the summer. There's a butcher block bar where you can wait and watch. The help is affable and on-the-ball. On the menu, it's burgers, soup, sandwiches, salads, bar appetizers, fried seafood, and daily dinner specials. Some of the names may be too cute, but the burgers make up for it. The French fries and onion rings are good, too. Alisson's also makes a noteworthy raspberry chocolate cake.

ARROWS
207-361-1100.
Berwick Rd., Ogunquit.
Closed: Mondays and
    December to March.
Price: Very Expensive.
Cuisine: Regional Ameri-
    can with ethnic accents.
Serving: D.
Credit Cards: CB, MC, V.
Reservations: Recom-
    mended.
Handicap Access: Limited.

In just a few years, Arrows has earned a reputation for being one of the best restaurants in New England, and in our opinion it certainly is one of the best restaurants on the coast. Their menu, which changes daily, is first rate and inventive. Start with Royal Osetra caviar served with fried potatoes, iced vodka and red onion. Then try their prosciutto — cured right there. Although purists may balk, it is good. Most of their greens are grown outside in the garden. The lemongrass smoked duck breast, served with ginger confit and mango chutney, was wonderful. Our venison was well seasoned and tender. Good wines are available by the glass, so you can sample a different one with every course. Their bottled selection has been praised by *The Wine Spectator*. Arrows is set in a manicured 18th century farmhouse surrounded by well-tended, well-lighted gardens, and can be found several miles west of the center of Ogunquit. If you think you've missed it, keep driving. Suddenly you'll see it on the right.

BILLY'S CHOWDER
   HOUSE
207-646-7558.
216 Mile Rd., Wells Beach.
Open daily in season;
    closed Dec. to late Feb.
Price: Moderate.
Cuisine: American,
    seafood.
Serving: L, D.
Credit Cards: AE, D, MC,
    V.
Handicap Access: Yes.

Friends of ours, a fisherman and an artist, know people from the Massachusetts' Berkshires who, when they hanker for fried clams or boiled lobsters, come here. Then they go home. All in the same day. Our friends understand this. They tell the story to make a point. The portions are huge. What you can't eat, you can take with you. The fried stuff is delicious and light — a true guilty pleasure that's so enjoyable you have a hard time believing it's bad for you. The service is bustling and efficient. This place has a hard New England beauty that you can't beat. Pine boards inside, wetlands and water outside.

CAPE NEDDICK INN
207-363-2899.
Rte. 1, Cape Neddick.
Closed: Mon. & Tues.
    off-season.
Price: Expensive.
Cuisine: Country gourmet.
Serving: D.
Credit Cards: AE, MC, V.
Reservations: Recom-
    mended.
Handicap Access: Limited.

From the outside, the Cape Neddick looks like a typical country inn. Inside, the decor is clever and rather modern with a split-level dining room, abstract sculptures, expressionistic canvases on the walls, Fiestaware, and funky vintage crockery on the tables. Starters may include Chef Michele Duval's pistachio topped farmhouse cheese, wrapped in grape leaves, then grilled and served with champagne grapes. For entrees we suggest you try the potato-crusted cod on cucumber noodles or the gin

Collecting maple syrup during the winter when the sap is running. Maine annually produces an excellent grade of the sweet sauce, which is sold at many roadside stands.

Tom Hindman

Special Features: Art gallery.
No smoking in the dining room.

CARSON'S FAMILY RESTAURANT
207-883-4400.
433 U.S. Rte. 1, Scarborough.
Open year round.
Price: Inexpensive.
Cuisine: Seafood, diner food.
Serving: B, L, D.
Credit Cards: D, MC, V.
Handicap Access: Yes.

and juniper marinated duck breasts in gooseberry sauce.

From the outside Carson's looks like one of those roadside stops that could be either a great find or a terrible mistake. It's a find. Frilly white and pink curtains lend a homey touch to classic diner booths. There's also a breakfast counter. The waitresses call you "honey" and treat everyone with a sisterly kindness. The menu is huge and put together with the traveling family in mind: hamburgers and cheeseburgers for the kids; meatloaf and center cut pork chops for those wanting to experience the cuisine of their childhood; salad plates for the dieter; a 12 oz. prime rib for the big eater, as well as a dazzling selection of fresh seafood. Ask for yours with a side of their great mashed potatoes. The pie and strawberry shortcake are homemade, and good.

CAP'N SIMEON'S GALLEY
207-439-3655.
Rte. 103, Pepperell Rd., Kittery Point.
Closed: Tues. in winter.
Price: Inexpensive to Moderate.
Cuisine: Seafood.
Serving: L, D, SB.
Credit Cards: AE, D, MC, V.
Handicap Access: Yes.
Special Features: Great view.

This is the perfect place to pop sweet scallops in your mouth or curl up with a nice French fry and gaze out the window at the sea. That's if you can get a window seat. The lobster — usually brought in earlier in the day to the docks below — may require more concentration, but it's worth it. The interior has the feel of an old boat that has been sealed up tight with yearly coats of shellac. There is nothing fancy going on in here with the food, either. These people know what they're doing and have been doing it for years. The purpose here is to see that you're properly filled full of fresh seafood and side orders, and to go on your way. But not before you're ready to leave.

CHAUNCEY CREEK LOBSTER POUND
207-439-1030.
Chauncey Creek Rd., Kittery Point.
Open: Mothers Day weekend–mid Oct.
Price: Moderate.
Cuisine: Lobster.
Serving: L, D.
Credit Cards: MC, V.
Special Features: Great no- frills lobster.

We can't think of any place we'd rather be up the creek. This old-fashioned lobster pond actually sits against the edge of an embankment rising from a creek. Across the way are thick woods, making this like a nice homey treehouse where you can lay waste to a lobster or two (there are no nautical distractions). They start serving at 10:30 a.m., and we've known friends to indulge in a late lobster breakfast now and then. The steaming mounds of clams and mussels are succulent and legendary. The service is to the point, probably because they don't indulge in any frills or side dish fanfare here. You want potato salad. Well, then, bring it yourself. The same goes for beer or wine. Chauncey's is out of the way (thoroughly removed from the shoppers' bustle in nearby Kittery) but well known and, for the crowd that comes back year after year, well worth the side trip.

CORNFORTH HOUSE
207-284-2006.
893 Portland Rd. (Rte. 1), Saco.
Closed: Mon. in season; Jan. & Feb.
Price: Expensive.
Cuisine: Continental.
Serving: D, SB.
Credit Cards: MC, V.
Reservations: Recommended.
Handicap Access: Yes.

The Cornforth House is an elegant sidelight on busy Rte. 1 — the last place you would expect to find a country inn. Once inside, the mood is romantic, with gilt-framed artwork and ornate fireplaces in the several small dining rooms. The service is warm, and maybe too eager. The menu ranges from classics such as steak au poivre, rack of lamb, prime rib, and veal marsala to more creative notions like veal sausage in puff pastry and pecan chicken. Desserts, made fresh daily, include a leprechaun-green creme de menthe mousse cake and a monster ice-cream-filled profiterole with hot fudge.

FLO'S HOTDOGS
Unlisted phone.
Rte. 1, York.
Open all year.
Price: Inexpensive.
Cuisine: American.
Serving: L.
Credit Cards: None.

It's not the hot dog. It's the sauce, the abuse, the atmosphere, and probably something deeper than all that. Just past Pie in the Sky on Rte. 1, this one-story shack with no real sign is the destination of experienced travelers, rich and poor, who come here from all over the country. There's no real parking lot. You just kind of pull over. Inside, not only is there no view, there are no windows, just a few old yellow wooden swivel stools and an order counter. "Here the customer is never right," says Gail, Flo's daughter-in-law. Ah, delicious.

HURRICANE
207-646-6348 or
    800-649-6348 in Maine
    only.
Perkins Cove, Ogunquit.
Open seven days a week.
Price: Moderate to
    Expensive.
Cuisine: Seafood and
    American with ethnic
    touches.
Serving: L, D.

Hurricane's chef gets his seafood fresh off the cove's fishing boats. He grills it, and often dresses it in an elegant sauce. It's that simple. The setting, like the food, is simple but dramatic. There are two fireplaces in the dining room and views of the Atlantic from every seat. Appetizers include fresh Maine lobster gazpacho, roasted corn and fresh Roma tomato soup, or the Hurricane House salad — fresh greens, roasted shallots, pistachios topped with a cracked peppercorn dressing.

It is apparent to serious shellfish eaters that in the great evolutionary scheme of things crustaceans developed shells to protect them from knives and forks.

—Calvin Trillin, *Alice, Let's Eat*

Lobsters in the ocean are the color of seaweed and walk along the floor. "A shoe with legs," is how poet Anne Sexton described them. Lobsters are caught by lobstermen who heave a string of box-shaped wooden or vinyl-coated wire traps over the side of their boat. They bait their traps with fish heads and tails and species that don't normally sell well at the fish market. (Somehow it's not surprising to learn that lobsters are carnivores.) With luck, when the lobstermen returns and pulls up the trap, there will be a legal-sized lobster in it. (A waterlogged trap may weigh as much as 70 pounds.) A "keeper" measures at least 3.25 inches and is no more than 5 inches from its eyes to the beginning of the tail. It may or may not weigh a pound or more.

Lobsters in a pot of boiling water turn red. Before the 1800s, lobsters were in such abundance you could simply pick them off the beach, take them home, and cook them. People who could afford it didn't. Lobsters were considered a low-class food. Nineteenth-century prisoners were forced to eat them three times a week, and on Boston's Beacon Hill the servants ate them, although there was a limit to the number they would eat a week.

Finally, in the mid-19th century, fishermen began lobstering by boat, and scarcity produced demand. In this modern age, the Maine fleet lands an annual lobster catch of approximately 30,000 lbs. or more.

The proper way to demolish a lobster.

How to Eat a Lobster

Always with gusto.

Rip off both claws, grab nutcracker, hammer, or rock. Crack open, remove meat, dip in butter, and eat.

Next, grab tail in one hand, body in other, and bend back until it cracks and the meat inside can be removed. Once removed, tear off end flippers, grab fork, or long narrow stick, insert, push out tail meat, and eat.

Next, tear off small claws, suck out the meat, and eat. Next, remove the body from the back, crack open sideways, remove the meat, and eat.

Finally, eat the green tomalley (liver), which many consider the best part.

Credit Cards: AE, D, DC, MC, V.
Reservations: Recommended.

There's an extra effort to make everything fresh here. Three or four varieties of fresh grilled fish are offered daily and may include pan roasted sea scallops with a sun dried tomato cream served over fresh linguine, or plank roasted haddock with black bean and Maine crab calalloo. Hurricane gives chicken, pizza, and beef equally fresh treatment and consideration. (Friends are crazy about the burgers — served only at lunch.)

JACKIE'S TOO
207-646-4444.
59 Perkins Cove, Ogunquit.

Jackie's Too is known for the generosity with which they pack their lobster rolls, among the least expensive in town, and a lobster dinner that

Open all year.
Price: Inexpensive to
  Moderate.
Cuisine: American.
Serving: L, D in summer; L
  in winter.
Credit Cards: MC, V.
Handicap Access: Yes.

includes steamed clams, mussels, knockwurst, and corn on the cob. The knockwurst is, we think, not only a brave break with tradition but a savory addition. In the summer, the best seats are on the deck, within a stone's throw of the rocky cove. The atmosphere is casual and comfortable. In the off-season, you get a spectacular, albeit protected, view of the water.

JOSEPH'S BY THE SEA
207-934-5044.
55 West Grand Ave.,
  Old Orchard Beach.
Closed: Nov.–March.
Price: Moderate.
Cuisine: French with
  regional touches.
Serving: B, D, SB.
Credit Cards: AE, MC, V.
Reservations: Suggested.

In a town of snack bars and pack-'em-in surf-and-turf joints, Joseph's is where to go for escargots served with native dulse, a wild mushroom torte and fettucini Genovese (fresh pasta with artichokes, shitake mushrooms, spinach, raisins, pine nuts, and lemon basil olive oil). Joseph's is known for its Angel Hair Pasta Maison (made with shrimp, scallops, and fish sautéed in sun-dried tomatoes, garlic, herbs, and cream). There's also a Saco Bay soup — scallops, mussels, and local fish in a bouillabaisse. Once a private house, its hardwood floors and handcrafted white birch archways, awnings, and mantels are well looked after. Most people prefer to eat outside on the screened-in porch, which overlooks a manicured lawn with gardens, the dunes, the beach, the ocean, islands, and sky. Our optometrist first told us about Joseph's. She didn't want to let too many others in on one of the region's best-kept dining secrets. We've broken her confidence, I'm afraid. This is too good a place to hide.

JONATHAN'S
207-646-4777.
2 Bourne Ln., Ogunquit.
Closed Mon. and Tues in
  Jan., Feb., and March
Price: Moderate.
Cuisine: New England and
  Continental.
Serving: D.
Credit Cards: AE, D, DC,
  MC, V.
Reservations: Yes.
Handicap Access: Yes.

For 18 years this has been a popular stop for area residents and returning visitors. Jonathan's offers a raw bar and an extensive menu that leans toward seafood and pasta but also includes dishes like Jaeger Schnitzel and Tennessee tenderloin of pork. Owner Jonathan West's art collection covers the dining room walls and represents well-known local painters, past and present. If they don't grab you, there's a 600-gallon tropical saltwater reef aquarium in the main dining room. Or you can take in the carefully tended gardens visible through the dining room windows. Jonathan's also provides an old-fashioned bright spot in the local nightlife with a convivial piano bar and nightly sing-alongs.

ROBERTO'S
207-646-8130.
82 Shore Rd., Ogunquit.
Closed: Dec.–April.
Price: Moderate to
　Expensive.
Cuisine: Italian.
Serving: D.
Credit Cards: AE. MC, V.
Handicap Access: Yes.

Roberto's specializes in simple Italian food, red and white checkered tablecloths, and collecting celebrities. Ask for table 14, the Paul Newman table, named for one who once ate here. This is an all natural, non-salt, high flavor Italian restaurant, and the dining room is pleasantly casual and busy. Specials change with the season: lighter in the warm days of summer and heavier in the fall. Garlic bread baked daily. Linguini, lasagne, canneloni, things parmigiana and marsala presented in a restored 1850s farm house. The wine list is limited.

YORK HARBOR INN
207-363-5119 or
　800-343-3869.
Rte. 1A, York Harbor.
Open all year.
Price: Moderate to
　Expensive.
Cuisine: American.
Serving: B, L, D.
Credit Cards: AE, MC, V.
Reservations: Recommended.
Handicap Access: Yes.

This 17th century white clapboard covered inn offers broiled scrod, milky clam chowder, a cluster of many small dining rooms, and a partial view of the harbor. Heavy wood beams, low ceilings, creaky wood floors provide that old new world feel. So does the menu. This is a good place for a dose of classic New England dining.

RESTAURANTS — CASCO BAY

BACK BAY GRILL
207-772-8833.
65 Portland St., Portland.
Closed: Sun.
Price: Expensive.
Cuisine: Regional
　American grill.
Serving: D.
Credit Cards: AE, D, DC,
　MC, V.
Reservations: Recommended.
Handicap Access: Yes.

This trendy grill in an untrendy part of town has a devoted following. The menu changes weekly, as do wines by the glass (there's an interesting selection); the beer list is not bad, either. The wait staff is extremely knowledgeable and efficient. No hemming and hawing when you want to know exactly what kind of vinegar is in the salad dressing. They grill almost everything here, including the vegetables and sometimes a dessert. Creme Brulee is a signature finish.

**BOONES FAMOUS
　RESTAURANT**
207-774-5725.
6 Custom House Wharf,
　Portland.
Open all year.

In the old days, this pier is where we would catch the ferry out to the islands. The ferry terminal has since moved down the street, but the hustle and bustle of coastal comings and goings have not been lost. We like this place for its atmosphere. The

Price: Inexpensive to
  Moderate.
Cuisine: Seafood,
  American.
Serving: L, D.
Credit Cards: AE, CB, D,
  DC, MC, V.
Handicap Access: Yes.
Smoking Section.
Reservations: For parties
  over 6.

outside deck is really the former ferry pier, and it's a good place to hang out on summer dog days because there's always a salty breeze and a cool harbor view. The menu, plain and simple New England seafood, is better at dinner than at lunch, but the service is more efficient earlier in the day. On a recent visit we found the haddock a little too buttery for our taste and the pie merely adequate. Still, on a hot day, a cold draught at the open air bar, complete with a well-preserved trophy tuna, is sure to make up for any shortcomings.

CHEBEAGUE INN
207-846-5155.
John Small Rd., Chebeague
  Island.
Closed: Mid-Sept.–
  mid-May.
Price: Moderate to
  Expensive.
Cuisine: Continental.
Serving: L, D.
Reservations: Recom-
  mended, even for lunch.
Credit Cards: AE, MC, V.
Handicap Access: Limited.
Special Features: Verandah
  with Casco Bay view.

The Chebeague Inn has an old-fashioned feel. Maybe it's the cane-backed rocking chairs on the porch, a perfect spot to while away a lazy (and hot) afternoon. Or because it's so remote (by ferry it's an hour or so from Portland and 13 minutes from Cousins Island). Or maybe it's the food. Old-timey fare like real Maine chowder with potatoes and bacon, baked ham sandwiches on thick warm-from-the-oven bread, tuna with celery and mayo, and homemade lemonade and iced tea. Desserts run along the same lines — a mile-high devil's food wedge being the attention grabber. The dinner menu, which is quite extensive, is a mix of country cooking and continental fare.

DELLA'S CATESSEN
207-773-2624.
92 Exchange St., Portland.
Open all year.
Price: Inexpensive.
Cuisine: American.
Serving: L, D.
Credit Cards: AE, MC, V.
Handicap Access: Yes.

Visitors order deli style here, but the atmosphere is more like a hip urban diner. The walls are painted in broad yellow and white stripes, and adorned with framed vintage *Life* magazine covers and autographed pictures of Roy Rogers, Dale Evans, and other Western greats. We eat here a lot and aren't afraid to champion our favorites. The meatloaf sandwich with spicy ketchup reminds us of mom's famous meatloaf. The turkey burrito is a lean and filling specialty. The melts are always good. Della herself presides with a smile over the friendly and welcoming staff. Take home dinner, ready to pop into the oven or micro, or choose from a selection of wines, gourmet foods, and regional specialties (Atlantic salmon, salt water taffy, rice noodles, exotic coffee beans). Also, this is the perfect place to pick up a boxed lunch for a day on the islands or a trip up the coast. Make sure one of Della's sinful desserts goes with you. We are particularly partial to the lemon squares and coconut-chocolate Magic Bars.

**DOLPHIN MARINA
    BASIN**
207-833-6000.
Basin Point., off Rte. 123,
    South Harpswell.
Open all year.
Price: Inexpensive to
    Moderate.
Cuisine: Seafood.
Serving: B, L, D.
Credit Cards: MC, V.
Handicap Access: Yes.

This is where the fishermen come to eat out. They're the ones sitting at the counter with meaty burgers piled with ketchup. You can get burgers in the city. Try the chunky lobster stew. Watch lobsterboats or sailboats tie up. Wash it all down with coffee and a slice of fresh fruit pie in season.

*Stacking lobster pots in
Frenchboro. Fresh lobster
is de rigeur for any Maine
coast visit.*

Herb Swanson

ESTES LOBSTER HOUSE
207-833-6340.
Rte. 123, South Harpswell.
Open Memorial Day to
    Labor Day.
Price: Inexpensive.
Cuisine: Lobster.
Serving: L, D.
Credit Cards: AE, D, MC.

It's about at this point on the coast that travelers have to start making choices about which isthmus or peninsula they want to explore. The advantage to overcoming any indecision you may have is that once you've acted, you feel like you've taken possession of the place — and its food. Temporary ownership has a terrific taste here. This is the sort of out-of-the-way place where you can watch fishermen work around their boats. It gives you a larger appreciation of that delicious haddock sandwich you're holding. If you want something naturally sweet, try a mess of clams.

FEDERAL SPICE
207-774-6404.
225 Federal St., Portland.
Open year round.
Price: Inexpensive.

If you're hankering for a burrito, this is just about the only place to go in Portland. What you will find are low fat renditions, with interesting seasonings and a good selection of exotic hot sauces to

Cuisine: Multi-ethnic.
Serving: L, D.

spice it up. Cheap and abundant, this is a healthy place to grab lunch and save your calories and appetite for dinner.

FIVE ISLANDS LOBSTER COMPANY
207-371-2150.
Off Rte. 127 at Five Islands, Georgetown.
Closed: Mid-Oct.–April.
Price: Inexpensive to Moderate.
Cuisine: Lobster in the rough.
Serving: L, D.
Special Features: Outdoor pier dining; BYOB.

This working pier happens to be an ideal spot to crack open a lobster and suck down some steamers. Picnic tables on the dock are about it for amenities. But the panorama — sailboats on the Sheepscot River and pine-blanketed islands — more than makes up for it. Order corn, steamers, and lobsters at the pound. Then step next door for coleslaw, french fries, burgers, etc. Five Islands also makes one of the best lobster rolls on the Maine coast, so if you're feeling lazy, go for it. They also specialize in grilled seafood. Dessert runs from double-dip ice cream cones to homemade blueberry cobbler.

FORE STREET
207-775-2717.
288 Fore Street, Portland.
Open nightly.
Price: Expensive.
Serving: D.
Credit Cards: AE, MC, V.
Handicap Access: Yes.

Fore Street is a place for sizable appetites and sophisticated tastes. The dining room is large and noisy — sometimes a bit too loud — with all the action centered around an open kitchen and the restaurant's impressive wood ovens. The menu changes daily and includes many items that have been apple wood smoked or grilled. Many of the appetizers and salads come from local farms and gardens in season. We enjoyed the tender hanger steak, grilled to just the right degree, and a braised fish and shellfish ragout. Best of all, we like to stop in here every once in a while for a cocktail or a light dinner in the small, elegant bar located just to the left as you come in door. The chairs are quite comfortable.

JAMESON TAVERN
207-865-4196.
115 Main St., Freeport.
Open year round.
Price: Moderate.
Cuisine: American seafood.
Serving: L, D.
Credit Cards: AE, D, DC, MC, V.
Reservations: optional.

The Jameson Tavern has been here practically forever, catering to the masses, most recently shoppers resting up from their L.L.Bean experience. This isn't wildly exciting food: lobster, seafood, burgers, and sandwiches. But it will fortify you before you head out to the outlets again, and it does offer something for almost everyone. The tavern is a local historical stop, where Maine's founding fathers gathered at the beginning of the 18th century and decided to separate from Massachusetts.

HARRASEEKET INN
207-865-9377 or
  800-342-6423.
162 Main St. (Rte. 1),
  Freeport.
Open daily.
Price: Expensive.
Cuisine: Regional
  American.
Serving: B, L, D.
Credit Cards: AE, D, MC,
  V.
Reservations: Recom-
  mended.
Handicap Access: Yes.
Special Features: Tableside
  cooking.

Chef Theda Lyden's menu is known for her innovations; her seasonal menu that draws heavily on local produce, fish, and meat; and her knowledge of wine and cheese. Decor is understated — white linens, fresh flowers and flickering candles. Menus change weekly, and there are nightly additions as well. Service is attentive, yet not as overbearing as it can be in places of this sort. Start with salmon Napoleon napped with light tarragon cream or potato soup with saffron. Salads, included with entrees, mix greens with edible flowers. Main courses run from rabbit with cider cream and wild mushrooms to lamb brochette with cumin. There are also classic dishes like rack of lamb and chateaubriand carved with great fanfare at your table. There is a good by-the-glass selection of wine, and the wine list is excellent. Dessert is a must — try the sundae with dense homemade chocolate ice cream and caramel and fudge sauce, apple pie with a scoop of rich vanilla, or the Harraseeket's fresh fruit sorbet. For those who prefer dessert a la Francaise, cheese and fruit are also on the roster.

**HARRASEEKET LUNCH
  & LOBSTER**
207-865-4888.
End of Main St., South
  Freeport.
Open: May to mid-Oct.
Price: Inexpensive to
  Moderate.
Cuisine: Seafood.
Serving: L, D.
Credit Cards: None.
Handicap Access: Partial.

Twenty minutes from downtown Portland and 10 from downtown Freeport, this is a favorite getaway, serving lobster on the deck with a protected view of boats, pine-topped islands and Wolf's Neck. During the height of the season the line is long, and the kitchen can get a little overwhelmed, but they always remain cheerful and courteous. Better yet, schedule your visit for anything but the height of the lunch or dinner hour. For those who can make do with just lobster, clams, and corn, there's another window around the side of the shack where there is rarely anyone waiting. All the seafood tastes heavenly, the fries have that nice, dry clean taste, and the corn is worth ordering two ears at a time. The pies are okay; the homemade ice cream is better.

KATAHDIN
207-774-1740.
Corner of Spring and High
  St., Portland.
Closed: Sunday.
Price: Inexpensive to
  Moderate.

This is a restaurant not afraid to serve carrots. We come here all the time, usually to get the Blue Plate Special and its accompanying mound of mashed potatoes. There's fun stuff on the walls and in the windows, no nonsense wait people who know what they're doing, and on any given night, the clientele is a good cross section of Portland,

Serving: D.
Credit Cards: D, MC, V.
Handicap Access: Yes
Reservations: No.

including all the so-called alternative groups. When we're not eating the blue plate, we like the stews or the buckwheat pasta, favored by a nurse friend who suggests a half order. Restaurants come and go in Portland. This one blew the local favorite out of the water a couple of years ago, and appears to be solidly entrenched.

MESA VERDE
207-774-6089.
618 Congress St., Portland
    04101.
Open: Mon. –Sat.
Cuisine: Mexican.
Price: Inexpensive.
Serving: L, D.
Credit Cards: V, MC, D.
Handicap Access: Yes.

Located in the heart of Portland's Arts District, Mesa Verde offers a relaxed atmosphere and a warm plate of food for those with a hankering for Mexican. The service is fast, and the food is about as good as Mexican gets in this northern New England town. The taco salad is crisp and delicious. The tostadas have the perfect blend of beans, rice, and vegetables, although we had hoped for a larger serving. What we love most about this restaurant isn't *la comida,* it's *los jugos,* the juices. Mesa Verde has a full juice bar and serves up some of the best combination juice drinks around. We like the strawberry-raspberry-banana smoothie with yogurt and the coffee mocha smoothie with bananas, iced coffee, rice milk, and almond butter.

NORM'S BAR B Q
207-774-6711.
43 Middle St., Portland.
Closed: Monday and
    Tuesday.
Price: Inexpensive to
    Moderate.
Cuisine: Bar B Que.
Serving: L, D.
Credit Cards: None.
Handicap Access: No.
Reservations: No

Ah, if not barbecue in Maine, then where? Actually, at times up here, we all get pretty tired of seafood, which may be why you'll find so many ethnic restaurants hidden away. The only fish you'll find at Norm's is catfish, barbecued catfish. Norm also sells homemade clam cakes, but that's it. The rest is ribs — pork, spare, country style, and beef short — barbecued chicken, meat sandwiches smothered in barbecue sauce, and barbecued duck salad, the chef's one bow to highbrow. Buttermilk biscuits and cornbread are baked fresh. Plus, try Norm's crunchy coleslaw or his fresh baked pies for dessert.

PEPPER CLUB
207-772-0531.
78 Middle St., Portland.
Open: Daily.
Price: Inexpensive to
    Moderate.
Serving: D.
Credit Cards: None.

Very organic and meatless, except for the hamburgers and an occasional chicken. In fact, the hamburgers are usually what we end up getting. They're big, juicy, and made from organic beef. This is Portland's version of southwestern-meets-Los Angeles — lots of huevos rancheros colors painted in jagged angles on the walls, and big

Handicap Access: Limited.
Reservations: No

black booths. All items are written in multi-colored chalk on the big blackboard, and are multi-ethnic in origin. They also make a nice pie.

SPURWINK COUNTRY KITCHEN
207-799-1177.
150 Spurwink Rd.,
  Scarborough.
Closed: Mondays; late
  Oct. through mid April.
Price: Inexpensive to
  Moderate.
Cuisine: Family.
Serving: L, D.
Credit Cards: D, MC, V.
Handicap Access: Yes.
No smoking.

The Spurwink is a low-slung beach bungalow smack dab in the middle of a coastal salt marsh and located near some of our favorite beaches. This is a local favorite, especially among families and the older Cape Elizabeth crowd. They serve simple Downeast classics, a few light items, a selection of half sandwich and cup of soup, and daily specials that you can rely on week to week. They also offer an occasional surprise, for instance their black beans and rice, which we like. Beer and wine are available by the glass. All desserts are homemade. The atmosphere is generally peaceful. They also have a kids' menu. Everything is available for take out.

RICHARD'S
207-729-9673.
115 Maine St., Brunswick.
Closed: Sun.
Price: Moderate.
Cuisine: German,
  American.
Serving: L, D.
Credit Cards: AE, D, MC,
  V.
Reservations: Recom-
  mended.
Handicap Access: Yes.

In recent years, Richard's has moved into town, taking up residence in an old steak house. German beers and victuals are the thing here. The beer roster is prodigious, with numerous offbeat selections. And beer is just what one needs to wash down hearty fare like wiener schnitzel, smoked pork chops, sauerbraten, wursts, potato salad, and sauteed cabbage. There's also an American menu for the unadventurous that includes chicken, haddock, and steaks. Located in the old Bowdoin Inn, the interior is brick and wood with high chandeliers, table clothes, flowers, and candles. The wait staff is particularly good-natured. Tortes and strudels for dessert.

ROSITA'S
207-729-7118.
212 Main St., Brunswick.
Open daily.
Price: Inexpensive.
Cuisine: Mexican.
Serving: L, D, SB.
Credit Cards: None.
Handicap Access: Limited.
Special feature: Huevos
  rancheros on Sunday.

Every college town needs a Mexican restaurant and Rosita's is the South of the Border outpost nearest to Bowdoin College. The term "casual" is an understatement here. Beer comes out of a cooler and one orders food cafeteria-style. But the folks behind the counter are eager to please and the place has a friendly feel. All the usual suspects are on the menu: burritos, tostados, nachos, tacos, enchiladas, chili, fajitas, and tamales. Besides the standard beef, pinto bean, and chicken trio, there are chorizo, the spicy Spanish sausage, and black beans, too. Salsas come in hot and mild strengths and the overall firepower of most fixings is quite tolerable. Sunday breakfasts are unusual, featuring bacon and egg tacos and huevos rancheros.

STREET & COMPANY
207-775-0887.
33 Wharf St., Portland.
Open daily.
Price: Moderate.
Cuisine: Seafood, pasta.
Serving: D.
Credit Cards: AE, MC, V.
Special Features: Patio dining.
Handicap Access: Yes.
Reservations: Recommended.

This was once a tiny restaurant with a few tables. We are glad to say that it has flourished and expanded, but not at the expense of menu, atmosphere, or service. Garlic from the open kitchen still perfumes the air at the casual, subterranean retreat, which sits on a funky cobblestone alley in Portland's Old Port. Dried flowers, rough wood, and family-sized cans of olive oil and tomatoes give the place an ethnic feel. They serve no red meat here, making Street & Co. a logical choice for visitors to this seaside metropolis. Salmon, swordfish, scallops, and shrimp are constants. There's also a soup of the day and changing specials like tuna Nicoise and sole meuniere. Pastas come with a variety of creative seafood sauces. Recent additions include a second dining room and a wine bar with one of the best wine selections in town. As we write, Dana Street is preparing to further expand his empire with a wood-fired oven restaurant a few blocks from here. It is rumored he'll be doing for steak what he's already done for seafood.

TABITHA JEAN'S
207-780-8966.
94 Free St., Portland.
Open daily.
Price: Moderate.
Cuisine: Eclectic.
Serving: L, D.
Credit Cards: AE, CB, D, DC, MC, V.
Handicap Access: Yes.
Reservations: No.

Stephen King's daughter is determined to make this place succeed. The location, several blocks from Portland's Old Port, has worked against her, which is a shame. Everything's well priced and superbly cooked. Entrees are evenly divided into light and large, and either way, healthy. The last time we were there they were having a wild mushroom blow out which was delicious. The decor is gold, black, woodgrain, and high modern.

THREE DOLLAR DEWEY'S
207-772-3310.
241 Commercial St., Portland.
Price: Inexpensive.
Cuisine: American, vegetarian.
Serving: L, D.
Credit Cards: MC, V.
Special features: Free popcorn.

This Portland landmark ale house recently moved to spiffy new quarters at the heart of the city's working waterfront district. The building is old, and that lends a nice flavor to the alehouse atmosphere. The kitchen here turns out an interesting menu of pub food mixed with a dash of spicy vegetarian. You can bring the kids during the afternoon and enjoy burgers at the long alehouse tables.

ZEPHYR GRILL
207-828-4033.
653 Congress St., Portland.
Open: Wed.–Sun.
Price: Expensive.
Cuisine: American eclectic.
Serving: D.
Credit Cards: AE, D, DC,
   MC, V.
Reservations: Suggested.
Handicap access: Dining
   room, yes; restrooms, no.

The Zephyr Grill is a lovely restaurant. The service is smooth, attentive, and unpretentious. The food is consistently excellent and always freshly presented. The menu changes regularly, but always maintains a solid core of our favorites. The mixed grill — handrolled sausage, lamb tenderloin and chicken breast — is one of those, and the seafood — however they serve it — is fresh and good. The Zephyr is a bit off Portland's beaten track, but it is well worth the trip. Are we gushing? We can't help it. We like this place.

RESTAURANTS — MIDCOAST

What to eat at The Breakfast Place in Damariscotta.

Herb Swanson

THE BREAKFAST PLACE
207-563-5434.
Main St., Damariscotta.
Open year round.
Price: Inexpensive.
Cuisine: Breakfast.
Serving: B.
Handicap Access: Limited.
Specialties: Bakery.

Just across and down the street from the historic steeple and clock on St. Andrew's, this morning coffee and baked goods joint also serves a good egg or two. It's been around for ages, serving as a wakeup stop for the local community. Recently it was bought by two ambitious transplants from Connecticut. They've raised the level of baking, but kept the hometown decor. Grab some of their tiny pecan and chocolate tarts for the road.

THE BROWN BAG
207-596-6372 or
   800-287-6372.
606 Main St., Rockland.

This place specializes in the most important meal of the day, breakfast, and the next most, lunch. They fresh bake daily an edible still life of warm

Open: Year round.
Price. Inexpensive.
Cuisine: Country eclectic.
Serving: B, L, D.
Credit Cards: MC, V.
Handicap Access: Yes,
through the back.

croissants, sticky buns, giant blueberry muffins, and fresh shredded wheat bread toast. Try a toad 'n holes — shredded wheat toast with an egg dropped in the center and grilled. The oatmeal is also home-made. So is the cinnamon swirl French toast. Also, excellent omelets. Lunch is hearty sandwiches and soups and chowders. Congenial customers line up to place their orders for huevos rancheros, brown bag pockets (their version is scrambled eggs with three cheeses in a whole wheat pita falafel with lemon tahini sauce, a roast beef/boursin sub (the beef is marinated and roasted on the premises), or daily fresh roasted turkey. The owners devote a whole blackboard to their changing dessert menu; their sea-sonal pies, cheesecakes, puddings, and cookies are all made from scratch. The Brown Bag also now serves dinner. The dining room is transformed into an upscale, candlelit bistro, where grilling is the order of the evening.

**CAPPY'S CHOWDER
HOUSE**
207-236-2254.
1 Main St., Camden.
Open all year. Closed Wed.
in winter.
Price: Moderate.
Cuisine: American.
Serving: B, L, D; call for
winter hours.
Credit Cards: MC, V.
Reservations: Large parties
only.
Handicap Access: Limited.

Right downtown, the compact size belies the huge staff required to make this place run. They claim sooner or later everyone shows up here, and they run it like they're ready for your arrival, morning, noon, and night. Great chowder, good burgers, a good short stack of ribs, and buoy-ant pancakes (at breakfast). They also are quite competent with locally caught fish. They're now serving more healthy selections, vegetarian and light items, while at the same time they've expanded their bakery. Many a time we have stood packed in the doorway or at the bar waiting for a table, or preferably a booth. Even once you've been seated in the varnished and bric-a-bracked joint, you feel like you're a character in a triple-decker sandwich.

CAPTAIN'S TABLE
207-596-6870.
Rte. 1, Rockland.
Open year round.
Price: Inexpensive.
Cuisine: American.
Serving: B, L ,D.
Credit Cards: D, MC, V.
Handicap Access: Yes.

Driving north into "downtown" Rockland on Rte. 1, don't miss the scruffy-looking residen-tial hotel on your left called the Wayfarer. The hotel's restaurant — the Captain's Table — is where the fishermen eat. From Brobdingnagian stacks of flapjacks to eggs with ham and fish cakes (potato, onion, and flaked fish formed into patties and grilled — delicious), this is the way to keep body and soul together through a morning of sightseeing, sailing, or any more strenuous activity.

There are also low-priced lunch and dinner specials, but come in the morning. The Ritz it ain't, but you've been living in the city too long if you can't enjoy this real slice of Maine life.

LE GARAGE
207-882-5409.
Water St., Wiscasset.
Closed: January.
Price: Expensive.
Cuisine: New England.
Serving: L, D.
Credit Cards: MC, V.
Reservations: Recom-
    mended.
Handicap Access: Yes.
Special Features: River
    view.

Candelabra, cathedral ceilings, and two half-sunk schooners set the scene at this former auto garage right on the river. The effect is dramatic — especially on one of those gray, misty days the coast for which the Maine coast is famous. As atmospheric as Le Garage is, the food is surprisingly down to earth, with starters like ratatouille; savory charbroiled items like chicken, steak, pork chops; fresh seafood; unusual pastas; light salads, and desserts. Homespun desserts include apple crisp, gingerbread, and birdnest meringue.

THE HAVEN
207-863-4969.
245 Main St., Vinalhaven.
Closed March and April.
Price: Moderate.
Cuisine: Seafood; exotic
    regional.
Serving: B, D; call for
    schedule.
Credit Cards: MC, V.
Reservations: Yes.

Favored by residents, summer people, and visitors, the Haven has been a popular gathering place for more than a dozen years. The menu changes often to incorporate the day's catch, ripening wild berries, or chanterelles harvested from the surrounding spruce woods. Two dining rooms are open in the summer. The back room offers a more traditional seafood-restaurant atmosphere. The front room, once a storefront, is a favorite place to dine, surrounded by the works of local artists, many of whom are well-known outside of this close-knit community. Haven's has a full bar.

JESSICA'S
207-596-0770.
2 South Main St. (Rte. 73),
    Rockland.
Open year round.
Price: Moderate.
Cuisine: Bistro.
Serving: D.
Credit Cards: D, MC, V.
Reservations: Recom-
    mended.

We have a soft spot for Swiss chefs, and chef/owner Hans Bucher has earned his way into that spot with consistently good food, prepared and served well. Jessica's is comfortable and inviting. The menu is a well-reasoned mix of Swiss, French, and Italian items. Lamb Bresale are tender lamb chops glazed with mustard, garlic, red wine, and herbs and served with portabello mushrooms. Bucher also serves a classic bistro steak, with rich tarragon butter melted atop. He rounds out the menu with daily fresh seafood specials and excellent desserts.

KRISTINA'S
207-442-8577.
160 Center St., Bath.
Closed: January.
Price: Moderate to
   Expensive.
Cuisine: American eclectic.
Serving: B, L, D, SB.
Credit Cards: D, MC, V.
Special Features: Bakery
   takeout.

Kristina's is consistently on everyone's list of coastal favorites, and for good reason. Upstairs, the low ceiling, modern dining room is casual and lounge-like; downstairs is bright, homey, and cheerful with butcher block tables and potted plants. They serve all three meals here, and while it might seem that a breakfast place would be unlikely to make an elegant dinner well, they do. Lunch is a meal of soups, salads, sandwiches, and burgers. Dinner runs from such standards as lamb chops and grilled salmon to more exotic Indian tofu. We like their steamed mussels, garlicky and rich, to start everything off. There's also a light menu that includes quiches and burritos. Stop by the bakery case on the way out the door and grab something good to take on the road. Their pies are good, so are their breads and cookies.

**LOBSTERMAN'S
   WHARF**
207-633-3443.
Rte. 96, East Boothbay.
Closed: Mid-Oct.–early
   May.
Price: Moderate.
Cuisine: American.
Serving: L, D.
Credit Cards: MC, V.
Feature: Kid-proof dining;
   deck with river view.
Handicap Access: Yes.

Wedged between two old shipyards, this family restaurant is fun. Best of all, there's plenty to keep the kids occupied. The long, paneled dining room has the look of an ocean liner, and just in case you don't get it, lobster traps, buoys, and paddles hang from walls and ceilings. In fair weather, dine on the deck overlooking the Damariscotta River. Otherwise, grab a table in the large dining room. Unlike places that are all gimmick and no substance, the Wharf has good food and an enthusiastic staff. Tasty biscuits and corn muffins. Savory starters like deep-fried artichokes. Bright salads. And interesting entrees. A mixed grill with kielbasa, sirloin, and chicken is a winner, as is the baked flounder stuffed with chunks of crab. There are occasional disappointments, but these can be avoided by sticking to basics. For dessert, brownie sundaes.

MOODY'S DINER
207-832-7885.
Rte. 1, Waldoboro.
Closed: Fri. & Sat. between
   midnight and 5 a.m.
Price: Inexpensive.
Cuisine: Diner food.
Serving: B, L, D.
Handicap Access: Yes.

What distinguishes a really great restaurant is when the locals refuse leave after it's been discovered by tourists. Everyone shares counter seats and booths at Moody's: Waldoborans, summer people, tourists, fishing boat captains, and yacht owners. The corned beef hash is legendary. The cheeseburgers and meatloaf are too, as is their walnut pie and any one of their cream pies.

The Pie State

The feast was a noble feast, as has already been said. There was an elegant ingenuity displayed in the form of pies, which delighted my heart. Once acknowledge that an American pie is far to be preferred to its humble ancestor, the English tart, and it is joyful to be reassured at a Bowden [sic] reunion that invention has not yet failed."
— Sarah Orne Jewett, *The Country of the Pointed Firs and Other Stories.*

The Maine coast is nothing if not for pie. And it wouldn't take much retooling to change Maine's nickname from the Pine State to the Pie State.

Maybe Maine's having a drowned coast, which resulted from those two tectonic plates crashing together before being smothered by the glaciers, explains why so many people here understand the importance of a good crust and pie a la mode.

Maine even has several filling seasons (see "Berry and Apple Picking" in Chapter Six, *Recreation*).

There are two kinds of Maine pies. Fruit and Cream.

The saying should be, "As American as blueberry pie." The Europeans brought the apples. The blueberries were already here. Cream pies probably were invented in Maine. Somebody looked out the window on a cold wintery day at the snow blanketing a blueberry barren and her thoughts turned to filling.

In 1825, David Robinson, a local ice dealer, supposedly invented ice cream and by extension, pie a la mode. Yorkie's, the best pie place in the history of civilization, flourished in Camden until the last decade. Sigh. Pie gone by.

Here are several pie places, some legendary, some secret and wrangled from friends and some our own favorites.

South Coast
Hattie's Deli (207-282-3435) in Biddeford Pool. Blueberry.

Casco Bay
Spurwink Country Kitchen (207-799-1177, Cape Elizabeth). We're happy to say that even though pastry chef Eileen Esposito is no longer baking there, the wild blueberry pie remains topnotch.

Midcoast
The Brown Bag (207-596-6372; 606 Main St., Rockland). Go with what's in season.

Dip Net Coffee Shop (207-372-6275; Port Clyde). This could very well be the true "Son of Yorkie's" (see above).

Kristina's Bakery and Restaurant (207-442-8577; 160 Center St., Bath). Try the orange-walnut.

Moody's Diner (207-832-7785; Rte. 1, Waldoboro). Famous for strawberry-rhubarb since 1927.

Weaver's Bakery (207-338-3540; 19 Main St., Belfast). Any flavor.

Down East/Acadia
The Fisherman's Friend (207-367-2442; School St., Stonington). Bonafide home-made.

The Left Bank Bakery & Cafe (207-374-2201; Rte. 172, Blue Hill). Good pie and good music.

East of Schoodic
Helen's (207-255-8423.; Rte. 1, Machias). Her famed strawberry.

THE NEWCASTLE INN
207-563-5685 or
800-832-8669.
River Rd., Newcastle.
Closed: Mon., June–Nov.;
Mon.–Wed. rest of year.
Price: Expensive to Very
Expensive.
Cuisine: Country gourmet.
Serving: D.
Credit Cards: MC, V.
Reservations: Required.

There's only one seating at the Newcastle Inn each evening. Such regimentation might be off-putting if the food were not so good and the experience enjoyable. The small dining room is lighted by candles and has white linens, fresh flowers, and classical strains. The five-course meal —there's a single set menu each night — is $37.50. Possibilities include Newcastle crab cakes, duck breast with pear and ginger, or champagne lobster.

Dessert might be an airy souffle or some other creation like luscious lemon-layered ice cream cake.

NICKERSON TAVERN
207-548-2220.
Rte.1, Searsport.
Closed: Call for fall and
winter hours.
Price: Moderate.
Cuisine: American.
Serving: D.
Credit Cards: D, MC, V.
Reservations: Recom-
mended.
Handicap Access: Limited.

The Nickerson is a favorite in the Midcoast area. Chef Jim Bouras runs a classic American restaurant. The raciest accents you will find are a nod to the French here, a nibble of Thai there. Mostly it's just good food — fresh seafood, roast duckling, lobster, salmon, lamb, veal, and filet mignon — served in the quintessential Maine coast setting, a handsome 1838 captain's home. My mother and father love to stop by here on their frequent trips to the region, and every time they are greeted with a fine meal and good service.

90 MAIN RESTAURANT
207-338-1106.
90 Main St., Belfast 04915.
Open all year.
Price: Moderate.
Cuisine: Eclectic.
Serving: L, D, SB.
Credit Cards: AE, D, MC,
V.

This place is a mix of Down East, New Age and New York — a common cultural crossroads in Belfast these days. Clean and woody upstairs and down, they offer just what you'd expect: local natural beef cheeseburgers, macrobiotic buckwheat soba noodles with a sweet and sour ginger sauce, blueberry chicken with a bagel and cream cheese on the side.

PERIWINKLE'S BAKERY
207-548-9910.
Rte. 1, Searsport 04974.
Season: Year-round except
January.
Cuisine: Bakery, tea.
Serving: Light lunch.
Price: Inexpensive.
Credit Cards: None.
Handicap Access: No.

This pretty little bakery and tea room, tucked into an old white farmhouse right on Rte. 1, is a good place to stop and catch your wind during a big day of antiquing in Searsport and nearby Belfast. There are plenty of tasty cookies, cakes, pastries, and tarts to sample. They also make good soup and sandwiches on thickly sliced homemade bread, and a nice homemade quiche. Enjoy breakfast, lunch, or tea inside, or outside at one of their

Processing wild Maine blueberries in Cherryfield. Much of the state's blueberry crop is harvested within thirty miles of here.

Herb Swanson

roadside picnic tables. These folks used to own a bakery in Philadelphia, and Philadelphia's loss is our gain.

THE SALT BAY CAFE
207-563-1666.
Main St., Damariscotta.
Open all year.
Price: Inexpensive to
    Moderate.
Cuisine: All American.
Serving: L, D.
Credit Cards AE, D, MC, V.
Handicap Access: Yes.

The Salt Bay serves typical American food with a polite nod towards lite and healthy. Big fat comfortable booths, a little too much carpet, non-threatening, been-there-forever help. This is *Murder, She Wrote* look-a-like country, and you can imagine Jessica Fletcher and the police chief sitting at the next booth over while the cook lies on the kitchen floor with a knife in his back. You've had this food many times before. It's a good place to come if you're homesick. Pie and bread pudding for dessert.

**SHAW'S FISH &
    LOBSTER WHARF**
207-677-2200.
Rte. 32, New Harbor.
Open: May to October.
Price: Inexpensive to
    Moderate.
Cuisine: Seafood.
Serving: L, D.
Credit Cards: MC, V.

What a wonderful view. Half the wharf is given over to fishermen and fishing boats, the other half to serving a prodigious supply of seafood, side orders, and pie. Lunch and dinner are self service, and you can pick your own table, outside, inside, or down on the wharf where at night there's also an outside bar. From the deck upstairs, you can look down on boats being made ready for next day's sail. If the young travelers don't want lobster, there's a wide selection of kid's sandwiches and three kinds of cookies at forty cents a pop.

THE SQUIRE TARBOX INN

207-882-7693.
Rte. 144, Westport Island.
Closed: Nov.–mid-May;
open seven days in
season.
Price: Expensive.
Cuisine: American.
Serving: D.
Credit Cards: AE, D, MC, V.
Reservations: Required.
Special Features: Goat
cheese made on
premises; dairy open
year round.

Dinner is served in the 1763 portion of this pretty farmhouse every night during the busy months. It's a hearty and lavish meal — five courses of good country cooking. The menu changes daily, but you can count on there being plenty of their homemade goat cheese on it — whether it's their spreadable and tasty farmstead chevre (fashioned after French-style goat cheese) or caerphilly, an aged, waxed cheese with a smooth texture and mellow flavor — smoked or plain. You never leave hungry, either, because they fill you up with great vegetables and a selection of dinner meats that can include roast fish, poultry, chops, or their goat salami (it's pretty tasty, too). Desserts include a chocolate torte with peach blackberry sauce and a bread pudding with fresh mango and strawberry sauce.

THE WATERFRONT

207-236-3747.
40 Bayview St., Camden.
Closed: January.
Price: Moderate.
Cuisine: American;
seafood.
Serving: L, D.
Credit Cards: AE, MC, V.
Handicap Access: Yes.
Special Features: View of
Camden Harbor.

Camden's harbor may be the most beautiful in the midcoast region, and the Waterfront is the place to watch it from. In summer, the restaurant opens its roomy terrace to salt breezes — all the better to enjoy your lobster and clams by. Seafood, in some cases with a stylish twist, is the kitchen's hallmark. Fresh fish, crab cakes, crab pie, linguine with sun-dried tomatoes, and fresh scallops share the menu with steaks and specials like breast of chicken with olive oil and blueberry vinegar. At lunch, sandwiches and salads are teamed with chowders and soups. This is a charming spot to while away a couple of hours. Crack open a chablis, dig into a halibut steak, and enjoy the water lapping at the docks.

THE WATER'S EDGE

207-389-1803.
Off Rte. 217, Sebasco
Estates.
Open year round.
Price: Inexpensive to
Moderate.
Cuisine: Seafood.
Credit Cards: MC, V.

The Water's Edge seems as if it sits perched at the end of the world. It is on the peninsula to the east and south of Phippsburg, and getting there takes a fair amount of winding in, out, and down country roads. There are tables outside where you can eat when the weather warms up. We were there late in the spring, and inside we found a woodburning stove to take the chill off. This place feels authentic with rough hewn wood, old nautical paintings, and an impressive collection of things that look like they've been washing up on the beach for years. The seafood is fresh from the family's wharf just below. On the day we were there, they had tiny, sweet mahogany clams steamed and served with butter, as well as a fine halibut filet. We finished with bread pudding.

ZADDIK'S PIZZA
207-236-6540.
20 Washington St.,
   Camden.
Open all year.
Price: Inexpensive to
   Moderate.
Cuisine: Italian and
   Mediterranean.
Serving: D.
Credit Cards: MC, V.
Handicap Access: Yes.

Zaddik's is probably the closest thing Camden has to a factory. If they're not busy producing, they're standing ready to produce. Zaddik's stresses the freshness of their ingredients. No vegetables in Number 10 sized cans. They also claim their pizza dough had its origins in Brooklyn and comes to them via Roslyn, Washington, where it won "Best in Eastern Washington State." Personally, that doesn't impress us, but their pizza is actually quite good, although the crust is thick and more chewy than crunchy. The menu also offers tastes of the Mediterranean east of Italy, as well as deep into Mexico, including gyros, humus, quesadillas, etc. There's wide open space with booths if you prefer to eat in rather than order out.

RESTAURANTS — DOWNEAST/ACADIA

THE BLUE HILL INN
207-374-2844 or
   800-826-7415.
Union St., Blue Hill.
Closed: Oct. 31–April; open
   Nov. weekends.
Price: Expensive.
Cuisine: Continental.
Serving: D.
Credit Cards: D, MC, V.
Reservations: Required.
Special Features: No smoking; six-course prix-fixe
   dinner.

With its many chimneys and six-over-six windows, The Blue Hill Inn has been a beacon in the night for travelers since 1840. One cool fall evening before dinner we sat in the common room enjoying warm brie, a glass of Medoc, and a crackling fire. When time for dinner came, we moved to the romantic dining room, candlelit by sconces and an enormous chandelier. The first course, butternut squash and apple soup, was rich and flavorful, warmed by nutmeg and thickened with creme fraiche. The second was a rainbow trout wrapped around a delectably smooth salmon mousseline, surrounded by a light mushroom sauce. After that they offered us a "breather" with grapefruit ice, a tart lead-in to the two main courses: noisettes of lamb, medium rare and juicy, served with sauteed red peppers and shallots; and lemon-and-bourbon-marinated quail with sides of scallions and summer squash. We especially liked the quail. It had no trace of gaminess and was crisp on the outside. We finished with a dark chocolate gateau and good strong coffee for the road. This is an inn as well, and we wished we had made arrangements to stay.

Apples ripen earlier here than in other New England states, and Maine Macs and Cortlands are often the nation's first taste of autumn.

Roy Zalesky

THE BURNING TREE
207-288-9331.
Rte. 3, Otter Creek.
Closed: Tues. except in
    August.
Price: Moderate.
Cuisine: American with
    Caribbean accents.
Serving: D.
Credit Cards: MC, V.
Handicap Access: Partial.
Reservations: Suggested

From the outside, The Burning Tree doesn't look like much. Although it is one of the best on the coast, you might be tempted to drive right by on your way to Northeast Harbor. This place is for those in the know—particularly those who know enough to be impressed by the restaurant's wonderful vegetable garden and compost pile in the back. We've heard Brooke Astor and other members of Mount Desert's old money summer residents come here. Most dishes take advantage of home grown herbs. The salmon appetizer is house smoked and served with a corn and caper relish.
They do not serve meat. Southwestern and Caribbean flavors and their characteristic colors predominate. Desserts include ginger orange cheesecake and chocolate applesauce cake with Kahlua frosting.

THE CASTINE INN
207-326-4365.
Main St., Castine.
Open daily early May–
    late Dec.
Price: Expensive.
Cuisine: New England
    regional.
Serving: B, D.
Credit Cards: MC, V.
Reservations:
    Recommended.
Handicap Access: Yes.
Special Features: Porch
    dining in good weather.

The restaurant at the Castine Inn is one of the best in Maine. The fare is New England regional — simple cooking with classic underpinnings, a tendency toward seafood and a good view of the harbor. Chicken and leek pot pie is a specialty here, as are crabmeat cakes with mustard sauce. The menu varies with the seasons, depending upon the harvest of local farmers and fishermen, and always offers half a dozen appetizers (the salmon ravioli with a tomato saffron sauce is excellent). Entrees include a delicious roasted squab with a morel torte. The dessert list is solid, too: raspberry creme brulee;

Aunt Becky's blueberry kuchen; assorted sorbets. Service is friendly and effi-cient. Smoking is permitted only in the pub, where appetizers such as Mussel Bisque or oysters on the half shell are served. Weather permitting, seating is available on the porch overlooking the handsome gardens.

CHARLIE'S LOBSTER HUT
No telephone.
Rte. 186, Prospect Harbor Rd., Gouldsboro.
Open Memorial Day to mid-Oct.
Price: Inexpensive.
Cuisine: Lobster.
Serving: Takeout.

Charlie would be out lobstering again if he had $100,000 for a boat, but he doesn't. So instead he sells lobsters, crabmeat, clams, and chips out of the cabin he was born in out here by the side of the road. You can get the lobsters live, or cooked in the big blackened half-barrel filled with water that con-tains his "secret solution." Although you might not think so, people from all over the world have stopped by. This is lobster to the right of rough. People say it tastes better here. Charlie says, "I know how I want it, so it suits me, and that's how I do it for everyone else."

CHASE'S
207-963-7171.
Rte. 186, Winter Harbor.
Open daily.
Price: Moderate.
Cuisine: American; New England diner.
Serving: B, L, D.
Credit Cards: AE, CB, D, DC, MC, V.
Handicap Access: Yes.

Chase's is Maine's answer to the diner: chowder, burgers, sandwiches, and broiled and fried seafood served in a no-nonsense, no-frills setting. The lights are bright and the chairs worn, but the food is right on the mark and the help on their toes. When was the last time you saw waiters carry three plates on an arm? Among the better picks: broiled fresh haddock, fried clams, chowder, and specials like a fried flounder basket. Bread pudding or pie for dessert. Afterwards, take a spin out to Schoodic Point and work it all off by climbing along the rocks.

DENNETT'S WHARF
207-326-9045.
1 Sea St., Castine.
Open: May–early October.
Price: Moderate.
Cuisine: American.
Serving: L, D.
Credit Cards: D, MC, V.
Handicap Access: Yes.

This place boasts the longest raw bar in New Eng-land. That may be one reason it's a favorite stop for cruising sailors, Maine Maritime cadets, tourists, and year-round residents. Dollar bills have been stuck to the high, barn-like ceilings, and the waiter says it costs a buck to find out how. The food is as good as the company and about as refined: seafood lasagna, grilled marinated swordfish steak. It can get particularly racy when sailors stop by during the regatta season. Great homemade desserts and decent coffee.

The crisp, casual atmosphere belies the serious —and excellent — cooking going on at Le Domaine.

Herb Swanson

LE DOMAINE
207-422-3395 or
  800-554-8498.
Rte 1., Hancock.
Closed: Oct. 15–late May.
Price: Expensive.
Cuisine: French.
Serving: D.
Credit Cards: AE, D, MC,
  V.
Reservations: Suggested.

Here is excellent French country cooking and an encyclopedic wine list (all French with many obscure regional labels) right in the heart of Down East. Everything that comes out of the kitchen is wonderful — dense rich chicken liver pate (now available by mail order as well), garlicky escargots, rabbit with prunes, stuffed Savoy cabbage. Vegetables (baby string beans and carrots) are from the garden, as are the salad greens. Desserts include Chestnut Coupe (a vanilla ice cream and chestnut parfait), bread pudding, mousses, and tarts. Even the dining room has a Provencal feel. A walk-in fireplace at one end dominates and doubles as a rotisserie. Copper pots, wine maps, and red-and-white linens give the place the feel of a bistro, while dark wood and classical music add an elegant touch. We know several well-traveled people who, if offered a last meal, would choose dinner from Le Domaine.

DUFFY'S
207-469-1100.
Rte. 1, East Orland.
Open all year.
Price: Inexpensive.
Cuisine: American.
Serving: B, L, D.
Handicap Access: Yes.

Homestyle food, muffins the size of softballs and a clientele that looks like a reunion of Norman Rockwell models. The silverware doesn't match and the chairs wobble. No extra charge for that. The motto on the menu says succinctly: "We here at Duffy's are a native orientated restaurant. We aren't fussy and we're certainly not fancy. If you are, Ellsworth is 12 miles east and Bucksport is 7 miles west."

**EATON'S LOBSTER
POOL**
207-348-2383.
Blastow's Cove, Little
Deer Isle.
Open: Mother's Day
through Oct.
Price: Moderate.
Cuisine: Lobster.
Serving: D.

FIREPOND
207-374-9970.
Main St., Blue Hill.
Closed: Labor Day–
Mid-Oct.
Price: Expensive.
Cuisine: Classic gourmet;
regional American.
Serving: D.
Credit Cards: AE, D, MC, V.
Reservations: Recom-
mended.
Special Features: Screened
porch overlooking creek.

**THE FISHERMAN'S
FRIEND**
207-367-2442.
School St., Stonington.
Open 7 days.
Price: Inexpensive.
Cuisine: Seafood, pie.
Serving: L, D.

**FISHERMAN'S INN
RESTAURANT**
207-963-5585.
7 Newman St., Winter
Harbor.
Open May through early
Dec.
Price: Inexpensive to
Moderate.
Cuisine: Seafood.
Serving: D.
Credit Cards: AE, D, MC, V.
Handicap Access: Yes.

Eaton's sits on one of those incredibly perfect Maine coves with small islands silhouetted against the horizon at dusk. Indoors or out, bibbed families lay waste to some of Maine's finest: steamed clams, lobster, chowder, French fries, coleslaw, blueberry pie, and coolers of beer (it's BYOB). When we were kids, Eaton's was exactly the same.

Lady Chatterley would have been fond of Firepond. A rushing stream below and roughhewn wood beams give it the feel of a romantic lair. But with lighted candles and pale linens this is more elegant than anything Lawrence might have dreamed up. The food encourages amorous visions, as well. Homemade breads and rolls, offbeat salads, smoked trout, pates, or baked brie with almonds begin the meal. Then there are the main courses, pork tenderloin marsala, steak au poivre, and lobster with fresh pasta and a three-cheese sauce. For dessert, look for fresh fruit tarts, homemade ice cream, or flourless chocolate cake.

There's no other place in the world like Stonington, and the Fisherman's Friend is a good place to take it all in. Besides, the food is great and the fish is certified fresh. Get there early on Friday for the all-day fish fry, just $6.50. Don't forget to get a slice of pie. It and all the other desserts are homemade.

Lobster served seven ways — from boiled and served whole to lobster pie and lobster rolls — and other local seafood, as well as staples like chopped sirloin with mushrooms and a salad bar with limited but crisp vegetables, lettuce, coleslaw, and potato salad. There are no frills in this modest dining room lined with spartan wooden booths and linoleum-topped tables. And the service could have been friendlier. But that was a little easier to overlook at the meal's sweet finale —hot, gingery Indian pudding and a nicely eggy custard pie.

GEORGE'S
207-288-4505.
7 Stephans Lane, Bar
  Harbor.
Price: Expensive.
Cuisine: Mediterranean
  with ethnic influences.
Credit Cards: AE, D, MC,
  V.
Serving: D.
Reservations: Suggested.

Behind the First National Bank and the most touristy section of Bar Harbor is George's, an excellent restaurant as well as an excellent alternative to the honky tonk of the high season in Bar Harbor. The interior is done in rich, very soothing colors. There are several dining rooms with many windows to look out at the canopy of old trees. It's like sitting on the ground floor of a treehouse here. The menu is limited, but excellent, and usually includes something on the following order: cream and smoked mussels; and a muscovy duck breast with rhubarb Zinfandel sauce and Ceylon cinnamon. They also serve game: the night we were there, char-grilled elk loin steak with fresh peach and plum salsa. What ports and sherries are to Redfield's (See Redfield's) single malt scotches and single barrel bourbons are to George's.

Tea on the lawn at Jordan Pond House in Acadia National Park.

Herb Swanson

JORDAN POND HOUSE
207-276-3316.
Park Loop Rd., Acadia
  National Park.
Closed: Late Oct.–May.
Price: Moderate.
Cuisine: American.
Serving: L, D, afternoon tea.
Credit Cards: AE, D, MC,
  V.
Reservations: Recom-
  mended.
Handicap Access: Yes.
Special Features: Tea and
  popovers on the lawn.

Yes, this is a touristy spot smack in the middle of Acadia National Park, but every once in a while tourists know the score. With an outdoor patio and a many-windowed dining room, the restaurant makes the most of its location on Jordan Pond. Tea, a repast of meltingly good popovers and raspberry preserves, is served at long tables on the lawn; lunch and dinner can be had on the patio or indoors. So what if the service can be a bit relaxed? Why would you want to rush off anyway? Look for lobster roll, curried chicken salad, sandwiches, and quiches at lunch; steaks, chicken, and lots of seafood at dinner.

KEENAN'S
207-244-3403.
Rte 102A, Bass Harbor.
Closed: Mon.
Price: Inexpensive to
   moderate.
Cuisine: Seafood.
Serving: D.
Handicap Access: Limited.

Don't come here unless you've hiked or biked Cadillac Mountain or something equally deserving. These two former teachers from Massachusetts offer great deals at cheap prices. The decor is late shack. It's a work in progress that leaves you thinking it'll be a long time coming. All of this, of course, adds to the dining experience. All seafood is cooked to order. You can have it baked, broiled, grilled, deep fried, sautéed, steamed, or blackened. The seafood sampler provides enough stuff to open your own fish market. Red beans and rice are also available.

**LEFT BANK BAKERY &
   CAFE**
207-374-2201.
Rte. 172, Blue Hill.
Open daily.
Price: Moderate.
Cuisine: Eclectic home-
   grown; some vegetarian.
Serving: B, L, D.
Credit Cards: D, MC, V.
Reservations: Recom-
   mended.
Special Features: Bakery
   takeout; live music after
   8 p.m.

The Left Bank has a counterculture feel not unlike those coffeehouses Bob Dylan and Joan Baez used to hang out in. A fieldstone chimney, pine paneling, and windows facing the garden (much of the food is homegrown) make for a rustic dining room. The help, although perfectly polite and efficient, has that I-was-at-Woodstock look. Not surprising then that the pickings are wholesome and homespun. Breakfast is a real eye-opener with more than a dozen options — challah-bread French toast; exotically stuffed omelets; pancakes; granola; oatmeal; homemade whole wheat bagels; muffins; cinnamon puffs, and smoked salmon. Lunch includes homemade pizzas; main course strudels and pies; sandwiches and pastas. Dinner may be a Thai noodle dish called Pad Thai, a curried orange chicken, fish stew, or a French country pizza. There's a children's menu as well.

**MAINE STREET
   RESTAURANT**
207-288-3040.
297 Main St., Bar Harbor.
Open: Daily.
Price: Inexpensive to
   Moderate.
Cuisine: Family.
Serving: L, D.
Reservations: No.
Credit Cards: D, MC, V.

The local working folks like this place. Partly because you can get it to go, partly because of the price, partly because it offers a little bit of everything. (Believe it or not, some people in Maine sometimes get a little sick of lobster.) In addition to lobster, you can have your soups, your salads, your burgers, your vegetarian dishes, as well as your usual choice of side orders, all served in a location that has a comfortable feeling recognizable everywhere.

THE OPERA HOUSE
207-288-3509.
27 Cottage St., Bar Harbor.
Open: May through Oct.

Where else can you listen to opera and eat Chateaubriand Ponselle? In Maine, anyhow. This is what Mainers call dining for adults. This place is so overdone it's come out the other side. The walls are plastered with opera stars and a couple of

Price: Moderate to
  Expensive.
Cuisine: Cajun opera.
Serving: B, L, D.
Credit Cards: AE, D, MC,
  V.
Handicap Access: Limited.

Norman Rockwells. Restaurant reviewers as far away as Germany have written this place up. All of them feel pretty much the same: Rococo on the half shell and well worth the visit. The owner is from Louisiana, obviously misses it very much, loves Maine as well, and indulges her passions. Have the creme brulee for dessert.

PORCUPINE GRILL
207-288-3884.
123 Cottage St., Bar Harbor.
Closed: Sun.–Thurs.;
  Oct.–June.
Price: Expensive.
Cuisine: Regional
  American.
Serving: D.
Credit Cards: MC, V.
Reservations: Recom-
  mended.

Antique oak, chic window swags, and oversized black-and-white photos of the Porcupine Islands give the place a big city look. Start with one of the classy cocktails — fresh fruit daiquiris, sparkling cider, peppered vodka. The wine and beer lists are interesting, too. Food is clever and modern: grilled salmon parfait, otherwise known as, "The leaning tower of Eastport," with sushi rice and mango salsa; homemade breads like poppy seed dill and cranberry walnut; offbeat salads like a Caesar with garlic fried clams; pork chops with cornbread stuffing, and homemade applesauce. Desserts, like chocolate fudge pie, are a good ending to it all.

PREBLE GRILLE
207-244-3034.
14 Clark Point Rd.,
  Southwest Harbor.
Closed: Sun., Mon. in the
  off season.
Price: Moderate to
  Expensive.
Cuisine: Mediterranean.
Serving: D.
Handicap Access: No.
Reservations: Suggested.

The place to eat in Southwest Harbor, this small, on-the-street spot offers the same famed crab cakes as its sister restaurant, The Fin Back in Bar Harbor. They share the same pink and turquoise color sense. Grilled polenta, baked asiago cheese, puttanesca—you get the picture. Also, for entrees, they have grilled pork chops glazed with applejack maple syrup and apple chutney. There is a full bar.

REDFIELD'S
207-276-5283.
Main St., Northeast Harbor.
Open: Mon.–Sat.
Price: Moderate to
  Expensive.
Cuisine: Continental.
Serving: D.
Credit Cards: AE, MC, V.
Reservations: Recom-
  mended.

Redfield's is very *Town & Country*, usually very crowded and caters to the wealthy summer crowd and local residents wise enough to book their tables well in advance. They've added a wine bar recently, and we remain impressed with the offering of sherries and ports. The menu changes nightly and is the sort you could find in many sophisticated cities — shrimp and pork dim sum with black bean garlic sauce to start, grilled chilled filet of beef with horseradish sauce or loin of lamb with rosemary Provençal sauce for entrees.

RESTAURANTS — EAST OF SCHOODIC

HELEN'S RESTAURANT
207-255-8423.
Rte. 1, Machias.
Open all year.
Price: Moderate.
Cuisine: American.
Serving: B, L, D.
Credit Cards: MC, V.
Handicap Access: Yes.

As the tour buses in the parking lot suggest, Helen's, famous coast to coast, is very good at hooking hungry travelers and putting up with any odd request you throw at them. For them it's faster to do it than think about it. All fried foods are cooked in cholesterol-free oil, which means you can then go ahead and get your dose from one of their fine cream pies. The strawberry pie is famous. We had a rib-sticking pork sandwich with home-made mashed potatoes and gravy because Helen's makes you feel that way. That feeling stuck all the way to Eastport. There's good parking.

MICMAC FARM
207-255-3008.
Off Rte. 92, which is off Rte.
   1, Machiasport.
Closed: Sun. and Mon.
Price: Expensive.
Cuisine: Country gourmet.
Serving: D.
Credit Cards: MC, V.
Handicap Access: Yes.
Reservations: Required.

This 18th-century farmhouse may be out of the way (that is to say, at the end of a rutted dirt road), but it's worth seeking out for the sheer romance of the place. Flickering candles give a refined glow to the rustic rooms with wide floor-boards and low beams. There are usually five din-ner choices; the night we were there they included filet mignon with Bordelaise sauce; shrimp-or-crab stuffed sole; lobster Graziella cream and wine and tomato sauce. Desserts are inspired creations on the order of their light-as-air Bavarian cream and meringue glace. Machiasport is dry, so if you want wine or beer with dinner, you'll have to bring your own.

The Waco Diner in Eastport, pronounced Wack-o.

Herb Swanson

WACO DINER
207-853-4046.
Bank Sq., Eastport.
Open every day.
Serving: B, L, D.
Price: Inexpensive.
Cuisine: American diner.
Handicap Access: Limited.

It's tempting to mispronounce the name of this place, but just try it and a dozen people will correct you. Wack-o is the right way to say it, and the name is suitable for this quirky little spot. Lunch counter standards — clam chowder, corned beef hash, grilled frankfurters, fish and chips, and all sorts of pies — make up the bulk of the menu, but there are some surprises: scallop stew, tuna noodle casserole, fried clam rolls, homemade English muffin toast, and Grapenut pudding. Best of all, the place looks as if it's been around for eons, with worn vinyl stools, old-timey booths, and counters all crammed in a space the size of a postage stamp. Service may be a little surly, but that only adds to the charm.

Maine Food Festivals

As we said before, Mainers love to eat. They also love to celebrate food. Here is a list of some of the annual food-centered celebrations on the coast:

Annual Winter Harbor Lobster Festival (207-963-7638; 800-231-3008 out-of-state). Mid-August. Almost as famous as Rockland's Lobster Festival (see below). The lobster boat races are a main attraction.

Bay Festival, Belfast (207-338-5900). Last week in July. This used to be called the Broiler Festival on account of its being a big chicken town. There used to be so much chicken here, you would think twice before visiting. These days, most chickens have moved out of town, but they still celebrate their broilers.

Maine Lobster Festival, Rockland (207-596-0376). First weekend in August. A parade, pageant, and the world's largest lobster cooker. This festival has been famous for more than 45 years.

Wild Blueberry Festival, Machias (207-255-4402). Mid-August. Two days celebrating one of the state's biggest crops. This is the home of the wild blueberry.

Yarmouth Clam Festival (207-846-3984). Third week in July. Every year for almost 30 years, the folks in Yarmouth pay tribute to the clam. They eat lots of fried ones, then they go take a ride on the roller coaster at the midway.

FOOD PURVEYORS

BAKERIES

South Coast

Whistling Wings Farm (207-282-1146; 427 West St., Biddeford). Berries from this farm and kitchen end up on tables all over the world. The jams, jellies,

People enjoying themselves at one of the many strawberry festivals on the coast.

and syrups contain no preservatives or juice concentrates, and in summer the bakery offers berry sweets for immediate consumption.

Chase Hill Bakery (207-967-2283; 9 Chase Hill Rd., Kennebunk). An unassuming gray clapboard house with old-fashioned bakery cases and a table or two. They sell comforting chicken pot pies, breads, cakes, and pastries.

Bread & Roses (207-646-4227; 28A Main St., Ogunquit). Fresh pastries and bread baked on the spot.

Casco Bay

The Port Bakehouse (207-773-2217; 205 Commercial St., Portland). You'll find their wholesome rolls and buttery cakes and tortes in stores and restaurants around Portland, or you can go straight to the source. They make a different bread every day of the week. Everybody likes the prairie bread because it's packed with nuts and grains and pumpkin seeds.

Midcoast

Kristina's (207-442-8577; 160 Center St., Bath). Pastries and tortes to fuel your way up the coast. They also make great French toast for a sit-down breakfast.

Down East/Acadia

Bah's (207-326-9510; Water St. behind the Co-op, Castine). Everybody likes to linger over breakfast at this bakery/deli, and then stay on for lunch. Scones, great looking bread, sweet rolls, and when we were there, boar's meat chili.

Cottage Street Bakery and Deli (207-288-3010; 59 Cottage St., Bar Harbor). You can have a sit-down meal here or you can grab a sweet to go. We weren't nuts about their muffins, but everything else was pretty good.

The Donut Hole (Main St., Winter Harbor). Homemade donuts, pies, and pastries. Also a good spot to grab a grilled cheese, take in the view of Henry's Cove and maybe run into Tom Selleck.

Left Bank Bakery & Cafe (207-374-2201; Blue Hill). Handmade, homemade bagels, peasant bread, and European pastries are baked fresh here every day.

East of Schoodic

The Sugar Scoop (207-546-7048; Main St., Milbridge). Pies, cookies, squares, and a heavenly bakery smell.

BREWERIES & WINERIES

There's been an explosion of microbreweries in Maine since we last wrote. D.L. Geary, maker of Geary's Pale Ale, one of the very first microbrews made, is still going strong, and has added a smokey London Porter to their roster. There are so many micros and such an appreciative audience that recently a microbrew (Shipyard Export Ale) sold more beer in Maine than Budweiser. Can you imagine that?

If you are looking for a good place to sample the full range of Maine micros, check out the *The Great Lost Bear* in Portland (207-772-0300; 540 Forest Ave.) or the *Water Works* in Rockland (207-596-7950; 3 Lindsey St.), a wonderful pub owned by two local windjammer captains.

South Coast

Kennebunkport Brewing/Federal Jack's Brew Pub (207-967-4322; 8 Western Avenue, Kennebunk). A brew pub and microbrewery at the site of a historic shipyard, and brewer of the aforementioned Shipyard Export Ale. The pub is okay. The beer is better.

Casco Bay

Allagash Brewing (207-878-5385 ; 100 Industrial Way, Portland).

Casco Bay Brewing (207-797-2020; 57 Industrial Way). Tours available.

Geary Brewing Company (207-878-2337; 38 Evergreen Dr., Portland). They brew a fine ale here, and if you can't make it to the brewery you can find it at almost any grocery store or gourmet shop in the area. Tours available.

Gritty McDuff's (207-772-2739; 396 Fore St., Portland;). This seems like just about everyone's favorite brew pub in New England. They are so popular, they now have a second brew pub (207-865-4321; 183 Lower Main St., Freeport), and they bottle a line of their "best" beers. We like this place, even though we find the brew can be watery.

Shipyard Brewing Company (207-761-0807; 86 Newbury St., Portland). The "sister" brewery to the Kennebunkport Brewing Co. The big beer guys at Miller were so impressed, they invested in it. This brewery was built on the site where, coincidentally, Henry Wadsworth Longfellow was born in 1807. They brew a fine winter ale in his honor. They also brew Old Thumper Extra Special Ale and more. Tours available.

Stone Coast Brewing (207-773-2337; 14 York St., Portland). There are many in this town who believe that you can't have enough beer or too many brew pubs. They have all been waiting for Stone Coast to open in the old brick warehouse at the edge of the Old Port. We'll keep you posted.

Midcoast

Andrew's Brewing (207-763-3305; High St., Box 4975, Lincolnville). Call ahead for directions and to make an appointment for a tour.

Sea Dog Brewing (207-236-6863; 43 Mechanic St., Camden). We like their India ale, although we aren't in love with the pub.

Down East/Acadia

Atlantic Brewing & the Lompoc Cafe (207-288-9392; 34-36 Rodick St., Bar Harbor). A good place to hang out and savor the local flavors. Brewery tours daily.

Bar Harbor Brewing (207-288-4592; Rte. 3, Otter Creek Rd., the Acadia Park Loop near Thunder Hole). Check out their Bar Harbor Peach, which tastes better than it sounds. Tours weekdays in the summer; less frequently during the rest of the year.

Bartlett Maine Estate Winery (207-546-2408; RR 1, Box 598, Gouldsboro). A tasting here is pretty relaxed. Honey wine, apple wine and wines of pear, blueberry, raspberry. Robert and Kathe Bartlett have been making their fruit wines since 1983. We especially like their dry pear and apple combination. Tours and tastings available.

Down East Country Wines (207-667-6965; Rte. 3, Bar Harbor). More than 40,000 bottles of fruit wines are produced in this old blacksmith's barn. Semi-sweet or medium dry wild blueberry, spiced apple, and blue blush, a blend of apples and blueberries. Tours are available.

Maine Coast Brewing (207-288-4914; 21A Cottage St., Bar Harbor). Tours by appointment.

CANDY AND ICE CREAM

South Coast

The Goldenrod (207-363-2621; York Beach). A vacation at the beach wouldn't be the same without saltwater taffy. They make it right here and call it "kisses." Watch it being made or grab an ice cream soda in their old-fashioned soda fountain.

Harbor Candy Shop (207-646-8078; 26 Main St., Ogunquit). European-style chocolates are made and sold here in a very elegant atmosphere.

Casco Bay

Beal's Old Fashioned Ice Cream (207-828-1335; 12 Moulton St., Portland; and 207-883-1160; 161 Pine Point Rd., Scarborough). The name may sound as if it's too good to be true, but it is. Standard flavors run the gamut from vanilla to deep, dark variations on chocolate. They also have someone out back who occasionally comes out with a surprise, like lemon-mint. It's really good.

Ben & Jerry's Ice Cream (207-865-3407; 83 Main St., Freeport). This grew from a one-room shack on the curb outside L. L. Bean to a much larger one room shack, big enough to accommodate long lines in all kinds of weather. Sometimes you need ice cream after a long day shopping.

Browns Apiaries (207-829-5994; 239 Greely Rd., Cumberland). They raise bees here and sell the sweet by-products. Honey, strained and with the comb, in half-pound to one gallon sizes, candles, honey candy, and bee keeping supplies. They're open year round, five days a week, but it's best to call ahead.

Haven's (207-772-0761; 542 Forest Ave., Portland). Every year they hire a new taffy puller and put him in the front window. Usually it's a high school boy, and the girls are hooked for the rest of the summer. Frankly, saltwater taffy is taffy, just about everywhere. Here, you should try the Bangor taffy, a Maine specialty, which has a buttery caramel flavor.

Wilbur's Chocolate Shoppe (207-865-6129; 13 Bow St., Freeport). All-natural chocolate — creams, berry flavors, or rich and dark.

Midcoast

The Downeast Ice Cream Factory (207-633-5178; 7 Bridge St., Boothbay Harbor). They make the ice cream, you make the sundaes. They also make homemade candies.

Fun? . . . You Bet! (207-882-9426; Rte. 1, Wiscassett). See it, make it, eat it. That's the motto here. Ice cream, fudge, and saltwater taffy in an interactive environment.

Miss Plum's (207-596-6946; Rte. 1, Rockport). A reporter friend of ours thinks this is the best ice cream on the coast. They also sell sorbet, frozen yogurt, and baked desserts.

Round Top Ice Cream (207-563-5307; Bus. Rte. 1, Damariscotta). For years they've made ice cream at this dairy. Now they also make art and music, but you can still find 30 flavors of the good stuff. Look for Round Top at stores and restaurants nearby.

Downeast/Acadia

Ben & Bill's Chocolate Emporium (207-288-3281; 66 Main St., Bar Harbor). This is like walking into a cartoon candy store: truffles the size of handballs; lobster ice cream (blechhhh). It's almost pornographic.

East of Schoodic

K-K-K-Katie's (207-454-8446; Rte. 1, Mill Cove, Robbinston). They hand dip all of their homemade chocolates and use recipes from well-loved Passamaquoddy Bay candymakers of old. Check out their Maine potato candy. It's an experience you won't soon forget.

DELIS AND TAKE-OUT

South Coast

Anthony's Food Shop (207-363-2322; 679 Rte. 1, York). Beer, apples, pizza, but best is a selection of great Green Mountain coffees like Columbian Supremo with real cream. There are small sizes for short hops and large sizes for long hauls. If you didn't get a decent cup of coffee for breakfast, stop here and rectify the situation.

Hamilton's (207-646-5262; 2 Shore Rd., Ogunquit). Eat-in or take out in this deli on the main drag. A favorite breakfast spot for residents.

Old Salt's Pantry (207-967-4966; Dock Sq., Kennebunkport). Don't be fooled by its size. This tiny deli offers a huge menu of take-out from sandwiches, subs, and burgers to gourmet tidbits, wine, and beer.

Casco Bay

Della's Catessen (207-773-2624; 92 Exchange St., Portland) Big, delicious sandwiches. Good soup. Great victuals for the road.

Portland Wine & Cheese (207-772-4647; Middle and Exchange Sts., Portland). Great deli sandwiches in the basement of an Old Port office building. Eat it there or get it to go. They also have a nice selection of wines.

Midcoast

Camden Deli (207-236-8343; 37 Main St., Camden). New York-style sandwiches, wine and beer, and great desserts.

Downeast/Acadia

Cottage Street Bakery & Deli Café (207-288-3010; 59 Cottage St. Bar Harbor). There's limited indoor seating. They serve a good box lunch which is not in their flyer and their pizza slices are large enough to feed a small family.

FAST FOOD

South Coast

Bob's Clam Hut (207-439-4233; Rte. 1, Kittery). Fried clams, sweet and steaming, are served here year round. The ultimate in finger-fast food.

Casco Bay

Mark's (corner of Exchange and Middle Sts., Portland). Mark is out there through all kinds of weather selling his dogs and smoked sausages from a little red cart. There's a park next door for you to sit in, if it's warm enough.

Midcoast

Brud's Hot Dogs (East Side, Boothbay Harbor). Hot dogs, fast and inexpensive. Since 1948. Sold out of a cart on the east side of town.

Cod End (207-372-6782; near town landing; Tenants Harbor). From Memorial Day through mid-October they serve up fresh, fast seafood, including good lobster rolls and chowder. Take it with you or eat it on their picnic tables.

Lady Millville Store (207-236-6570; 113 Washington St., Rte. 105, Camden). Fresh dough pizza, subs, burgers, hot dogs, even fast food seafood and chicken.

Wasses (207-594-7472; 2 North Main St., Rockland). *The Washington Post* likes their hot dogs. Their "waffles" are pretty good, too — vanilla ice milk, Spanish peanuts, and thick fudge in a crispy waffle cone.

Herb Swanson

Seaside Takeout on the Pier in Seal Harbor, Mount Desert Island.

Down East/Acadia

Bubba's (207-288-5871; 30 Cottage St., Bar Harbor). Soups, sandwiches, and a full bar, for those who choose to linger. You wouldn't guess by the name that this would be a small art deco palace, would you?

The Deacon Seat (207-244-9229; Clark Point Rd., Southwest Harbor). They serve breakfast and lunch here from 5:00 a.m. to 4:30 p.m. every day except Sunday. Eat it as fast as you want.

Epi Sub & Pizza (207-288-3507; 8 Cottage St., Bar Harbor). Homemade calzones, pizza, pasta, and other quick stuff like crabmeat rolls, quiche, and salads.

Seaside Takeout (Town Pier, Seal Cove on Mount Desert Island). Steve Smith serves a dynamite chowder from this tiny joint. The view's not too shabby, either.

East of Schoodic

The Crossroads (207-726-5053; Rte. 1, Pembroke). Located at the site of an old iron works, this little carry-out attached to a roadside motel serves the best lobster roll around.

GOURMET FOOD STORES

Casco Bay

Micucci's (207-775-1854; 45 India St., Portland). A tiny Italian grocer at the foot of Munjoy Hill, they have all the fixings for an authentic Italian feast, including fresh mozzarella on Wednesdays.

Midcoast

Ducktrap River Fish Farm (207-338-6280; Belfast). Naturally smoked Atlantic salmon and rainbow trout raised here and at fish farms nearby. Open year round, Monday through Friday. We like their smoked bluefish and scallops best.

Foggy Ridge Gamebird Farm (207-273-2357; West Branch Rd., Warren). They raise, dress, and smoke game birds. They also sell live ones. Pheasants, partridges, and quails. Call for an appointment.

Great Eastern Mussel Farms (207-372-6317; Long Cove Rd., Tenants Harbor). They've taken the lowly mussel and cultivated it. Call ahead and ask for a tour of their plant. They'll let you taste them as well.

Kohn's Smokehouse Inc. (207-372-8412; Rte. 131, St. George). They make and sell fine smoked meats and seafood. Bacon, sausage, bratwurst, salami, even poultry. In the winter they're open Monday through Saturday; in the summer seven days a week.

An inviting window display at a Maine island general store.

State Development Office

Morse's Sauerkraut (207-832-5569; Rte. 220, Waldoboro)Every once in a while they run a simple ad in the paper that says, "Kraut's ready." Maybe eating sauerkraut wouldn't be considered a chore if it were all as good as the fresh stuff made here. Also available are your knockwurst, bratwurst, kielbasa, and the humble dog. Sandwiches available.

Mystique (207-832-5136; Friendship St., Waldoboro). Open June to Dec. They sell French-style goat cheeses, as well as feta.

State of Maine Cheese Company (207-236-8895; 321 Commercial St., Rockport). Peter Kress, cheesemaker, is responsible for these distinct cheeses: Penobscot cheddar, Katahdin cheddar, Cumberland smoked, Aroostook Jack, and more, all made from all natural Maine milk.

Weatherbird Trading Company (207-563-8993; Elm St. Damariscotta). Pates, imported beers, and French scents in a 1754 saltbox cape.

Wicked Wild Maine Preserves (207-882-7772; Rte. 27, North Edgecomb). Jams and jellies for toast or cooking; some are made with no sugar at all. Especially interesting are their hot sauces and their run-for-water mustard. Call ahead.

Downeast/Acadia

Penobscot Bay Provisions (207-367-2920; W. Main St., Stonington). Let them get you ready for the boat ride to Isle au Haut. Smoked seafood, cheese, fresh fruit salads, good baked goods.

Periwinkles (207-288-9685; 59 Cottage St., Bar Harbor). Wild Maine blueberry jam, relish, syrup, and jelly. Also local cookbooks and other made-in-Maine specialties.

Herb Swanson

Salmon pens on Cobscook Bay near Eastport. Aquaculture is a thriving industry downeast, and many restaurants feature locally raised Atlantic salmon.

East of Schoodic

J. W. Raye & Co. (207-853-4451; Rte. 190, Eastport). They've been making mustard here since 1903, first for the sardine canning industry that used to flourish here, now for the mass market. Visit their gift shop or get a tour and learn how they make the stuff at the Mustard Museum.

Jim's Smoked Salmon (207-853-4831; 37 Washington St., Eastport). Jim smokes Atlantic salmon raised on farms in Cobscook Bay. He will also wrap your salmon gift in a beautifully crafted wood box that he builds himself. Also, smoked mussels and rainbow and steelhead trout.

Maine Wild Blueberry Company (207-255-8364; Elm St., Machias). These people have the biggest wild blueberry business in the world. You can buy frozen, canned, and dried blueberries right from the factory. They call the dried ones "wild chews." They taste like very sweet blueberries and have the consistency of raisins.

HEALTH FOOD AND FARM MARKETS

Casco Bay

Portland Green Grocer (207-761-9232; 211 Commercial St., Portland). Terrific fruit and vegetables. Great bakery breads, wine, and an ever-improving selection of cheeses and gourmet deli meats.

Wolf Neck Farm (207-865-4469; Wolf Neck Rd., off Flying Point Rd., Freeport). Lean, delicious organic beef and lamb raised on a beautiful saltwater farm run by the state university system. They ship to New England and elsewhere, but it's better yet to take the trip down the long dirt road and get a slab to thaw out for a seaside barbecue. This farm has been operating for more than one hundred years and selling natural beef since 1959.

Midcoast

Belfast Co-op Store (207-338-2532; 69 High St., Belfast). Whole foods, local produce, fresh bread, and other baked goods. Bona fide good things brought to you in a macrobiotic town.

Camden Farmers' Market (Colcord Ave., near Union St., Camden). Every Saturday morning, rain or shine.

Fresh Off The Farm (207-236-3260; Rte. 1, Rockport). Native produce and berries in season; apples and cider in season; natural foods, vitamins, herbs, jams, jellies, maple syrup and candy, pickles, relishes, blueberry syrup, chutney, mustards, dried beans, and local honey year round. Lots of things to take home to your friends.

The Last Stop Poultry Farm (207-273-4029; Rte. 1, Warren). In case you're running low. Fresh native broilers and roasting chickens. Fresh native turkeys. Homemade chicken and turkey pot pies.

School House Farm (207-273-2440; Rte. 1, Warren). Late June through Thanksgiving. Seven days a week. They raise and sell 24 varieties of apples, six of plums, and four of pears. They also have fresh vegetables in season. Fresh homemade donuts as well as their renowned cider donuts in the fall.

Down East/Acadia

Darthia Farm (207-963-7771; West Bay Rd., Rte 186, Gouldsboro). They offer a selection of organic fruits, vegetables, and herbs, as well as homemade jams, vinegars, pesto, yogurt, herb cheeses, and fresh butter.

Hay's Farm Stand (Rte. 172, Surry Hill, Blue Hill). From July to October, Monday through Saturday, they sell certified organic vegetables, strawberries, raspberries, tomatoes, corn, potatoes, and lamb. They also sell farm sausage, jams, and their homemade Old Goat Soap.

H.O.M.E. (207-469-7961; Rte. 1, Orland). It stands for Homeworkers Organized for More Employment and, in addition to crafts, they sell fresh vegetables in

The joys of a farmer's market in Maine.

Tom Hindman

season and storage crops like potatoes and squash. They also have a good selection of locally grown spices, flour in bulk, grains, and dried fruit.

East of Schoodic

Cross Road Farm Stand (Off Rte. 187, Jonesport). Organic isn't a fad here. They've been farming that way for more than 20 years and are certified. More than 200 types of vegetables, 50 kinds of potatoes, unusual salad greens, squashes, and onions.

Arnold Johnson digs potatoes on his farm near Perry.

Herb Swanson

CHAPTER SIX
By the Sea, By the Sea
RECREATION

Herb Swanson

The beach at Ogunquit on a cloudy day.

Many of the recreational opportunities along the coast and on its islands center around, you guessed it, water. Your time spent here will likely include swimming in water; sailing, canoeing or kayaking on it; windjamming through it; camping by it, or biking, hiking, climbing, horseback riding or cross-country skiing to get a view of it. Of course, there are many other things to do. The coast also has its share of skating rinks and bowling alleys, and in this chapter we will explore many different possibilities for you and your family.

Fun on the coast used to be a one-season affair. Nineteenth-century tourists came here to enjoy cool breezes when cities to the south — Boston, New York and Philadelphia — sweltered in the summer sun. French Canadians early on discovered Old Orchard Beach, the closest sand beach of note to Montreal and Quebec. Today the Maine coast holds plenty of chances to enjoy yourself the year round. Although most people choose to hike and camp here in the summer, many know to take advantage of the off seasons and avoid the crowds. Leaf peeping has become a popular pastime for autumn visitors. Several resorts and parks have extensive cross-country ski trails. There's even downhill skiing at the Snow Bowl in Camden. Spring is mountain bikes and kayaks and the chance to have Acadia National Park all to yourself.

Whatever season you visit, remember the weather. The outlook often changes quickly, and the combination of ocean wind and water can make 40 degrees Fahrenheit seem much colder. Bring along a good selection of warm clothes and rain gear (See "Climate and What to Wear" in *Information*, Chapter Eight).

Railroad buffs rejoice. After much controversy among conservationists and residents of a nearby retirement home, the Maine Narrow Gauge Railway opened for business during the winter of 1994–95.

Maine's only two-foot common carrier is a beauty — especially as it chugs along 1.5 miles of track on Portland's Eastern Promenade. The railway was an instant hit. During its first summer, more than 11,000 passengers rode on the relic (see "Family Fun," below).

Plans to extend the railway across the bridge to Falmouth or around the peninsula of Portland to the Sea Dogs ballpark are still brewing. The real miracle is that the entire enterprise is staffed entirely by volunteers. They lay the track, run the train and answer all your questions at the museum.

AUTO RACING

The chance to see auto racing is rare on the coast. **Beech Ridge Motor Speedway** (207-885-0111, automated race information at 207-885-5800; 70 Holmes Rd., Scarborough) features four divisions of stock car racing on a $^1/_3$ mile track. Starting time April through September is 6:30 p.m. every Saturday evening. Call for times of special events.

Acadia National Park

Acadia National Park on Mount Desert Island is the most visited place in Maine. It has more than 100 miles of trails through forests and past lakes; eight climbing peaks, most suitable for family hikes; great biking on old *carriage trails*; camping facilities; wonderful views; good rock climbing, canoeing and cross-country skiing; lovely beaches and the only fjord on the eastern seaboard.

You can wander through the *Wild Gardens of Acadia* and see over 200 species of plants, trees and shrubs indigenous to the island; climb to the summit of *Cadillac Mountain*, the highest point on the eastern seaboard, and enjoy the grand views, including of Frenchman Bay; swim at freshwater *Echo Lake* or saltwater *Sand Beach*; see the high tide surge at *Thunder Hole*, a tidal cavern carved by wave action with water spouts as high as 40 feet, and sea kayak along the New England coast.

Part of Acadia National Park is on the *Isle au Haut*, a lightly populated island that is eight miles out to sea from Stonington, where there is good biking, hiking, swimming and fishing.

A third section of Acadia is *Schoodic Point*, at the tip of the Schoodic Peninsula near Winter Harbor, where there are great views of the rocky coastline from hiking trails that ascend to overlooks, and a scenic 13-mile biking loop.

BALLOONING

Most balloon flights originating near the coast are overland. Balloonists talk about one pilot who often dares saltwater flights. He and his passengers have been rescued three times.

Even if the winds are blowing inland, you are almost assured a good view from the White Mountains to the shore. Spring flights are tricky — and often canceled — due to the changeable Maine weather. September and October tend to be the busiest months because of foliage flights, so be sure to make your reservations early. Experienced balloonists say winter flights are the most spectacular, when the air takes on a crystalline clarity. Dress warmly, though; it will be much colder at an 800-foot altitude than it is on the ground.

The Casco Bay region is a hotbed for balloonophiles: *Balloon Rides* (207-761-8373 or 800-952-2076; 17 Freeman St., Portland) boasts of having "Coastal Maine's oldest balloon company." Pilot Bob Schuerer of *Freeport Balloon Company* (207-865-1712; Tuttle Rd., Pownal) offers intimate champagne flights (just two passengers and the pilot). Also, call *Hot Fun* (207-799-0193; Cape Elizabeth) and *Balloons Over New England* (800-788-5562; Kennebunk)

BASEBALL

Win or lose, the *Portland Sea Dogs*, the Double A affiliate of the Florida Marlins, keep Hadlock Field (207-879-9500; 271 Park Ave., Portland) filled to capacity throughout the season. This is a young team with an exceptionally loyal following, including former President George Bush who, when he goes, often is asked to throw in the first ball.

The Sea Dogs are so popular that getting a ticket to witness Eastern League baseball in one of the 6,500 seats is virtually impossible for most games. Monday nights are your best bet. Still we suggest calling well in advance.

BEACHES

Maine's beaches are the crown jewels of the coast. Almost all are flanked by the rugged terrain that gives the coast its distinct beauty and character — jagged outcroppings of metamorphic rock, sheer cliffs and exhilarating Atlantic surf. More than 40 percent of the visitors to the coast make the South Coast their destination. That's where most of the sand beaches are, and *Old Orchard Beach* and the long, broad stretches of sand at *York* and *Ogunquit* are the most famous southern Maine beaches. These beaches have lovely sandy bottoms perfect for swimming. Non-residents often find the water a little cool.

We have our favorites. The swimming is great at *Ferry Beach*, in Scarborough, where water over a long, shallow sandbar warms up early in the summer and is kept protected by Prouts Neck. *Higgins Beach* in West Scarborough is a beautiful, broad stretch of sand bound by a modest, old-fashioned summer village (there is no boardwalk in sight and dogs run free after 4 p.m.). Then there's *Jasper Beach* near Bucks Harbor, where the surface is littered with almost perfectly round, palm-sized pieces of granite and crystalline quartz. Further Down East, the beaches become colorful. At *Perry*, the beach is deep red; at *Bailey's Mistake* it's black, and at *Jonesport*, it's brilliant white. These beaches are separated by only 40 miles.

Below, we've listed the *major* beaches, but not all of Maine's beaches. Travelers will find dozens of lovely little sand beaches tucked here and there, many of them with public access. Just keep your eyes open.

South Coast

Crescent and Seapoint beaches; Seapoint Rd., Kittery. Crescent Beach, a 625-yard sand beach and its 550-yard sister beach Seapoint across a small peninsula are nice, but have limited parking.

Drakes Island and Laudholm beaches; Rte. 1 to Drakes Island Rd., Wells. This is really one beach with two names, in addition to being a well-kept secret among South Coast beach goers. It's comparatively quiet here in the height of the summer, even when nearby Moody is jammed. It is 940 yds. with accompanying saltwater farm and nature center; limited parking.

Ferry and Western beaches; Rte. 207 to Ferry Rd., Scarborough. Actually three beaches, including two that wrap around a rocky point and lead up to tony Prouts Neck. The tide rips right at the point, and at high tide you can almost reach out and touch the lobster boats in the harbor. You can let your dog run free after 4 p.m. Total of more than 1,700 yds.; limited parking, for a fee.

Ferry Beach State Park; Rte. 9, Saco. A fine sand beach that stretches more than 4,500 yds. It is part of a 117-acre state park with all the facilities, including picnic tables, toilets and bathhouse. Fee is charged at gate. Parking.

Fortunes Rocks Beach; Rte. 208, Biddeford. Long sand beach that's great for swimming. 3,740 yds.; parking limited.

Gooch's Beach; Rte. 9 to Sea Rd., then left onto Beach Ave. past Kennebunk Beach, Kennebunk. The beach of choice for Kennebunkport residents and summer people including surfers, this is a crescent-shaped sand and shingle beach with a rocky point; 1,300 yds.; parking is limited to those with permits, so take the trolley. It's well worth the ride.

Goose Rocks Beach; Rte. 9 to Dyke Rd., then left onto King's Hwy., Kennebunkport. Lovely beach that attracts both swimmers and birdwatchers (there's a salt marsh at the southeast end); 3,600 yds.; parking limited.

Hills Beach; off Rtes. 9 and 208, Biddeford. An excellent, if short, swimming beach, on a 530-yd. sand spit protecting Maine's largest tidal basin. People like to birdwatch here (see below). Facilities nearby; parking limited.

Kennebunk Beach; Rte. 9 to Sea Rd., then left onto Beach Ave., Kennebunk. Sand and shingle beach popular among families and surfers. It's hard to park here, and illegal if you don't have a sticker; take the trolley instead; 820 yds.

Long Beach; Rte. 1A, York, and **Short Sands**; Rte. 1A, York Beach. Long Beach, at 2,180 yds., and Short Sands, 410 yds., are two of the South Coast's most popular beaches. The surfers like the waves. Parents like Short Sands, because it is near the heart of York Beach, so tired young beach bums can easily refuel with a snack. There are lifeguards and rest rooms at both. Parking is limited, so arrive early.

Moody Beach; Rte. 1 to Bourne Rd., then right onto Ocean Ave., Wells. A couple of years ago in a heated courtroom battle, residents tried to cut off public access to the beach. In a blow to the coastal aristocracy, they failed. Moody Beach is 2,750 yds. and surrounded by a honeycomb of summer cottages; facilities nearby; fee for parking which is none plentiful.

Ogunquit Beach; Rte. 1 to Beach St., Ogunquit. People love the sand here. It's refined, white and abundant (1,620 yds.). One local newspaper describes this as "very popular with the gay community"; another publication says that it is "near summer art colony." We call it fun. Facilities; fee for parking.

Old Orchard and Surfside beaches; Rte. 9, Old Orchard Beach. Some call this the Canadian Riviera, and more often than not the language spoken here is French. Lovely fine white sand beaches with a total length 3,320 yds. Bathhouse. Fee for parking.

Parsons and Crescent Surf beaches; Rte. 9 to Parson's Beach Rd., Kennebunk. You get to these two pretty beaches along a private way owned by the Parson family. Total is 1,700 yds.; no facilities; limited parking.

Pine Point and Grand beaches; Rte. 9, Scarborough. Two fine white sand beaches and sand spit totaling 2,500 yds. Facilities nearby; fee for parking.

Scarborough Beach; Rte. 207, Scarborough. This is a barrier beach and dunes that protect a freshwater marsh. It's so popular among swimmers and surfers that it often fills to overflowing by noon on a hot day; 2,060 yds.; picnic tables, grills, bathhouse, fishing; fee for parking.

Wells Beach; Rte. 1 to Mile Rd., then left onto Atlantic Ave., Wells. Motels and condos line the beach; 4,000 yds.; facilities; fee for parking.

Casco Bay

Crescent Beach State Park; Rte. 77, Cape Elizabeth. The Maine Times calls this "one of Maine's best family beaches." Sand and stone beach; 1,560 yds.; picnic tables, snack bar, fishing. Entrance fee.

Winslow Memorial Park; Rte. 1 onto South Freeport Rd. (at the Big Indian) and follow to Staples Rd., South Freeport. Nestled in the middle of a pretty, immaculate town-run park and camping area, this is another great beach for the family. The small, man-made beach is sheltered although untended by a lifeguard. Picnic tables, playground, rest rooms; entrance fee charged.

Midcoast

Crescent Beach; Crescent Beach Rd., Owl's Head. Popular swimming beach near summer colony. Length, 1,100 yards. Nearby facilities; limited parking.

Pemaquid Beach Park; off Rte. 130, New Harbor. About a half-mile long and backed by dunes. There's a bathhouse, picnic tables, rest rooms. Entrance fee.

Popham Beach State Park; Rte. 209, Phippsburg. Not only fine sand, but a fine beach. In fact, one of the finest. More than two miles long; there are picnic tables, rocky outcrops and tide pools and plenty of parking, which fills up quickly on a hot day. Entrance fee.

Reid State Park; Rte. 127 to Seguinland Rd., Georgetown. A half-mile open barrier spit, this is another great beach. There's a salt marsh, sand dunes, rocky ledges, tidal pools, a bathhouse, picnic tables, fireplaces and a snack bar. Decent parking. Entrance fee.

Sandy Point Beach; Stockton Springs. About a mile long; there's not much here except beach. No facilities and little parking.

Sand beach in Acadia National Park is one of the few sand beaches east of Portland.

Courtesy: State of Maine

Down East/Acadia

Lamoine Beach; Lamoine State Park, Rte. 184, Lamoine. Best swimming beach in the area with great views of Mount Desert Island across the bay. Picnicking; camping; no bathhouse; parking; entrance fee.

Sand Beach; off Park Loop Rd., near Cadillac Cliffs, Acadia National Park. Possibly more people have driven by this famed pocket beach than any beach in the country. It's on the Loop Road. There are no facilities. There are so few parking spaces and so many people who want to stop, they sometimes have to close it off during the height of the summer. It's a beauty. The sand is actually shell fragments. Entrance fee to national park.

East of Schoodic

Jasper Beach; off Starboard Rd., Bucks Harbor. This beach is made up entirely of polished pebbles. It's beautiful, even if it makes for difficult swimming.

Roque Bluffs Beach; Roque Bluffs Rd. off Rte. 1, Roque Bluffs. There's also Simpson Pond next door for freshwater swimming, a playground, picnic tables, grills, a bathhouse, bathrooms, and parking. Sand and shingle beach; 910 yds.

BERRY & APPLE PICKING

Wild blueberries, wild red and black raspberries, and berries of the cultivated kind, including strawberries, somehow taste better in Maine. Maybe it's because spring here is usually a long, cold, and damp affair. Maybe it's because you get to pick them yourself, sneaking a taste now and then to determine whether the big ones or smaller ones are sweeter this year. Whatever the reason, berry season in Maine is heavenly, beginning with strawberries in late June to early July, and with wild blueberries in late July right through August Down East.

Good wild berrypicking spots, like fishing holes, are well-guarded secrets passed down from parent to child. Better-known berry spots are the tops of **Blue Hill** and **Schoodic Mountain**. Knowing those two will put you ahead of millions of visitors, but get there early. If you want to do better than that, we recommend you find a local family willing to adopt a berry picker.

Here are some places that, for a fee, will let you pick cultivated berries to your heart's content. We've also listed a few apple orchards for fall visitors in search of a crisp Mac or Cortland. Call ahead for picking prospects.

South Coast

Jordan's Farm (207-799-1466; Wells Rd., Cape Elizabeth). Strawberries. End of June through August 1. Mon.–Sat., 7–7.

Harvesting wild Maine blueberries near Cherryfield.

Herb Swanson

Spiller Farms (207-985-2575; store: 207-985-3383; Rte. 9A, Wells Branch). Strawberries and raspberries. June 20 to end of season. Apples. Daily 9–5.

Whistling Wings Farm (207-282-1146; 427 West St., Biddeford). Raspberries. July to Labor Day. Daily 8–5.

Casco Bay

Hilltop Raspberry Farm (207-737-4988; Post Rd., Bowdoinham). Raspberries. July 15–Oct. Daily 9–6.

Juniper Edge Strawberries (207-725-6414; Harpswell Rd., Rte. 123, Brunswick). Strawberries. June 15 to end of season. Daily 8:30–5:30.

Maxwell's Farm (207-799-3383; off Rte. 77 near Two Lights, Cape Elizabeth). Strawberries. Mid-June–mid-July. Mon.–Sat., 7 a.m.–8 p.m. Closed Sun. Call ahead.

Prouts Vegetable (207-666-5604; Brown Point Rd., Bowdoinham). Strawberries. Late June–mid-July. 7 a.m.–dusk. Closed Sundays.

Midcoast

Spear Farm & Greenhouse (207-273-3818; Rte. 1, Warren). Strawberries. Open Friday, Saturday, and Sunday 9–12, Wednesday 6 p.m–8 p.m.

Down East/Acadia

Richard's Orchard (207-667-7287; Oak Point Rd., Trenton). Blueberries. Call for information.

Silveridge Farm (207-469-2405; McDonald St., Bucksport). Strawberries. Late June to end of season; daily, 8–8, conditions permitting.

BICYCLING

Cycling on a Maine coast country road.

Herb Swanson

First, here's what The Law says:

You need to have brakes so you can stop within a reasonable distance. (Seems fair.)

You need a head lamp if you're riding at night; night being that time when cars by law should have their headlights on.

The head lamp has to produce a white light someone in front of you can see from at least 200 ft.

You need a rear red reflector visible from at least 200 ft. and reflector strips on your bike pedals and handlebars.

Helmets are not the law for cyclists in Maine. However, we strongly suggest them. Coastal paved roads, dirt roads, and trails open to cyclists are often narrow and winding as they follow the terrain. Traffic at the height of summer can make those byways even more dangerous. Wearing a helmet will help protect you from injury should you hit a bad piece of road or path. It also could save your life should you encounter a car wanting more than its share of the road. We'd also like you to consider that biking — and any other outdoor activity in Maine — requires paying careful attention to weather conditions. Be sure to dress properly. Even if it promised to be a warm day, take along a windbreaker that will help you ward off a sudden damp fog.

Now, here's a roundup of biking on the coast.

There are three highways closed to cyclists: the Maine Turnpike, the interstate highway system and Rte. 1 between Brunswick and Bath.

Otherwise, go crazy. Great areas to pedal through include: *Cape Elizabeth,* which has excellent bike lanes on Rts. 77 and 207 leading through coastal marsh areas and past several great beaches; the stretch of ***U.S. Rte. 1 between Belfast and Bucksport*** which is littered with old sea captains' homes; the perimeter of ***Megunticook Lake*** and on to Lincolnville around ***New Harbor*** and the ***Pemaquid Peninsula***; the carriage paths and Park Loop Rd. in ***Acadia National Park***; the Park Loop Rd. on ***Schoodic Peninsula***; the lovely, rolling, uncrowded terrain ***East of Schoodic***; ***Islesboro***; ***Monhegan***, and any other island with paved roads. During the summer of 1990, state ferries carried 5,000 cyclists to Maine's islands. That's about the same number of cars traveling along Acadia's Loop on a busy day or two. Bike and rider fares range from $4 to $47.

Several chambers of commerce offer bike tour maps of their areas, including the Rockport–Camden–Lincolnville Chamber of Commerce. (See "Tourist Information" in Chapter Eight, *Information*.) If you want to make your own way, the state publishes excellent, inexpensive highway maps. Write for information from the Maine Department of Transportation, State House Station 16, Augusta, 04333-0016. Margaret Vandebroek is the state's bicycle coordinator.

DeLorme Mapping Company offers an inexpensive pamphlet titled *Bicycling*. It can be found at bookstores and large supermarkets in the magazine/map/recreation areas. Another excellent guide for cyclers is *25 Bicycle Tours in Maine* by Howard Stone (Back Country Publications, P.O. Box 175, Woodstock, VT 05091). Both books offer excellent maps and directions for touring cyclists.

Bike clubs, whether off-road or touring, come and go. In the last few years, however, the ***Casco Bay Bicycle Club*** has maintained a steady following of all kinds of cyclists. Their information line (207-828-0918) will astound you with choices. Or you can write to them at: 84 Gloucester Road, Cumberland 04121. Otherwise, the best bet for updates on new groups, trails, tours, and races is to call the local bike shop. Often one shop in town will be the hub for roadies, while mountain bikers will call the other one home. All are friendly.

BICYCLE DEALERS

You're on the road bright and early on your first day, and bam, you hit a bump, wipe out, and break a spoke. That's not to say the roads and trails in Maine are any rougher than those you're used to at home. We just say it to remind you that accidents do happen, and let you know that help is not far away.

Here's a list of bike shops on the coast. Several rent bikes; all repair them. Some are great places to go to replace the water bottle you left behind, as well as pick up information on roads and trails favored by local cyclists, tours, and clubs.

South Coast

Bicycle Habitat (207-283-2453; 294 Main St., Saco).

Bikes, Blades & Boards (207-967-3601; Shipyard Complex, Lower Village, Kennebunkport).

Breton's Bike Shop (207-646-4255; Rte. 9B, Wells).
Cape-Able Bike Shop (207-967-4382; Arundel Rd., Kennebunkport).
Quinn's Bike Shop (207-284-4632; 140 Elm St., Biddeford).
Wheels and Waves (207-646-5774; Rte. 1, Wells).

Casco Bay

Allspeed Bicycles (207-878-8741; 1041 Washington Ave., Portland).
Back Bay Bicycle (207-773-6906; 333 Forest Ave., Portland).
Brad's Bike Rental and Repairing (207-766-5631; 115 Island Ave., Peaks Island).
Brunswick Bicycles (207-729-5309; 11 Center St., Brunswick).
CycleMania (207-774-2933; 59 Federal St., Portland).
Haggett's Cycle Shop (207-773-5117; 34 Vannah Ave., Portland).
Joe Jones Ski and Sports (207-885-5635; Payne Rd., opposite Wal-Mart, Scarborough).
L. L. Bean Bicycle Dept. (207-865-4761; Main St., Freeport).
Rodgers Ski and Sport (207-883-3669; 332 Rte. 1, opposite Scarborough Downs, Scarborough).

Midcoast

Au Clair Cycle and Ski (207-633-4303; Boothbay House Hill, Boothbay Harbor).
Bath Cycle and Ski (207-442-7002; Rte. 1, Woolwich).
Birgfeld Bicycle Shop (207-548-2916; Rte. 1, Searsport).
Fred's Bicycle (107-236-6664; Chestnut St., Camden).
Maine Sport (800-722-0826; Rte. 1, Rockport).

Down East/Acadia

Acadia Bike and Canoe and Coastal Kayaking (207-288-9605; 48 Cottage St., Bar Harbor).
Bar Harbor Bicycle Shop (207-288-3886; 207-288-3886; 141 Cottage St., Bar Harbor).
Southwest Cycle (207-244-5856; Main St., Southwest Harbor).

BIRDWATCHING

The black-billed cuckoo taps out his hollow message in code. . . .

— E. B. White

FOR EXPERIENCED BIRDERS

Bird life in the woods, bogs, ponds, open lands, rocks, and beaches of the Maine coast is amazingly rich. Though there are few year-rounders, innu-

Herb Swanson

The great blue heron, a frequent visitor to the coast of Maine.

merable birds drop by. Maine is the last stop for many migrants, both from the north in winter and from the south in summer.

Accordingly, human migrants from the north will be attracted in late summer to the abundant shorebird life of marshes and mudflats like **Scarborough Marsh** and **Biddeford Pool**, where they may hear the coocoo of the least bittern or catch sight of a little blue or a black crowned night heron, a snowy egret, glossy ibis or even a marbled godwit.

Southern birders, on the other hand, will head well-bundled in winter for a shore lookout like **Quoddy Head** to see flying murres, kittiwakes and other alcids, a swimming harlequin duck or a king eider. Or they may hope to see a northern three-toed woodpecker in the spruce forests along the rocky northeastern shore, the year-round habitat of gray jays, northern ravens, and boreal chickadees.

Any birder north of Portland will look for bald eagles nesting. All will want to visit the extraordinary flocks of ocean birds that breed in early summer among the more than 2,000 sheltering islands and the plankton-rich waters fed by the icy Labrador current. The puffin is the most famous; other notable breeds include black headed gulls, razorbills, black guillemots, and Leach's petrels, hard to spot because they fly at night.

Arctic terns arrive in mid-May like a snowstorm over the sea. In late summer they're off east again over the Atlantic, starting their incredible annual trip through Europe and Africa to the Antarctic. All these nesting creatures pose the birder's familiar dilemma: how to observe the birds without disturbing their habitat.

The ferry from **Bar Harbor to Yarmouth** is an excellent place from which to observe coastal bird life. So are many shorter ferry rides (See "Ferries" in *Transportation*, Chapter Two, and "Whale Watching," below). Take a boat ride around **Matinicus Rock** (offshore from Matinicus Island), the southernmost known breeding place for puffins on the East Coast. *Seal Island* near Machias has pathways and blinds set up for birders and is worth a special trip in June. You can land for a few hours but not stay overnight.

Wonderful places to see the fall migration of shore birds are the quiet beaches near the Canadian border. One birder we've heard of spotted 100 species in one day in **Dennysville** on the Dennys River. The **Lubec and Eastport flats** host an enormous number and variety of traveling sanderlings, sandpipers, knots, willets, and other beach feeders.

FOR NON-BIRDERS

If you've never watched birds, Maine raises your awareness of them. As your car crosses an inlet or shallow river your eye is suddenly caught by a four-foot-tall great blue heron — still as a post, ankle deep in running water, coiled to spear his lunch on a six-inch yellow beak. On a Maine beach you see a familiar flock of sandpipers do their tiny quickstep all together, slow down to stoop and feed together along the curl of a retreating wave, soar away together with a flash of white along each wing. It's hard to imagine these tiny creatures may have spent the winter in Palm Beach and have Arctic plans for the summer.

Keep watching. You might see among them one with longer legs or, higher up the beach, a plumper bird with a reddish back looking under seaweedy pebbles. A fellow beachgoer with binoculars will tell you the plump one is a ruddy turnstone and the tall one a yellowlegs. If you ask to borrow the binoculars to see the color of the long-jointed legs, you've taken the first step to a new interest.

Irresistible in harbor waters in winter are the diving buffleheads, chunky little black and white birds that tip up like toys, all in one motion. In tidal inlets and freshwater ponds you see not only birds shaped like farm ducks but also swimming birds of less familiar shape, maybe one with a tuft of feathers on the top or back of the head, a grebe or merganser.

Finally, there are the sea birds on the rocky shores. Even if you haven't learned to distinguish the soaring seagulls from the smaller terns that hover and dive along the surf, you may want to take the boat to **Matinicus** in June or July. Then you can tell friends back home you've seen the unmistakable puffin, standing tall like a penguin on its large orange feet, its back black, its round stomach white, its broad beak blue, yellow, and red.

FOR ALL BIRDERS

If you want to know the latest action on the wing call the *Maine Audubon* bird alert hotline at 207-781-2332. The hotline operates from 5 a.m.–8 p.m. daily. All of the beaches listed above come with birds. Following are a few places well worth looking into. Some are full-fledged nature preserves or refuges. Others are just great spots for locating birds. When possible, we have provided addresses and phone numbers.

South Coast

Biddeford Pool (Rte. 208, Biddeford). A one-mile wide tidal basin and broad mud flats at low tide. There is excellent birdwatching here, because many species of shore birds stop here en route to northern and southern climes. Open Mon.–Fri., 8–4:30.

Rachel Carson National Wildlife Refuge (207-646-9226; 321 Port Rd., Wells). This famous refuge includes 1,600 acres of salt marsh, white pine forest and many, many birds. It is managed by the U. S. Fish and Wildlife Service, which offers limited access to birders and naturalists interested in viewing extensive bird life. Maps and guides to the preserve are available.

Scarborough Marsh Nature Center (207-883-5100; Pine Point Rd., Scarborough). The Maine Audubon Society operates an education center on this 3,000-acre saltwater marsh. They offer guided tours, including Full Moon Canoe tours during the summer when participants can experience the marsh at night. There's also a self-guided tour (you follow directions in a pamphlet available at the center). You can rent a canoe for your trip through the marsh on your quest for birds until 4 p.m. Art programs and walks are available for kids. In the early morning on Wednesdays, a bird-watching walk is offered. Open 9:30–5:30.

Seapoint Beach (Seapoint Rd., Kittery). Good birdwatching on a tiny peninsula that sticks out into the Atlantic Ocean, just southwest of Brave Boat Harbor.

Webhannet River Marsh (off Rte. 1, Wells). Good birders vantage for spotting shore birds and migrating waterfowl.

Wells National Estuarine Research Reserve (207-646-1555; Laudholm Farm Rd., Wells). This reserve has seven miles of trails on estuaries, rivers, and beaches. Wednesday mornings there is bird banding at 8 a.m. Children's programs. Visitor's center, 10–4 p.m. Trails, 8–5 p.m. Parking fee July and August.

Casco Bay

Maine Audubon Society (207-781-2330; 118 U.S. Rte. 1, Falmouth). The Gilsland Farm Sanctuary is home to the society, as well as whoever stops by. More than 60 acres of salt marsh, fields, and forest also serve as a workshop and touring ground for naturalists. There is a great bookstore for naturalists here, with the best selection of optics and guides around. Early morning bird walks and the children's discovery room are open to the public.

Midcoast

Hog Island Audubon Camp (Muscongus Bay). Osprey drop in here, so do eagles. Audubon annually sponsors two six-day field ornithology sessions. The Todd Wildlife Sanctuary on the island hosts a variety of nesting birds. Workshops include a one-day trip to Matinicus Rock. For more information, see "Schools" in *Culture*, Chapter Four.

Salt Bay (Rtes. 215 and 1 through Damariscotta Mills, Newcastle, and Damariscotta). If you don't want to leave your car, Salt Bay is a good spot. Rte. 215 borders the bay along its southwest edge; Rte. 1 leads along the bay to the east. Birds like to rest and feed in the large shallow bay and its mud-flats laid bare at low tide.

Swan Island (Merrymeeting Bay near Richmond). The state operates this 2,000-acre preserve and allows a few visitors to camp at shelters in the path of a wide variety of migrating and nesting birds, including the Canada or wild goose. Tours are available, provided you obtain the necessary (and inexpensive) permit. Write Swan Island Reservation Clerk, Maine Department of Inland Fisheries and Wildlife, 8 Federal St., Augusta 04330.

Down East/Acadia

Matinicus Rock (Criehaven Township). A mass of granite that rises 60 ft. above sea level is home to the southernmost colony of puffins. It's also favored by many other birds, including the rare razorbill auk.

Stanwood Museum and Birdsacre Sanctuary (207-667-8460; Rte. 3, Ellsworth). A 160-acre sanctuary and museum that is the former home of Cordelia Stanwood, a famed ornithologist and nature writer. In the museum there are stuffed birds, eggs, and photos any birder will love.

Keeping track of the birds near the lighthouse on Petit Manan, one of the best places in the country to view the European whimbrel.

Tom Hindman

East of Schoodic

Petit Manan National Wildlife Refuge (Milbridge). An 1,841-acre preserve
that includes Bois Bubert, Petit Manan and Nash islands is said to be one of
the best spots in the state to view the whimbrel, a small European curlew.
There are nature trails on the mainland. The islands (with the exception of
the northern end of Bois Bubert) are open to the public and can be reached
by private boat.

BOATING

*During the summer on
Mount Desert Island
narrated nature cruises
introduce visitors to the
wonders of Maine's birdlife,
geography, and seals.*

Diana Lynn Doherty

Wooden Boats

Pleasure boats and working boats come and go in all shapes and sizes in Maine,
but there's something particular about a wooden boat. Museums are devoted to
the wooden boat, and a magazine industry flourishes here thanks to wooden boats.
There are also schools to help keep the craft of wooden boat building alive. Best of
all you can still look out at the harbor — or practically anyplace else on the coast —
and see them in abundance.

In spite of all the extra work wooden boats demand of their owners, many Mainers would not go down to the sea in anything else. They are a living part of the sea.
A boat, said someone probably before the invention of fiberglass, is a hole in the
water into which you throw money. Nowhere else do people throw money into
their wooden boats so willingly as in Maine.

The wooden boat has as important a place in Maine's history as the glacier. The
Passamaquoddy Indians cruised the coast in birch bark canoes. The graceful lines of
those canoes still live in the famed Old Town canoes made in Bangor. The first
wooden ship built in America was constructed in Maine by the colonists of Popham
Colony in 1607. It was a 30-ton pinnace called the *Virginia*, and it carried cargo
between England and Virginia for 20 years.

At first, Maine boat builders relied on the forests at their back door. As lumber

(continued)

along the South Coast became scarce, more boat builders moved Down East to take advantage of cheaper building materials. The industry grew. Soon it seemed like the whole coast was one big shipyard, building good, cheap cargo ships.

The earliest Maine ships were built in the tradition of their British forebears, but by the time of the Revolutionary War, Maine shipwrights had developed their own designs and style of shipbuilding. Speed became important to the merchant marine, and shipbuilders responded with the sleek, fast clipper ship; 83 clippers were built and launched in the state during the mid-1800s. The last of the famous wooden cargo ships built in Maine was a three-masted square rigger ship called the Down-Easter that was almost as fast as the clipper, but had a deeper, more spacious hull and enabled merchants to haul more with every trip.

Schooners were also built in Maine. Merchants prized them because they were even larger than the clippers and Down-Easters and more economical to operate. Today they operate out of Rockland and Camden serving the tourist trade (See "Windjammers," below).

The end of the wooden boat as a merchant trading vessel came with the invention of the steamers. Steamships didn't rely on changeable winds and currents. They ran on time, and even the fastest clipper couldn't compete. Ironically, renowned Bath shipbuilder Arthur Sewall built the first steel sailing vessel, *Dirigo I*, in 1894. It weighed more than 2,800 tons.

Maine wooden boat builders took a new tack, building smaller boats for fishermen and pleasure sailors. The style of boat often depends on where it comes from: Peapods come from Penobscot Bay; Quoddy boats from Passamaquoddy Bay; the pretty, gaff-rigged Friendship Sloops from the town of Friendship on Muscongus Bay. There were also punts built to navigate a harbor or any small, calm waterway; dories to ferry people and small loads to and from shore; and pulling boats that were manned by oarsmen who literally hauled large ships that had been becalmed on windless water. Today those same pulling boats are used by Outward Bound students, their courses set on personal development.

For an invigorating taste of Maine's wooden boat heritage hard at work, watch the **Friendship Sloop Races,** held every year in late July in Rockland. Sponsored by the Friendship Sloop Society, the sloop races are really a week of wooden boat activities, including three days of racing and events at the Maine Maritime Museum in Bath. For more information, contact the Rockland–Thomaston Chamber of Commerce (207-596-0376). Also in Rockland are the spectacular **Schooner Days,** a three-day festival with all the trimmings — food, entertainment, arts, and marine demonstrations — crowned by the Parade of Sail, which features more schooners every year, including the National Historic Landmark *Stephen Taber.*

Windjammer enthusiasts head to Boothbay Harbor in late June for **Windjammer Days.** The festival includes concerts, a boat and a street parade, fireworks, and a chance to tour visiting military vessels. The Boothbay Harbor Chamber of Commerce has all the information (207-633-2353; P.O. Box 356, Boothbay 04009).

Smart enough to realize that you can't get too much of a good thing, the Rockport-Camden-Lincolnville Chamber of Commerce (207-236-4404) promotes another windjammer fix later in the summer. Pretty Camden Harbor hosts **Windjammer Weekend** every Labor Day weekend, when over two dozen windjammers from ports along the mid-coast are on display — except for the *Victory Chimes*, which at 132 feet is the largest windjammer in the fleet and too big to stick around after the parade.

Boating on Maine's shore was once exclusively the activity of members of the Abenaki tribe cruising the coast in well-made birch bark canoes. Today few people venture on saltwater in modern fiberglass and aluminum canoes, let alone birch bark. Most recreational boating is now done in sailboats, motor boats, and kayaks. Some will argue that ferries — a way of life for many Mainers — are also a form of recreational boating. They certainly are a good way to gain access to some of the best sights on the coast (See "Ferries" in Chapter Eight, *Information*). Windjammers and sightseeing cruises to view puffins and whales are two types of boating we list later in this chapter.

Whatever boat you choose, watch the weather. Spring often brings weather systems moving through the Gulf of Maine at a fast clip. Summer fogs can last for days. Fall and winter nor'easters can combine driving winds and rain with a high tide to make life on the water miserable if you are unprepared.

CANOEING AND SEA KAYAKING

A surfer and kayaker ride the waves off Kennebunk Beach.

Herb Swanson

Canoeing is rare off the Maine coast these days. Most boaters prefer something larger or smaller and more self contained. Where canoeists reign is on the small inland waterways, fresh and saltwater ponds, and salt marshes.

Extended solo sea kayak trips are not the stuff for amateurs. It's not so much the kayak as the elements that can cause problems. Weather changes quickly, currents and tides can be dangerous and tricky. Knowing how to handle your kayak properly will give you an edge out on the water. You can learn the basics in a couple of hours on a few weekends. You begin with wide, stable kayaks, then you learn how to flip. After a while, it won't feel too tippy.

The varied coastline of **Deer Isle** is a wonderful place to canoe and kayak. **Camden Harbor** is also a favorite stopping place for kayakers on the way east or west. There you see them bouncing in the waves dwarfed by the moored windjammers and giant pleasure yachts. The inlets and harbors of *Mount Desert Island* are popular, too. So are the islands of *Casco Bay*. A great reference for kayakers is *Sea Kayaking Along the New England Coast* (AMC Books, $14.95). It contains an excellent round-up of information on everything about coastal kayaking conditions throughout New England, including the *Maine Island Trail* (see sidebar in this chapter).

The following places offer gear, lessons, rentals, and two hour to five-day trips.

South Coast

Kittery Rent-All & Sales (207-439-4528; Rte. 1, Kittery). Canoe rentals.

Scarborough Marsh Nature Center (207-883-5100; Pine Point Rd off Rte. 1, Scarborough). Hourly canoe rentals and self-guided canoe tours of the marsh. Also guided tours, including "full-moon" tours during the summer. The center is open from 9:30 a.m.–5:30 p.m.; last canoe rental at 4. Open from mid-June until Labor Day.

Casco Bay

Far Horizons Kayak Center (888-375-2738; 13 Main St., S. Freeport 04078). Kayak equipment and instruction.

H2Outfitters (207-833-5257; P.O. Box 72, Orrs Island 04066). Canoe and kayak instruction for groups or individuals, as well as three-hour guided tours of waters near Bailey and Orrs islands. Classes offered year round.

L. L. Bean Outdoor Discovery Program (207-865-4761, ext. 6666; Main St., Freeport). Throughout the summer, the L.L. Bean store staff gives canoe and kayak lessons on a nice, easy stretch of the Royal River in Yarmouth. The academic wing of the outdoor store also hosts an annual Sea Kayak Symposium in early August and the Annual North American Canoe Symposium in early June.

Maine Island Kayak Co. (207-766-2373 or 800-796-2373; 70 Luther St., Peaks Island 04108). Trips and instruction.

Norumbega Outfitters (207-773-0910; 58 Fore St. Portland). Canoe and kayak rentals, instruction, and gear, as well as guided trips on Casco Bay.

Paddleworks USA (207-833-5342; Rte. 24, Harpswell).

Midcoast

Dragonworks (207-666-8481- RR1, Box 1186, Bowdoinham 04008) Boats, tours, instruction on Merrymeeting Bay.

Indian Island Kayak Co. (207-236-4088; 16 Mountain St., Camden). Guided tours specializing in 3–5 day tours, "bed and paddle" (See Chapter Three, *Lodging*), instruction and sales.

Island Hopping (603-466-2721; or write Summer Workshop, P.O. Box 298, Gorham, NH 03581). The Appalachian Mountain Club offers experienced canoeists the chance to spend three days exploring the water routes the Abenaki Indians used as they traveled among the islands of Penobscot Bay.

Maine Sport Outdoors School (800-722-0826; Rte. 1, Rockport 04856). Sea kayaking guided tours from two-hour harbor trips to six-day excursions, and all levels of instruction from beginners' clinics to five-day trips. They also rent sea and lake kayaks, canoes, and bicycles (see "Bicycling").

Tidal Transit Ocean Kayaking Co. (207-633-7140; 49 Townsend Ave., Boothbay Harbor). Hourly lessons and custom trips for sea kayakers.

Down East/Acadia

Coastal Kayaking Tours (207-288-9605, 207-288-8118 or 800-526-8615; 48 and 106 Cottage St., Bar Harbor). Canoe and kayak rentals. The store also offers sea kayaking tours for coastal waters.

National Park Canoe Rentals (207-244-5854; Long Pond, Acadia National Park). There are 30 canoes available, but reservations in June and July are suggested as all canoes are often rented by 9 a.m. Open daily 8:30–5. Paddles, life jackets, and basic instruction provided.

Phoenix Centre (207-374-2113; Rte. 175, Blue Hill). Kayaking only, but they offer special tours like the Fantasy Island escape for two, a romantic weekend led by a guide who sets up camp and prepares fancy meals for you, and a Mother-Daughter trip. Their daily guided tours are for a maximum of

---

Reversing Falls

Maine with its dramatic tides has several good reversing falls, favorite proving grounds for kayakers and canoeists. What makes reversing falls interesting is the water speed and direction change as the tide changes. The rapids run inland as high tide approaches, and they run out to sea as the tide ebbs. Here are some favored by small boaters in Maine:

Bagaduce Falls (Brooksville). It's easy to park and find these reversing falls between Snow Cove and the Bagaduce estuary.

Blue Hill Falls (under Rte. 175 bridge, Blue Hill Falls). The best time to negotiate these rapids, which are only about 100 yds. long, is about 3 hours before high tide. The coast near here also offers some good exploring for people in small boats. Parking is limited, and access to the falls is hampered by traffic. Be careful walking to and from the water.

Damariscotta Reversing Falls (Damariscotta/Newcastle; Rte. 1 bridge or Rtes. 129 and 130 bridges). Two locations to practice your whitewater canoe and kayak skills.

Goose Falls (Brooksville). Reversing falls at outlet of Goose Pond.

Sullivan Falls (Sullivan). Great scenery at these reversing falls between Taunton Bay and Sullivan Harbor.

Maine Island Trail

The Maine Island Trail Association was founded in 1988. The waterway is a kind of Appalachian Trail for boaters. It begins with islands in Casco Bay and follows the coast Down East past Machias, a distance of 325 miles. The trail includes 77 islands where travelers can put ashore and camp for the night. Thirty are privately owned islands; the rest are owned by the state and governed by the Bureau of Parks and Lands.

"What makes the Maine Island Trail a pleasure is its 'connect the dots' character, the 'dots' being islands. Without access to islands along the way, there would be no trail," wrote kayaker Michael Burke in *Yankee* magazine.

Members have access to prudent use of the islands on the trail — as well as a stewardship handbook and guidebook. Members receive a copy of *The Maine Island Trail Book*, a guidebook packed with charts and information. There are about 2,000 members of MITA, 300 of whom regularly monitor usage and erosion on forays to islands they have "adopted."

For information about the organization, write to the Maine Island Trail Association, P.O. Box C., Rockland, ME 04841 or call 207-596-6456.

---

eight people, and all trips include equipment, gear, instruction, food, and transportation to the launch site.

CRUISING

For the sailboat or motorboat cruiser, the coast could be considered a paradise. There are hundreds of deepwater anchorages, beautiful fishing villages like Jonesport and quaint, albeit sophisticated, towns such as Camden (a true pleasure sailor's town). Islands make for great side trips. The smallest are great places to anchor and enjoy a swim on a warm summer day and lobster on the rocks; the largest offer almost all the amenities of the mainland.

An excellent guide for pleasure boaters in Maine is *A Cruising Guide to the Maine Coast* by Hank and Jan Taft (International Marine Publishing; Camden, ME; $32.50). It's packed with charts, tips, and history for those viewing the coast from the water. If you don't have your own boat, here is a list of dealers who sell and rent sailboats and motorboats.

CHARTERS AND RENTALS

There are not a lot of people willing to rent you their boats. More are willing to take you. Boat people are like that.

South Coast

Lazyjack (207-967-8809; Schooner Wharf, Kennebunkport). Capt. Richard Woodman is an obliging captain known to perform many ceremonies at sea

Learning how to sail on the Lazyjack.

Herb Swanson

for his guests aboard his pretty schooner. He's done weddings, burials, and an occasional "pirate cruise" complete with eye patch. Two-hour and four-hour crewed sails, two-person minimum; private charters also negotiable.

Casco Bay

Palawan (207-773-2163; Custom House Wharf, Portland). Half-day, full-day, and evening trips aboard a gorgeous vintage 58-foot ocean racing sloop.

Midcoast

Sloop Surprise (207-372-6366; Tenants Harbor). Capt. Steve Daley sails his Friendship sloop from the East Wind Inn's pier around the islands of Tenants Harbor.

Down East/Acadia

Black Jack Charters (207-276-5043; Northeast Harbor).

Chance Along Sailing Center (207-338-1833; Belfast). Sailboats from the tiny (Sunfish) to the small yacht (23 foot). Half-day, full-day, and week rentals.

Hinckley Yacht Charters (207-244-5008 or 800-HYC-SAIL; South West Harbor). Bareboat sailboat charters to qualified sailors. Thirty-two boats available from 30 to 49 feet. Reservations suggested.

Machias Bay Boat Tours (207-259-3338; Machiasport). Half-day trips around Machias Bay afford views of salmon aquaculture pens on Cross Island, sheep on Chance Island, a lighthouse, and many harbor seals. Lobster traps also are hauled onto this 34-foot lobster boat during the tour. Sea kayaking and basic instruction offered as well.

Mansell Boat Rental (207-244-5625; Main St., Southwest Harbor). Day sailors and canoes and power boats for the day. Sailing lessons.

SAILING LESSONS

Bay Island Yacht Charters and Sailing School (207-596-7550; Bay Island).

Chance Along Community Sailing Center (207-338-6003or 800-286-6696; 278 High St. Belfast). Lessons to get around the harbor or down the coast. Rentals from Sunfish to 23 ft. boats; half day, full day , or weekly rates.

Sawyer's Sailing School (207-783-6882 or 800-686-9703; Dolphin Marina, S. Harpswell). Three-day instructional cruises aboard a 25-foot sloop.

Spring Point Sailing School (207-799-3976; Southern Maine Technical College, South Portland). Classes for beginning and advanced sailors, including private lessons by appointment.

WoodenBoat School (207-359-4651; Brooklin). One- and two-weeklong instructional programs, part of the boat-building school and run by *WoodenBoat* magazine. June–late Sept.

BOWLING

There are two types of bowling. Tenpin is known to most of the world as "bowling." In New England — and Maine — candlepin is most often the game of choice.

Candlepin bowling is a great way to spend a rainy — or any other — day. Unlike the tenpin's duck pin shape, the sticks in candlepin are cylindrical and tapered at both ends. Candlepin balls are the size of coconuts and, because there is no need, there is no place to insert your fingers. The balls travel much faster. There is none of the lumbering, none of that crowding the pins back off the alley. When one of the small balls hits the pins, they fly out of the way like just-split wood, but you know the ball has pretty much given it all it's got. Even with three chances every frame, candlepin scores are lower. That's the challenge.

South Coast

Big 20 Bowling Center (207-883-2131; Rte. 1, Scarborough). 20 candlepin lanes.

Vacationland Bowling Center (207-284-7386; Rte. 1, Saco). 32 candlepin lanes.

Casco Bay

Champion Lanes Bowling (207-797-2699; Elmwood Ave., Westbrook). 14 tenpin; 12 candlepin lanes. Open Wed., Fri., and Sat. or by appointment.

Columbus Club Bowling Bowl (207-725-5241; 7 Dunlap Rd., Brunswick).

Yankee Lanes of Brunswick (207-725-2963; Bath Rd., Brunswick). 32 tenpin lanes.

Midcoast

Candlepin Lodge (207-863-2730; Vinalhaven). Six candlepin lanes.

Oakland Park Bowling Lanes (207-594-7525; Rte. 1, Rockport). 12 candlepin lanes.

Down East/Acadia

Bucksport Bowling Center (207-469-7902; Rte. 46, Bucksport). 12 candlepin lanes.

Eastward Bowling Lanes (207-667-9228; Eastwood Plaza, Ellsworth). 12 candlepin lanes.

East of Schoodic

Eagel Lanes (207-255-6699; Marshfield).

CAMPING

There are hundreds of private and public campgrounds along the coast. Many offer priceless views of the water at campers' prices. Some are no bigger than a modest parking lot. Others are mammoth. Because the summer camping season is short in Maine, we recommend calling well ahead for reservations — especially if your camping plans include staying in Acadia National Park over the July 4 weekend. Once Labor Day weekend ends and school begins, most coastal campgrounds become lovely, quiet, and wonderfully available.

Below we've listed some of the best municipal, state, and federal campgrounds on or near the coast. For a complete list of private campgrounds, contact the ***Maine Campground Owners Association*** (207-782-5874; 655 Main St., Lewiston 04240). The ***Maine Publicity Bureau*** also publishes a camping guide. Call or write for one (207-623-0363 or 800-533-9595 out-of-state; P.O. Box 2300, Hallowell 04347).

Casco Bay

Recompense Shores Camp Sites (207-865-9307; Burnett Rd., Freeport). This small oceanside campground is run by the state university system. Tent and RV campsites, showers, electrical hookups, and one of the best views in the area. Next door is a state-run organic beef farm. Ask when you check in, and you may purchase a couple of thick steaks to grill during your stay.

Winslow Memorial Park (207-865-4198; Staples Point Rd., Freeport). Small, municipally run park with camp and picnic sites and a lovely man-made beach.

Midcoast

Camden Hills State Park (207-236-3109; two mi. off U.S. Rte. 1). Often this lovely campground is full. It's near one of the most popular sea-coast

*Camping in beautiful
Camden Hills State Park.*

Herb Swanson

towns in Maine, as well as within striking distance for hikers headed up Mount Battie. You should have a reservation to make sure you have a spot during July and August. But you're almost certain to get one the rest of the season if you arrive before 1 p.m. Showers. Nominal fee. Open May 15–October 15.

Down East/Acadia

Acadia National Park There are two campsites in the national park. The larger of the two, **Blackwoods**, is located off Rte. 3, five mi. south of Bar Harbor. Call Mistix 800-365-2267 for reservations. Call well in advance. **Seawall**, the other camp, is on Rte. 102A, four mi. south of Southwest Harbor. Sites are first come first serve. Both have attractive, wooded sites, and most amenities during the season (electrical hookups excluded; showers and a camp store are within $^1/_2$ mi.). Blackwoods is open all year. Seawall is open between Memorial Day and the end of September. Campsites are easier to come by during the off season.

Lamoine State Park (207-667-4778; off Rte. 1 on Rte. 184, Lamoine). This is one of the best-kept secrets for campers visiting Acadia during the high season. While sites in the national park are crammed, there are usually available waterside spots in this pretty little campground with 61 sites, as well as great views of Cadillac Mountain and Mount Desert Island. There's a lovely pebble beach nearby, too.

East of Schoodic

Cobscook Bay State Park (207-726-4412; six mi. south of U.S. Rte. 1 at Dennysville). This is a jewel of a campground with 106 camping sites. Most are for tents and many with water views. There are even showers (unusual in a

Maine state campground). The 864-acre park has picnic benches, hiking, and cross-country ski trails (see below). Mid-May–mid-October.

McLellan Park (Wyman Rd., Milbridge). Washington County operates this family recreational area. You can camp here. There are also picnicking facilities and hiking trails.

CLAMMING

How to clam. Get a bucket, a pitchfork or a clamming rake, which looks like a gardener's claw with a long handle — that kind of thing — then go down to the beach, preferably at low tide, when your clam is at its most vulnerable. Stomp on the beach. If you see a stream of water squirt up, start digging. Warning: before you begin, look around for signs warning not to dig because of red tide. Clams and mussels drink in this rust-colored algae and collect it in a concentrated form. Cooking the clam or mussel won't help. If you eat some you can develop paralysis.

CROQUET

Croquet. The game that makes mergers and acquisitions look like sandbox play. If you don't believe it, go watch the annual *Claremont Croquet Classic*, played during early August on the lawns of the Claremont Hotel (207-244-5036; Southwest Harbor). You're invited.

FAMILY FUN

There's recreation and then there's recreation. When you get tired of going to the beach, the perfect remedy is a stroll down *the boardwalk at Old Orchard Beach* where you can get your fortune read, ride the Ferris wheel, and eat more than one man's share of fried things — French fries, fried clams, and fried dough. If you're somewhere else on the coast and looking for family fun, herewith is some more good stuff, kids.

South Coast

Aquaboggan Water Park (207-282-3112; Rte. 1, Saco). Can't miss it. Kids love it. Water slides, splash pools for kiddie tots, bumper boats, races cars, shuffleboard. A real fun time.

Fun-O-Rama (207-363-4421; 7 Beach, York Beach).

Funtown–SplashtownU.S.A. (207-284-5139 or 800-878-2900; Portland Rd., Saco). Need we say more?

Jellystone Park (207-324-7782; Rte. 109, Sanford/Wells). Family camping at Yogi Bear's place! Wacky fun all night long!

Maine Aquarium (207-284-4511; Rte. 1, Saco). Fish under glass.

Pirate's Cove Adventure Golf (207-934-5086; First Street, Old Orchard Beach). 36 holes. "Explore the wonderful and mysterious hideout of pirates!"

York Wild Kingdom (207-363-4911; Railroad Ave., York). Contained wild animals and more.

Casco Bay

Hot Shots (207-883-1500; 450 Payne, Scarborough). Family fun for a rainy day. Indoor mini-golf, video games, air hockey, bankshot basketball. Enough to hold you and the kids over until the sun comes out.

Maine Narrow Gauge Railroad Co. & Museum (207-828-0814; 58 Fore St., Portland) This train is immensely popular with travelers young and old. A well-preserved two-foot narrow gauge train follows about 1.5 miles of track on Portland's Eastern Prom. Train rides and tours of the adjacent museum are available seven days a week, mid-May–mid-Oct.

Westerly Winds (207-854-9463; 771 Cumberland St., Westbrook). Pitch n' Putt golf course, driving range, miniature golf, and pitching machines for hardball and softball.

Down East/Acadia

Odyssey Park (207-667-5841; Bar Harbor Rd., Trenton).

Pirate's Cove Adventure Golf (207-288-2133; Rte. 3 near Hulls Cove, Mount Desert Island). 36 holes of miniature golf.

FISHING

People have fished in Maine's waters since before recorded history. Tribes of the Algonquin nation used to erect weirs — traps of net and wood that fish swim into, but can't get out of — in the bays and inlets of the coast. The Portuguese are believed to have fished here long before the coast of Maine was first "discovered" by the British and French. The cold waters off the coast were famous for their abundant supply of bluefish, striped bass, mackerel, and tuna. Today, the waters are not as populated as they once were. Commercial fisheries during this and the last century have depleted much of the natural supply of saltwater fish.

While large schools of fish are now rare on the coast, there are many opportunities both for salt and freshwater fishing. Former President Bush's fishing tackle master Bob Boilard, one of the most knowledgeable sports fishermen in

Flyfishing for striped bass at Willard Beach.

Herb Swanson

the Saco Bay area, suggests bottom fishing for cod, pollock, and mackerel. Well-known spots for saltwater fishing are Saco Bay off York, Ogunquit, Kennebunkport and Saco; Casco Bay from Portland to South Freeport; Boothbay Harbor; the waters off Rockland; and Passamaquoddy Bay near Eastport. (Bush often fishes in a small boat off Parsons Beach in Kennebunk.)

Beach and shore fishing is also popular in the fall when sunbathers have left. Good beach or shore fishing spots are Popham Beach near where the Kennebec River empties into the Gulf of Maine near Bath; the Presumpscot, Saco, and Mousam rivers in the South Coast; and the southern beaches including Crescent, Laudholm, Moody, and Ogunquit.

If you're a competitive fisherman or you like to be there when the pros weigh their fish, there are two saltwater tournaments held on the coast. *Tuna Tournament & Small Fish Rodeo* usually takes place from late July to early August. Fair game include codfish, bluefish, mackerel, and cusk. For more information contact the Boothbay Chamber of Commerce (207-633-2353) or Breakaways Sports Fishing (207-633-6990; P.O. Box 28, Boothbay Harbor 04538). *The New England Bluefish Open* is held every year in mid-August in the waters near Bath. For more information, contact Downeast Sports Fishing (207-443-8940; 118 Front St., Bath 04530).

When your taste runs more to trout and bass, try the rivers near the coast. Late spring and early summer are traditionally good seasons for freshwater fishermen. Then hungry fish come to the surface to feed on insects and their larvae. Atlantic salmon fishing is big in the rivers of Washington County, including the Dennys River. The season usually runs from mid-August through September.

Freshwater fishing licenses may be bought at the Kittery Trading Post in Kittery, L. L. Bean, and Peregrine Outfitters in Freeport, as well as many other

Maine sporting goods stores (no licenses are required for saltwater sport fishing). The rate for a one-day license is about the price of a movie. The longer you plan to fish, the cheaper it gets. Junior licenses are available for those ages 12 to 16. For more information call or write the **Department of Inland Fisheries and Wildlife** (207-287-8000; 284 State St., 41 State House Station, Augusta 04333). They also can give you dates for the freshwater fishing season and send maps showing waters open and restricted to fishing.

If you want to learn how to fish, you can learn from the pros at "fly fishing school." L.L. Bean's **Outdoor Discovery Program** every year offers intense fly fishing instruction in addition to frequent free programs about fishing. For more information about those classes call the outdoor school (207-865-4761 or 800-341-4314, ext. 26666).

DEEP SEA FISHING BOATS

Following is a partial listing of boats that offer full- and half-day deep sea fishing excursions. Some provide rods, reels, and bait, but it's good to check when you make reservations.

Breakaway (207-633-6990; Pier 6, Fisherman's Wharf or The Pier at Ocean Point). Sport fishing charters. Full- or half-day trips.
Bunny Clark (207-646-2214; Perkins Cove, Ogunquit). Mid-March–mid-November. Full- and half-day trips as well as 12-hour "fishing marathons."
Enterprise (207-363-7407; York). Capt. Kirk Snader. Sport fishing charters. Six passengers. Full- or half-day trips.
Ugly Anne (207-646-7202; Perkins Cove, Ogunquit). April–November. Half-day trips only July–Labor Day. Full-day trips April–July and Sept.–Nov.

GOLF

The first golf courses built in Maine were built along the coast at the turn of the century, just as the game was beginning to take hold in this country. The 18-hole course at **Kebo Valley Club** in Bar Harbor, built in 1892, has the distinction of being the oldest operating golf grounds in America. Mark Twain, who once said that "Golf is a good walk spoiled," learned how to play golf at a course in York County. Former President George Bush continues to master the intricacies of the game on a course in York County.

Many of the courses listed here are set right on the shore. If you don't make par, at least you've scored a great view. Call for current rates and hours.

South Coast

Biddeford-Saco Country Club (207-282-5883; Old Orchard Rd., Saco). 18 holes, 6,200 yds., par 71, cart and club rental, pro shop, clubhouse, lessons, snack bar.

Cape Arundel Golf Club (207-967-3494; Old River Rd., Kennebunkport). 18 holes, 5,869 yds., par 69. Cart and club rental, pro shop, clubhouse, lessons.

Dutch Elm Golf Course (207-282-9850; Brimstone Rd., Arundel). 18 holes, 6,230 yds., par 72. Cart and club rental, pro shop, clubhouse, lessons.

Old Orchard Beach Country Club (207-934-4513; Ross Rd., Old Orchard Beach). 9 holes, 2,762 yds., par 36, cart & club rental, pro shop, clubhouse.

Pleasant Hill Country Club (207-883-4425; 38 Chamberlain Rd., Scarborough). 9 holes, 2,400 yds., par 34. Cart and club rental, pro shop, clubhouse, snack bar.

Webhannet Golf Club (207-967-2061; Kennebunk Beach). 18 holes, 6,136 yds., par 71. Cart rental, pro shop, lessons. Call 24 hours in advance.

Willowdale Golf Club (207-883-9351; Willowdale Rd., Scarborough). 18 holes, 5980 yds., par 70. Cart and club rental, pro shop, snack bar.

Casco Bay

Brunswick Golf Club (207-725-8224; River Rd., Brunswick). 18 holes, 6,600 yds., par 72. Cart and club rental, pro shop, clubhouse, lessons. On weekends, private until 10 a.m.

Freeport Country Club (207-865-4922; Old County Rd., Freeport). 9 holes, 2,955 yds., par 36. Cart and club rental, pro shop, clubhouse.

Riverside Municipal Courses (207-797-3524 or 797-5588; 1158 Riverside Dr., Portland). Two courses: 18 holes, 6,520 yds., par 72; and 9 holes, 3,152 yds., par 36. Cart and club rental, pro shop, clubhouse, lessons.

Sable Oaks Golf Club (207-775-6257; 505 Country Club Dr., South Portland). 18 holes, 6,359 yds., par 70. Cart and club rental, clubhouse, pro shop, snack bar, lessons.

South Portland Municipal (207-775-0005; 155 Wescott Rd., South Portland). 9 holes, 2,171 yds., par 33. Cart and club rental, pro shop, snack bar.

Val Halla Golf Course (207-829-2225; Val Halla Rd., Cumberland). 18 holes, 6,200 yds., par 72. Cart and club rental, pro shop, clubhouse, lessons.

Midcoast

Bath Golf Country Club (207-442-8411; Whiskeag Rd., Bath). 18 holes, 6,260 yds., par 70. Cart and club rental, pro shop, clubhouse, lessons.

Boothbay Region Country Club (207-633-6085; Country Club Rd., Boothbay). 9 holes, 2,668 yds., par 35. Cart and club rental, pro shop, clubhouse.

Bucksport Golf Club (207-469-7612; Duckcove Rd., Bucksport). 9 holes, 3,352 yds., par 36. Cart and club rental, pro shop, clubhouse, lessons, snack bar.

Golfing in Portland.

Herb Swanson

Goose River Golf Course (207-236-8488; Simonton Rd., Camden). 9 holes, 3,049 yds., par 35. Cart and club rental, pro shop, clubhouse.

North Haven Golf Club (207-867-2061; Iron Point Rd., North Haven). 9 holes, 2,060 yds., par 35. Cart and club rental, lessons.

Northport Golf Club (207-338-2270; Bluff Rd., Northport). 9 holes, 3,047 yds., par 36. Cart and club rental, pro shop, clubhouse, lessons.

Rockland Golf Club (207-594-9322; Old County Rd., Rockland). 18 holes, 6,121 yds., par 70. Cart and club rental, pro shop, clubhouse, lessons.

Samoset Resort (207-594-1431 or 800-341-1650, ext. 511; Warrenton St., Rockport). 18 holes, 5,620 yds., par 70. Cart and club rental, pro shop, clubhouse, lessons.

Down East/Acadia

Bar Harbor Golf Course (207-667-7505; Rtes. 3 & 204, Trenton). 18 holes, 6,667 yds., par 71. Cart and club rental, pro shop, clubhouse, lessons.

Castine Golf Club (207-326-8844; Battle Ave., Castine). 9 holes, 2,977 yds., par 35. Cart and club rental, pro shop, lessons.

Causeway Club (207-244-3780; Fernald Point Rd., Southwest Harbor). 9 holes, 2,302 yds., par 32. Cart and club rental, pro shop, lessons.

Grindstone Neck Golf Course (207-963-7760; Grindstone Ave., Winter Harbor). 9 holes, 3,100 yds., par 36. Cart and club rental, pro shop, lessons.

Island Country Club (207-348-2379; Rte. 15A, Sunset). 9 holes, 3,865 yards, par 31. Pull cart and club rental, pro shop, clubhouse, lessons.

Kebo Valley Club (207-288-3000; Eagle Lake Rd., Bar Harbor). 18 holes, 6,131 yds., par 70. Cart and club rental, pro shop, clubhouse, lessons.

Northeast Harbor Golf Club (207-276-5335; Sargent Drive, Northeast Harbor). 18 holes, 5,430 yds., par 69. Cart and club rental, pro shop, lessons.

White Birches Golf Course (207-667-3621; rte 1., Ellsworth). 9 holes, 2,800 yds., par 34. Cart and club rental, pro shop, snack bar.

East of Schoodic

Great Cove Golf Course (207-434-2981; off Rte. 1 in Jonesboro, Roque Bluffs). 9 holes, 1,694 yds., par 30. Cart and club rental, snack bar, clubhouse.

HANG GLIDING

Island Soaring (207-667-7627; Hancock County-Bar Harbor Airport, Trenton). Soar over Mount Desert Island and Acadia National Park. Avoid the crowds and the entrance fee to the Loop.

HARNESS RACING

Standardbreds pulling a two-wheeled sulky and driver compete against each other for your betting pleasure. There's only one harness racing track on the coast of Maine — *Scarborough Downs* (207-883-4331; exit 6 off the Maine Turnpike, Scarborough, just southwest of Portland). It also happens to be the largest of its kind in New England. Races run Wed, Fri., and Sat., 7:30 p.m.; Sun. 4 p.m. The season varies; call for schedule.

HEALTH CLUBS

Here is a list of health clubs along the coast. Health clubs come and go. Call first to find out about guest and visitor policies, and check the phone book for new clubs that may have opened.

South Coast

Maine Coast Fitness (207-883-3858; 605 Rte 1., Scarborough). Weights, lifecycles, stair masters, and fitness machines.

Saco Sport and Fitness (207-284-5953; 329 North St., Saco). Pool, sauna, whirlpool, racquetball, aerobics, weights, lifecycles, stair masters, and fitness machines.

YMCA (207-283-0100; Alfred Road Business Park, Biddeford). Aerobics, fitness machines, Bio climbers, Nautilus, rowing machines, lifecycles, pool, and sauna.

Casco Bay

The Maine Event (207-729-8433; 120 Harpswell Rd., Brunswick). Tennis and racquetball, walleyball, yoga, karate.

The Maine Event (207-729-0129; 126 Main St., Topsham). Pool, tennis, aerobics, weights, racquetball, sauna, whirlpool, fitness machines, and lifecycles.

The Racquet and Fitness Center (207-775-6128; Congress St., Portland). Racquetball, tennis, aerobics, weights, fitness machines, lifecycles, and sauna.

Union Station Fitness (207-879-9114; 274 St. John St., Portland). Aerobics, weights, treadmill, stair master, lifecycles, rowing machines, Versa climber, spin bikes, cardio kick-boxing, and Nautilus.

YWCA (207-874-1130; 87 Spring St., Portland). Pool, aerobics, sauna, weights, yoga, water aerobics, and self defense.

YMCA (207-874-1111; 70 Forest Ave., Portland). Pools, sauna, squash, racquetball, aerobics, fitness machines, and basketball gym.

Women's Fitness Studio (207-729-5544;14 Maine St., Brunswick). Aerobics, Nautilus.

Midcoast

Oceanside Health and Fitness (207-338-1692 or 800-626-1692; 9 Field St., Belfast). Fitness machines, weights, aerobics, and lifecycles.

Samoset Resort (207-594-2511 or 800-341-1650; Waldo Ave., Rockport). Pools, hot tubs, sauna, weights, lifecycles, fitness machines, and aerobics.

Trade Winds Health Club (207-596-6889 or 800-596-6889; 2 Parkview Dr., Rockland). Pool, sauna, whirlpool, steambath, Nautilus, weights, fitness machines, lifecycle, stairmasters, and treadmill.

YMCA (207-443-4112; 26 Summer St., Bath). Aerobics, pool, whirlpool, sauna, racquetball, weights, and basketball gym.

YMCA (207-633-2855; Townsend Ave., Boothbay Harbor). Pool, aerobics, weights, racquetball, sauna, and cardiovascular equipment.

YMCA (207-236-3375; 50 Chestnut St., Camden). Aerobics, racquetball, weights, pool, sauna, and fitness machines.

Down East/Acadia

Fitness East Health and Racquet Club (207-667-3341; Rte. 1, Trenton). Pool, tennis, aerobics, racquetball, weights, sauna, whirlpool, lifecycles, rowing machines, Nautilus, and stairmasters.

YMCA (207-288-3511; 20 Park St., Bar Harbor). Aerobics, weights, fitness machines, Nautilus, pool, rowing machines, Nordic track, toning classes, and indoor running track.

HIKING & WALKING

A hiker takes in the view.

Herb Swanson

Hiking and walking can be the best way to see the coast, burn off lunch or blow off the cobwebs after sitting in the car all morning. A hike on the coast can entail anything from walking a scenic island perimeter road to climbing **Cadillac Mountain** in Acadia, which at 1,530 ft. is the tallest peak on the Atlantic coast. Another favorite hiking spot is **Camden Hills State Park**. Walkers have several options there from the tame to rigorous short climbs. A map and guide to the various hikes are available at the park entrance.

DeLorme Mapping Company offers an inexpensive booklet titled *Hiking: Volume 1 Coastal & Eastern Region*. It is available in most bookstores and larger supermarkets and has several routes mapped with experience levels clearly marked. Here are some of the more popular coastal hikes and walks:

South Coast

Marginal Way, Ogunquit. Begin near Rte. 1 in Ogunquit and follow the paved footpath over cliff and ledges all the way to Perkins Cove. It's about a mile and is perfect for a morning constitutional or an evening sunset stroll.

Rachel Carson National Wildlife Refuge, Wells. Follow the signs off Rte. 9 to parking area and trail head. This is another short and pretty walk rich with coastal flora and fauna. The refuge borders the Wells National Estuarine Sanctuary, a 16,000-acre preserve.

Casco Bay

Back Cove, Portland. This 3.5-mile walk around Back Cove in Portland is a popular one on a warm spring or summer evening. What's that smell?

Baked beans? That's the B & M Baked Bean factory across the way putting the final touches on a new batch of the sweet beans.

Bradbury Mountain State Park, Pownal. A little north and west of Freeport on Rte. 9, this small state park is a great place to get out of the car and stretch the legs. You'll get a good view of Casco Bay and the White Mountains from the summit of this small, bald mountain.

Wolfe's Neck Woods State Park , Freeport. Just a few miles from the commercial craziness of downtown Freeport, this is truly a cool haven in the spring and summer. The 200-acre state park is on a small peninsula jutting into Casco Bay. The park has four miles of well-marked trails that lead along Casco Bay past Googins Island (where a pair of osprey return from South America to nest every year) through a stand of white pine and along the Harraseeket River.

Midcoast

Bald Rock Mountain, Lincolnville. From the summit, you can see Mount Desert and the Penobscot Bay islands. From Ski Lodge Rd., this is an easy ascent on a well-traveled path to the top. It is a one-half mile walk with an elevation gain of 1000 feet.

Monhegan Island. Take the Burnt Head trail along the 150-foot cliffs and through Cathedral Woods — one of the few existing stands of virgin pine in Maine. This is a good day trip. The island has about 17 miles of hiking trails and is ruled by walkers (no vehicles are allowed). Ferries leave for Monhegan from Boothbay Harbor, New Harbor, and Port Clyde.

Mount Battie, Camden. There aren't many prettier walks than this one. From various lookouts you can see Mount Desert Island, Blue Hill Bay, Camden village, harbor, coast, and Megunticook from the mountain's exposed summit. There's also a stone tower at the top. This walk is even prettier in the fall when the leaves change. A park nature trail joins with a short, steep trail that climbs parallel to the auto toll road. One-mile climb with a 600-foot elevation gain.

Mount Megunticook, Camden. The highest of the Camden Hills, the ridge is ascended by park trails from several directions. The views are more limited on this walk, but there are several good vistas from exposed ledges en route. The Megunticook Trail offers most direct ascent. It begins near the park entrance and passes a grotto and stream, then rises steeply to Ocean Lookout and panoramic views. Base to Lookout is a one-mile climb with an elevation gain of 1,100 feet.

Mount Megunticook/Mount Battie, Camden. More ambitious walkers can plan to do both hills in one day. The trip begins at the parking lot, continues over Mount Megunticook, across to Mount Battie, and back to the parking area. The total walk is about 4.5 miles, and the top of Mount Battie is a great place for a picnic.

Ragged Mountain, Camden. An easy trail that weaves in and out of the trail and ski lift at Snow Bowl. The elevation gain is about 400 feet, and the trail is about one mile from base to summit.

Down East/Acadia

Blue Hill, Blue Hill. A one-mile climb up a Jeep trail. The path leads through open areas and woods. Look for blueberries. (500 feet.)

Hiking in Acadia National Park

There are eight climbing peaks in Acadia National Park on Mount Desert Island. All of them are relatively easy. The tallest and most often climbed is Cadillac, probably because most people choose to climb Cadillac in their cars. On foot, it's less crowded, and many of the best sites come before or after you make it to the top. Below we list favorite hikes in the park. You can get trail information at the park entrance.

Cadillac Mountain, Mount Desert Island. This is a gradual climb that belies the fact that it is the highest peak on the coast. From the park loop road it is about 3.5 miles with a 1,200 foot elevation gain. Make it a round trip, and you have an excellent day's hike.

Dorr Mountain, Mount Desert Island. Stone steps lead directly up this mountain passing through woods. There are some great views of Frenchman Bay and Cadillac Mountain from its ledges. Base to summit, this is a 1.5 mile walk with a 1,200 foot elevation gain.

Flying Mountain, Southeast Harbor. Short, brisk climb through pleasant woods to a plateau and outlook, with great views of Somes Sound and Cadillac. (Possible loop, descending via Valley Cove; slippery in spring.) Fernald Cove to overlook, 1/2 mile; elevation gain 200 feet. (Loop, 1.25 miles.)

Gorham Mountain, Mount Desert Island. This is a great hike for amateur geologists. Combined with a side trip to Cadillac Cliffs, you will walk among overhangs, arches, and caves. From the summit, you can see many of the park highlights, including the Beehive, Sand Beach, Great Head, Otter Cliffs, and The Bowl. If you want to continue on, a trail leads along the ridge to Champlain Mountain. This is a one-mile hike to the summit with a 500 foot elevation gain.

Pemetic Mountain, Mount Desert Island. This is one of the best hikes on the coast and perhaps the very best on the island. It lets you warm up on a nice, easy stretch, then gets tougher as the trail gets steeper. It passes through what some call a "storybook forest" to great views of Mount Desert's hills and the nearby islands and ocean. The climb begins at Bubble Pond and continues for one mile with an elevation gain of 1,000 feet. You can make this walk into a 3.75 mile loop by following the trail down to Jordan Pond, then the carriage trail back to Bubble Pond.

Penobscot and Sargent Mountains, Mount Desert Island. A wonderfully varied walk with excellent views of Cadillac and the island panorama. This begins tough with a somewhat difficult ascent up Jordan Cliffs, but the rest is relatively easy. After the cliffs, follow the trail from the summit of Penobscot about 1.5 miles past a pretty lake to Sargent, the island's second highest mountain. The climb is about 1,200 feet from Jordan Pond to the top of Sargent.

Schoodic Mountain, Winter Harbor. An easy climb that offers a short backward-looking view of Frenchman Bay and the more populated section of Acadia. It's a winding road to the top of this rocky headland (400 feet).

East of Schoodic

West Quoddy Head State Park, south of Lubec. This is the easternmost point of the United States, an elemental and majestic beginning. A two-mile trail outlines the 100-ft. cliffs and Carrying Place Cove. Several miles out, you can see Grand Manan, looking like a giant humpback whale.

HORSEBACK RIDING

The thrill of learning to ride a pony.

Diana Lynn Doherty

South Coast

Bush Brook Stables (207-284-7721; 463 West St., Biddeford). Lessons, boarding, indoor riding arena.

Horseback Riding Plus (207-883-6400; Scarborough). Public trails.

Long Horn Equestrian Center (207-883-6400; Scarborough). Indoor arena, lessons, boarding.

Casco Bay

Highland Dressage Center (207-797-6207; 77 Babbidge Rd., Falmouth). Lessons, training, riding, driving, boarding, indoor and outdoor rings.

Midcoast

Cherrydale Horse Farm (207-443-6782; Old Brunswick Rd., West Bath). Trails, boarding.

Gallant Morgan Horse Farm (207-443-4170; Days Ferry Rd., Rte. 128, Woolwich). Lessons, boarding, training, indoor facilities, tack shop, girls' riding camp.

Hill-N-Dale Farm (207-273-2511; Bradford Rd., Wiscasset). Lessons, trail rides, indoor arena, day camp, and carousel tack shop.

Ledgewood Riding Stable (207-882-6346; Bradford Rd., Wiscasset). Trail rides.

Fall Foliage in Maine

Leaf peeping is relatively new to Maine. For years, devoted foliage aficionados have chosen New England neighbors to the south and west of Maine. That wasn't for any lack of color, say state tourism officials, but merely because the state had failed to promote the fall season. The truth is the coast does have a lovely foliage season, and it is often less crowded than coinciding seasons in New Hampshire and Vermont.

The change begins almost immediately after Labor Day, when the temperature begins to drop. The big change comes about a month later, when warm days and cool nights cause trees to begin storing energy to get them through the winter. Trees extract sugars, starches, and other nutrients from their leaves, causing leaves to turn from green to red, yellow, and orange. First trees inland change, then those on the coast.

Down East from Acadia to Washington County is the first region on the coast to turn — generally around the end of September or early October. The western coast stretching from Kittery to Bucksport usually turns about a week later. Peak foliage usually lasts for about three to four weeks. This can all change from year to year, depending on the prevailing temperatures, the rainfall and other weather factors. For an inside tip on color conditions, call the *Foliage Hotline* (207-582-9300; out-of-state 800-533-9595) after September 15. The state publishes a leaf peepers' guide with several coastal leaf routes between 100 and 250 miles long; ask for it at any of the state information centers listed in *Information*, Chapter Eight.

If you want to find your own way, here are some tips on colorful routes. *St. George's Peninsula* near Port Clyde usually has great color. So does the *Blue Hill Peninsula. Acadia* is a favorite spot, particularly if you drive the park loop road or hike up Cadillac or the other Mount Desert hills.

The *Camden Hills* are another excellent site for autumn foliage. The *Saco River* near Biddeford and the *Royal River* in Yarmouth are two great canoe trips for viewing the foliage. One of our favorite sights is the *blueberry barrens* that cover the hillsides way Down East. As the weather cools, they turn a brilliant scarlet. We also think the shortcut (See "Shortcuts" in Chapter Two, *Transportation*) on Rte. 182 between *Ellsworth and Cherryfield* is one of the prettiest autumn drives in New England.

MOTORCYCLING

Annually, motorcycle clubs do a lot of socializing in Maine. During the summer of 1997, around 5,000 motorcyclists rolled into Portland for a Harley Davidson convention. Bikers enjoy the beauty of Maine's back country roads and the excitement of the downtown water district. Also during a recent season, bikers went on a lobster run in Brunswick, a surf & turf run from Biddeford, held a swap meet in Portland and a Halloween Party in Hallowell. See a local bike shop for scheduled gatherings.

The state urges all riders to wear helmets, though helmets are *required* only for passengers under 15, those driving with a learner's permit, and those who have had their licenses less than one year. The law requires lights to be on during the day as well as at night.

NATURE PRESERVES

The state may seem vast and unpopulated to visitors from the north and south, but the fact is that less than four percent of Maine's lands are publicly held. That makes Maine 47th in the union in the preservation of public access lands. Three groups are actively trying to increase the supply of lands protected from commercial development.

The Maine chapter of the ***Nature Conservancy*** (207-729-5181; Fort Andross, 14 Maine St., Suite 401, Brunswick 04011) has been able to convert more than 103,000 acres of Maine wilderness to protected preserves since it was founded in 1956 at the urging of naturalist Rachel Carson. The group's recent projects included a close study of the saltwater ecosystem of Cobscook Bay, one of the most biologically diverse ecosystems on the East Coast — the group's first research and preservation efforts focused below the tidal waterline. The Nature Conservancy owns and manages more than 20,000 acres of nature preserves, including 50 Maine islands and several coastal preserves. Day use of the Conservancy's lands are welcome, including the string of nature preserves called the Rachel Carson Sea Coast.

The ***Maine Audubon Society*** (207-781-2330; PO Box 6009, Falmouth 04105) operates several nature centers on the coast as well as inland. Founded in the early 1970s by Peggy Rockefeller and Tom Cabot, the ***Maine Coast Heritage Trust*** (207-729-7366; 167 Park Row, Brunswick 04011) has worked to preserve and protect more than 66,000 acres through conservation easements. That includes 173 entire islands and 250 miles of shore line.

These and several smaller conservation organizations have established a network of nature preserves that grace the coast like pearls on a loosely strung necklace. Beginning in the South Coast with the ***Wells National Estuarine***

Sanctuary and the *Rachel Carson National Wildlife Refuge*, these few small preserves are rich with avian and plant life, and they are fragile havens for birdwatchers, ecologists, and the garden variety of nature lover. Spring, summer, and fall are good times to walk the trails and observe nature in action. Many of the preserves turn over their trails to cross-country skiers in the wintertime (see below).

South Coast

East Point Sanctuary, Biddeford Pool. A 30-acre sanctuary on the largest tidal pool in Maine. Two trails ring the water and give views of nesting and migratory birds as well as harbor seals at high tide.

Laudholm Farm, Wells. Part of the Wells Reserve that also links the Carson Refuge, this is a saltwater farm that boasts soils more fertile than the richest Iowa farmland. More than 300 years ago the first European farmers in the New World tilled land like that found at Laudholm Farm. Visitors can tour buildings and grounds to get a taste of this endangered agricultural tradition.

Rachel Carson National Wildlife Refuge, Rte. 1, Wells. The naturalist summered on the coast, and during her lifetime she was instrumental in establishing the national environmental movement with the writing of environmental classics including *Silent Spring* and *The Edge of the Sea*. Her estate was willed to the Sierra Club and the Nature Conservancy. Today, this refuge is a living reminder of her crusade — and a wonderful place to observe nature. The mile-long trail built by volunteers in 1988 is handicap accessible.

Refuge at Brave Boat Harbor, Seapoint Rd., Kittery Point. Small refuge on a tidal inlet with good birdwatching and an interesting trail through a salt marsh.

Scarborough Marsh Nature Center, Scarborough. Maine Audubon operates this nature center on the coast's largest saltwater marsh. Self-guided nature walk, as well as several special events and educational programs. You can rent a canoe here, too, to visit marsh animals in their natural habitat. This is a great way to "get into" coastal biology.

Wells National Estuarine Research Reserve, Rte. 1, Wells. An educational and research facility set on 1,600 acres of coastal marshland and woods with seven miles of nature trails. There are guided nature, birding, sky watch, and wildflower tours in the summer. Admission is free, but there is a nominal fee for guided tours and parking in July and August.

Casco Bay

Fore River Sanctuary, Portland. A 76-acre preserve on the Fore River Estuary. This small pocket of nature includes a portion of the old Cumberland and Oxford Canal and Jewel Falls, the city's only waterfall; 2.5 miles of nature trails lead through hemlocks, red oaks, and white pine.

Gilsland Farm, Rte. 1, Falmouth. The headquarters for Maine Audubon sits on

60 acres of salt marsh just minutes from Portland with 2.5 miles of trails. Good walks, great cross-country skiing, and one of the region's best selection of natural history books in the society's gift shop. Open year round.

Mast Landing Sanctuary, Freeport. Another of the small refuges set aside by Maine Audubon, this one winds through the hills, fields, woods, and salt marshes near busy downtown Freeport. There are self-guided nature walks, and you can tent, camp, and picnic here.

Wolfe's Neck Woods State Park, Freeport. This small park is truly one of nature's gems. Well-marked, self-guiding nature trails through coastal woods on Casco Bay and the Harraseeket River. Lovely picnic area. Nominal fee in summer time.

Midcoast

Fernald's Neck Preserve, off Rte. 52, Camden-Lincolnville. Four miles of trails through woods, bog, and along 200-ft. cliffs on a 315-acre preserve near Lake Megunticook. Managed by the Nature Conservancy.

Josephine Newman Wildlife Sanctuary, Rte. 127, Georgetown. A 119-acre preserve on the ocean with more than two miles of natural trails. The sanctuary is bounded on two sides by salt marsh and contains a small pond. Managed by Maine Audubon.

Lane's Island Preserve, Vinalhaven. The Nature Conservancy manages a 43-acre refuge here made up of rolling moors and shoreline pounded by rough surf. Trails lead to several beaches. Access is by a stone causeway from Vinalhaven (a car ferry from Rockland services the island of Vinalhaven).

Merryspring (Conway Rd. off Rte. 1, on the Camden-Rockport town line). A private foundation manages this 66-acre nature park. While there are several cultivated gardens, the park also features a 10-acre arboretum and the group's ongoing efforts to preserve native wildflowers.

Rachel Carson Salt Pond Preserve, Rte. 32, Bristol. Part of the Rachel Carson Sea Coast, the network of protected lands willed to the public by the late naturalist Rachel Carson. A great place to observe marine life from the point of view of a tidal pool. Good views of Muscongus Bay. A map published by the Nature Conservancy (207-729-5181) points out interesting rock formations along the shore.

Robert P. Tristram Coffin Wildflower Sanctuary, Rte. 128, Woolwich. The New England Wildflower Society owns and operates this 180-acre refuge. It is home to more than 200 species of flowers, grasses, trees, and other plants. Nature trails follow the edge of Merrymeeting Bay.

Down East/Acadia

Crockett Cove Woods, Stonington. A 100-acre preserve managed by the Nature Conservancy, this is a good example of an eastern coastal rain forest. It is a great place to visit on a foggy summer day. Self-guided nature trail.

Indian Point-Blagden Preserve, Mount Desert Island. One of the few forested portions of Mount Desert Island that survived the disastrous 1947 fire, this 110-acre preserve is managed by the Nature Conservancy. Pick up a map and guide from the caretaker and explore the intertwined trails leading through spruce, fir, and cedar forests, and along the water. Seals like to sun on nearby islands.

Ship Harbor Nature Trail, Rte. 102A, Mount Desert Island. Thirteen stations describe the geology, flora, and fauna of the island along a 1.4-mile trail. This is a good, self-guided trail for the family. The trail is named for the famous 1739 shipwreck of the Grand Design from Ireland.

The Wild Gardens of Acadia (Rte. 3, Sieur de Monts Spring entrance, Mount Desert Island). Maintained by the Bar Harbor Garden Club, this is an exquisite collection of plants native to Mount Desert Island.

East of Schoodic

Great Wass Island Preserve, Rte. 187, Beals Island. Almost 1,600 acres of land with two wooded trails through spruce and fir forests edging a long, narrow cove. Magnificent views of the ocean and eastern islands. Managed by the Nature Conservancy.

Petit Manan National Wildlife Refuge, Rte. 1, Milbridge. A pleasant trail leads 1.5 miles through a wild blueberry barren and woods to a rugged shoreline. Part of a 1,841-acre refuge that includes Petit Manan Peninsula, Petit Manan, and Nash islands, and part of Bois Bubert Island. The islands — except for the northern end of Bois Bubert — are open to the public and can be reached by private boat.

PUFFIN WATCHING

Their feathers once graced the heads of fashionable women during the 19th century, so much so these colorful sea birds were almost plucked from the species list. Their eggs were also a favorite meal of gourmands. Also known as sea parrots because of their colorful curled beaks, their population is on the increase with help from their friends at the Audubon Society, which launched a major campaign in 1973 called ***Project Puffin***. The project has been successful to date, although puffins may never reach their pre-1800 population. The society relies on private donations to fund the repopulation. To make one, write to Project Puffin, National Audubon Society, HC 60, Box 102-P, Medomak, ME 04551.

The struggle to repopulate puffin colonies off the coast is understandable. Puffins prefer to nest on the remote islands stretching from mid-Maine to Canada. They don't reproduce until after their fifth year, and each mating pair produces only one egg each year. Today puffins flourish to the north in Newfoundland, Iceland, and Britain. In Maine, colonies of the birds nest on Matinicus Island, Machias Seal Island, Eastern Egg Rock in Muscongus Bay, and Seal

Island in Penobscot Bay. Early summer is the best time to see them. Several tour boat operators split ticket sales with the National Audubon Society, which watches over these puffin sanctuaries.

Midcoast

Pink Lady, **R. Fish and Son** (207-633-3244; Pier 1, Boothbay Harbor).
Hardy III, **Hardy II Tours** (207-677-2026; Rte. 32, New Harbor).
Mary Donna, **Offshore Passenger & Freight** (207-366-3700; Maine State Ferry Service, Rockland).

East of Schoodic

Barna Norton (207-497-5933; Jonesport).
Seafarer, **Butch Huntley** (207-733-5584; Lubec).

ROCK CLIMBING

In spite of this being the rock-bound coast, rock climbing is not one of the most popular pastimes. Consequently, good rock climbing spots have not yet been well mapped. The coast of Maine offers climbers both challenges and solitude. *Acadia National Park* is the obvious place; the Precipice, Great Head, and Otter Cliffs offer a handful of quality climbs. *Camden Hills State Park* provides moderate climbs as does *Fort Williams Park* in Cape Elizabeth just south of Portland. These places are easily accessible. Want to get in a good climb, but the weather stinks? Check out the *Maine Rock Gym* (207-780-6370; 127 Marginal Way, Portland). The gathering place for the lithe athletes, the gym has been such a hit that they built a brand new climbing tower outside. For further information or gear, call or stop by one of the nearby sporting goods stores (see "Sporting Goods" in Chapter Seven, *Shopping*).

RUNNING

Don't let us stop you. Seriously, *Runner* Magazine readers voted the *Schoodic 10K Road Race* on the Schoodic Peninsula as one of the five best in the country. The terrain is relatively flat, the scenery beautiful, the air and the light clear. Here is a short list of some of the more popular annual runs and the approximate time of year they are held. Call the number supplied for further information.

5K Road Race & Fun Run, Bar Harbor (207-288-3511) Early June.
Maine Lobster Festival 10K Road Race, Rockland. (Contact Rockland-Thomaston Area Chamber of Commerce, 207-596-0376.)

Old Orchard Beach, which stretches for seven miles, challenges visiting runners. The snow fence is to protect new grass.

John Metzger

Shipbuilders Triathlon, Bath (Contact Annie Walker, 207-443-5402 or Joe Gross 207-725-1085) Early July.

10 K, Camden (207-236-7120) Early June.

13-Miler, Bar Harbor and Acadia National Park (207-288-3511) Mid-September.

Tin Man Triathlon, Camden (207-236-7120) Late Aug.

SKATING

If it has to do with water — frozen included — it's available on Maine's coast. Skating is popular on the coast during the winter. Outdoor listings are free. Indoor listings cost a couple of dollars. Call for times and fees.

South Coast

The Arena (207-283-0615; Alfred Rd., Industrial Business Park, Biddeford). July 31–April 14. Indoors.

Casco Bay

Brunswick Parks & Recreation (207-725-6656; on the Mall, Brunswick). December–March. Outdoors.

Deering Oaks Park (207-775-5451, Ext. 300; State St. and Park Ave., Portland). December–February. Outdoors.

Mill Creek Park (207-799-7996; Cottage Rd., South Portland). December–February. Outdoors.

North Yarmouth Academy Ice Arena (207-846-2406; Rte. 1, Yarmouth). Indoors. Mid-Oct.–late Dec., Jan.–Mar; Sunday afternoons, 3:40–4:40 p. m.

Payson Park (207-775-5451, Ext. 300; Baxter Blvd., Portland). December–February. Outdoors.

Portland Ice Arena (207-774-8553; 225 Park Ave., Portland). Open through April. Indoors.

Yarmouth Community Services Park (207-846-9680; Main St., Yarmouth). Check out the skating nearby on the Royall River, too. December–February. Outdoors.

Midcoast

Camden Snow Bowl Ski Area (207-236-3438; Hosmer Rd., Camden). Open December–March. Outdoors.

Walker Park Ice Rink (207-236-9648; Sea St., Rockport). Outdoors.

SKIING

DOWNHILL SKIING

There are not many people who come to the coast to go downhill skiing; the state's biggest ski areas are inland near Bethel and Rangeley. But you can be one of the few to escape the crowds and feel the ocean breezes at the *Camden Snow Bowl* (207-236-3438; Camden). There the vertical drop is about 950 feet, the mountain has ten trails and is serviced by a double chairlift and two T-bars — one 4,100-ft. long. Best of all, lift tickets are inexpensive.

CROSS-COUNTRY SKIING

Cross-country on the coast is another story. There are dozens of summer hiking trails that are converted to cross country ski trails with the first snowfall. Skiing the carriage roads at *Acadia* is a beautiful way to experience the park; further Down East, *Cobscook Bay State Park* offers great oceanside ski trails. We also recommend the *Lincoln House* in Dennysville for a good cross-country ski B&B (See *Lodging*, Chapter Three). The inn has its own trails cut through almost 100 acres of woods, and they serve a wonderful dinner as well. Almost every town along the coast has a park and trails that cross-country skiers take over in the wintertime. We've listed some of the better-known areas, but you can find out more by contacting the local chamber of commerce where you plan to visit.

Most of the areas listed below are unstaffed. Remember that it can be unsafe to ski alone. Stay on the trails, and be prepared for Maine's mercurial weather. Also, don't forget to carry out your trash. Call beforehand for snow and trail conditions.

South Coast

Vaughan Woods State Park (207-384-5160; Old Fields Rd. off Rte. 236, South Berwick). 4.5 miles of snow-covered hiking trails that take you by Salmon Falls River and Cow Cove. Two miles are classified "easy," the other four miles are more difficult.

Casco Bay

Bradbury Mountain State Park (207-688-4712; 6 mi. west from the Freeport exit of I-95, Pownal). From the top of Bradbury Mountain (460 feet) you can see past L.L. Bean to the ocean. There's ten miles of trails; two difficult paths, two intermediate, and four trails for beginners. Trail maps are available at the entrance.

Gilsland Farm (207-781-2330; 118 U.S. Rte. 1, Falmouth). This is the home of the Maine Audubon Society. Three-and-a-half kilometers of trails through their country backyard. Open 7:30 to dusk.

Mast Landing Sanctuary (207-781-2330; Upper Mast Landing Road, Freeport). Also owned and operated by Maine Audubon Society. Five kilometers of estuary trails through forests and orchards. Open from dawn to dusk.

Wolfe's Neck Woods State Park (Wolf Neck Rd, Freeport). This small park is officially closed during the winter, but skiers like to ski the snow-covered walking trails which wind for about 4 miles through the woods and follow along the edge of Casco Bay and the Harraseeket River.

Midcoast

Camp Tanglewood at Camden Hills State Park (207-789-5868; off Rte. 1, Lincolnville). Ten miles of ungroomed trails, graded for entry level to the most skilled skiers. Ask for a map available at the gate. January through March, dawn to dusk.

Samoset Ski Touring Center (207-594-1431; P.O. Box 78, Rockport). 4.5 kilometers of groomed trails split evenly between entry level and more difficult.

There are more than 40 miles of well-marked cross-country ski trails in Acadia National Park on Mount Desert Island.

Roy Zalesky

Down East/Acadia

Acadia National Park (207-288-3338; Mount Desert Island). Forty miles of well-marked carriage roads and trails. A trail map can be had from park headquarters on Rte. 233. Wilderness facility.

Holbrook Island Sanctuary State Park (207-326-4012; Cape Rosier, Brooksville). Seven kilometers along wood roads and hiking trails through upland forests and fields offering views of Penobscot Bay.

East of Schoodic

Cobscook Bay State Park (207-726-4412 for snow and trail conditions; off Rte. 1, Edmunds). Six miles of roads through woods with terrific views of the bay.

Moosehorn National Wildlife Refuge (207-454-3521; Calais). Fifty miles of service roads closed to automobiles in the winter. Moderate to difficult.

SURFING

It's a South Coast sport. That's where the best waves are, and, in the fine tradition of Moon Doggie and Gidget, that's where the best beaches are. Don't plan on sunbathing when you surf. The truth is that the best surfing is in the fall and winter. Even then surfing here is mostly for beginners. Here are some prime surf apprentice spots.

Fortune Rocks, Biddeford. Surf on the incoming tide. Then the waves are steep, hollow and break to the right.

Gooch's Beach, Kennebunkport. Best surfing is at low to mid-tide. The waves are steep, thick waves, and they break both right and left.

Moody Beach, Wells. Best waves at high tide. They break close to shore.

Old Orchard Beach, Old Orchard Beach. There is a designated surfing area on the north side of the pier.

Wells Beach, Wells. Surfing best during the incoming tide. The waves break both right and left over sandbars.

York Beach, York Beach. Best waves are at low to mid-tide, and they break right and left.

TENNIS

For a tennis vacation try these resorts: The *Samoset Resort* (207-594-2511 or 800-341-1650, Rockport) has both indoor and outdoor courts, so you can play year round; *Sebasco Estates* (207-389-1161 or 800-225-3819) near Phipps-burg boasts two courts with a great view of the ocean; the ***Whitehall Inn*** (207-236-3391 or 800-789-6565; 52 High St, Camden) is an old-style Yankee resort with tennis courts perched on the hillside above Penobscot Bay.

Below are some public and private courts where play is free or at least available to visitors for a small fee. In addition to those listed, call the local town hall for the location of other free municipal tennis courts. Also several motels and hotels make their courts available to the traveling public for a small fee.

South Coast

Biddeford (207-283-0841; Mayfield Park, May St.). Three courts with night lights. Also Clifford Park, Pool St., has two courts.

Kennebunk (207-985-6890; Parsons Field, Park St.). Two courts, plus courts at Kennebunk High School. Total of four courts with night lights.

Ogunquit (207-646-3032; Agamenticus Rd.). Three courts.

Old Orchard Beach (207-934-2500; high school, T for Turn Rd.). One court; two courts at Ocean Park and two more at Memorial Park.

Wells (207-646-6171; Congdon's Resort, Rte. 1). Three courts.

York Recreation Area (207-363-1040; Organug Rd.). Four courts; two at the high school and two with night lights at the middle school.

Casco Bay

Bath (207-443-8360; Congress Ave.). Four courts with night lights.

Brunswick (207-725-6656; Stanwood St. Courts). Five courts with night lights; bring change. The Maine Event (207-729-8433; 120 Harpswell Rd.).

Falmouth (Tennis of Maine, 207-781-2671; 196 Rte. 1, Falmouth).

Portland (207-874-8793; Deering Oaks Park). Eleven courts, and six more across town at Deering High School; four courts on the Eastern Promenade; four courts at Payson Park on Baxter Blvd.; the Racket & Fitness Center (207-775-6128; 2445 Congress St., Portland).

Midcoast

Boothbay Harbor (207-633-2855). Two courts.

Damariscotta (207-563-3477; YMCA). Two indoor courts.

Down East/Acadia

Bar Harbor (207-288-5801; Atlantic Oaks, Rte. 3). Four courts. Night lights.

Trenton (Fitness East Health and Racket Club, 207-667-3341; Rte. 3). Three indoor courts.

WHALE WATCH

Whales are frequent summer visitors off the coast of Maine.

Tom Hindman

Whales are frequent summer visitors off the coast of Maine. Finbacks, pilots, minkes, rights, and humpbacks cruise the coast along the continental shelf. From early spring through late fall from shore you can see whales from *East Quoddy Head Lighthouse, West Quoddy Head Lighthouse* and *West Quoddy State Park* looking out toward Grand Manan Island. The Gulf of Maine is also home to dolphins, harbor porpoises, seals, osprey, storm petrels, puffins, and other sea birds (see Birdwatching, above) and fishermen. Most of the charters listed below run through the summer and into mid-September or October. Reservations are recommended.

South Coast

Indian Whale Watch (207-967-5912; Arundel Wharf Restaurant, Ocean Ave., Kennebunkport).

Casco Bay

Odyssey Whale Watch (207-775-0727, 207-642-3270, or 800-437-3270; Long Wharf, Commercial St., Portland).

Down East/Acadia

The Acadian Whale Watcher (207-288-9794 or 800-247-3794; Bar Harbor).
Whale Watcher Inc. (207-288-3322 or 800-508-1499; 1 West St., Bar Harbor).

Capt. Butch Huntley (207-733-5584; Lubec). If he can't make it, he'll tell you who can. Butch also does puffin trips.

WINDJAMMERS

Today the only cargo these sea trains carry are tourists. Life on a windjammer was never the cruise it is today. Work for the crew was never optional; private cabins were unheard of for all but the captain; and there were never gourmet meals served at respectable hours.

At 132 feet and capable of carrying 44 passengers, the _Victory Chimes_ is the biggest of the windjammer fleet (no wonder many of those passengers hail from Texas). The _Lewis R. French_, built in 1871, is the oldest. _Angelique_, a steel-hulled ketch launched in 1980, is the youngest member of the fleet. That new ships still are being built and the industry is prospering is testament to the enjoyment windjammers provide. The newest windjammers are built true to old ways, only with a few added comforts. In fact, most of the old fleet has been rebuilt or refurbished to serve the cruise business in the style to which its tourists are accustomed. Some of the old ones are still pushed by yawl boats to open water.

Every year near Rockland, home to much of the fleet, there is an annual _Great Schooner Race_ in early July. People with timely reservations take part. There are Windjammer Days in Boothbay Harbor around the end of June, and _WoodenBoat_ magazine's annual sail-in during mid-September.

If you aren't lucky enough to visit during one of these events, there are always the cruises. They last from three days in the off-season to six days during the summer. Most windjammer cruises cost between $325–$650. On some windjammers you can take a two-hour ride for less than $20 per person. For more information about the old sailing vessels, you can contact the Maine Windjammer Association, 800-807-9463.

Midcoast

American Eagle (207-594-8007 or 800-648-4544; Capt. John Foss, P.O. Box 482, Rockland 04841).

Angelique (207-236-8873 or 800-282-9989; Capts. Mike & Lynne McHenry, Box 736, Camden 04843).

Appledore (207-633-6598; Capt. Andrew Grainger, Fisherman's Wharf, Boothbay Harbor 04538.) Two and a half hour cruises to the outer islands. June through September.

Appledore (207-236-8353 or 800-233-PIER; Sharp's Wharf, Camden 04843). Four two-hour sails daily, late June through mid September. Three daily, mid-September through mid-October

Grace Bailey (207-236-2938 or 888-MWC-SAIL; Maine Windjammer Cruises, Owners Ray and Ann Williamson, P.O. Box 617, Camden 04843).

Heritage (207-594-8007 or 800-648-4544, 800-542-5030; Capts. Doug and Linda Lee, P.O. Box 482, Rockland 04841).

Isaac H. Evans (207-594-8007 or 800-648-4544; Capt. Ed Glaser, P.O. Box 482, Rockland 04841).

J & E Riggin (207-594-2923 or 800-869-0604; Capt. Dave Allen, Box 571, Rockland 04841).

Lewis R. French (800-469-4635; Capt. Dan and Kathy Pease, Box 992, Rockland 04841).

Mary Day (207-236-2750 or 800-992-2218; Coastal Cruises, Owners Steve Cobb and Barry King, P.O. Box 798, Camden 04843).

Mercantile (207-236-2938 or 888-MWC-SAIL; Maine Windjammer Cruises, Owners Ray and Ann Williamson, P.O. Box 617, Camden 04843).

Mistress (207-236-2938 or 888-MWC-SAIL; Maine Windjammer Cruises, Owners Ray and Ann Williamson, P.O. Box 617, Camden 04843).

Nathaniel Bowditch (207-273-4062 or 800-288-4098; Capt. Gib Philbrick, P.O. Box 459, Warren 04864

North Wind (207-236-2323; Capt. John Nugent, P.O. Box 432, Camden 04843).

Roseway (207-236-4449 or 800-255-4449; Yankee Schooner Cruises, Capt. George Sloane, Box 696, Camden 04843).

Stephen Taber (207-236-3520 or 800-999-7352; Capts. Ken and Ellen Barnes, Windjammer Wharf, 70 Elm St., Camden 04843). This is the only windjammer to be listed on the National Historic Register.

Summertime Cruises Inc. (800-562-8290; Capt. Bill Brown, 115 South Main St., Rockland, 04841).

Surprise (207-236-4687; Drawer H, Camden 04843). Owners Jack and Barbara Moore.

Timberwind (800-759-9250; Capt. Rick Miles, Box 643, Rockport, ME 04856).

Victory Chimes (207-594-0755 or 800-745-5651; Capt. Kip Files and Paul DeGaeta, P.O. Box 1401, Rockland 04841). Three- and six-day cruises on the state's largest windjammer, built in 1900.

Wendameen (207-594-1751; Capt. Neal Parker, Box 252, Rockland 04841). Overnight cruises on a 67-foot schooner.

Down East/Acadia

Sylvina W. Beal (207-288-4585 summer, 207-546-2927 winter; Downeast Windjammer Cruises, Capt. Steven F. Pagels, P.O. Box 8, Cherryfield 04622).

Whale Watching Inc. (207-288-3322 or 800-508-1499; 1 West St., Bar Harbor 04609). Twenty-one trips a day from whale watching to windjamming.

Young America (207-288-4585 summer, 207-546-2927 winter; Downeast Wind-jammer Cruises, Capt. Steven F. Pagels, P.O. Box 8, Cherryfield 04622). Sails from Bar Harbor Inn Pier, Bar Harbor.

WINDSURFING

This is not an easy sport to learn. It's even harder in the ocean. Lakes are the place for lessons. *Back Cove* in Portland is a popular spot. It's lake-like enough to learn on, and the wind can blow like the ocean in a storm. *Pine Point* in Scarborough is another good spot. So are *Eagle Lake*, *Echo Lake* and *Long Pond* on Mount Desert Island. The beaches in the south are popular and are a good place to catch the breeze once you've mastered the sport. Wherever you windsurf in Maine, a wet suit is required because the water can be very cold.

SEASONAL SPORTING EVENTS

Beyond the annual events mentioned in the above categories, the coast has dozens of events that lure sportsmen and women from around the world. Following are a few favorite events you should know about.

South Coast

Beach Olympics, mid-August. On the beach in Old Orchard (207-934-2500). Kids and adults enjoy this three-day event to benefit the Maine Special Olympics. Round-robin volleyball, water-balloon races, ice cream eating contests, and more. Live music and entertainment at night.
Great Inner Tube Race, early August. On the river in Ogunquit. (207-646-2939 for information).
Kite Flying Contest, early Sept. On the beach in Ogunquit (207-646-2939).
Sand Building Contest, mid-July. On the beach in Ogunquit, the time of this contest is governed by the tides (phone 207-646-2939 for information).

Casco Bay

Peaks Island-to-Portland Swim, early Aug. Strong-armed swimmers often finish the two-mile swim from Peaks Island beach to East End Beach in Portland in under one hour (contact YMCA, 207-874-1111).

Midcoast

Friendship Sloop Days and **Friendship Sloop Races**, late July in Friendship. Beautiful wooden boats compete for attention and prizes (contact the Friendship Sloop Society, 207-354-8036).

The Great Schooner Race, early July. Sponsored by the Maine Windjammer Association, this all-day race begins at North Haven and ends in Rockland (contact the Rockland Chamber of Commerce, 207-596-0376).

Maine Retired Skipper's Race, mid-August. You have to be at least 65 to enter (contact the Retired Skipper's Race Committee, Castine, 207-326-8579).

The Monhegan Island Yacht Race, mid-August.

Owls Head Transportation Rally, early August. Planes, high-wheeled bicycles, and automobiles. More than 300 of them (contact the Owls Head Transportation Museum, 207-594-4418).

Schooner Days, early July (Rockland area Chamber of Commerce, 207-596-0376).

Windjammer Days, late June. Windjammers of all shapes and sizes (contact the Boothbay Harbor Chamber of Commerce, 207-633-2353).

Windjammer Weekend, late August. Parade of sail, fireworks, day sails (contact the Camden Chamber of Commerce, 207-236-4404).

East of Schoodic

The World's Fastest Lobsterboat Races, early July. Takes place near Moosabec Reach (contact the Jonesport 4th of July Committee, P.O. Box 106, Jonesport 04649; 207-497-2804).

Something Old, Something New
SHOPPING

Maine these days is known for its outlets as well as its inlets. The outlet trail stretches north and eastward from Kittery all the way to Ellsworth, near Bar Harbor. Maine's outlets may be traced back in history to the first L.L. Bean store in Freeport, a shopping mecca for hunters, fishermen, and outdoors people. The descendants of L. L. Bean, the man who invented the Maine Hunting Boot, still keep shop in Freeport on Casco Bay and in two "factory stores," one in Ellsworth and another in Freeport.

Herb Swanson

Restored brick shop fronts on Water Street in Eastport

Mainers have been commercially adept since the early 1600s. The Pilgrims of Plymouth Colony sent their most industrious members north to establish a fur trade out of Bagaduce (now known as Castine) on the Blue Hill peninsula. They paid off the debts for their voyage in just a few years, evidence of the resources they found there.

The earliest trade with Europe and their fellow colonists was in furs and lumber, then ships and granite. Later, coastal residents began selling manufactured goods to the rest of the world: fabric woven in textile mills to the south; shoes from leather tanned and handsewn at factories inland; paper made at pulp mills on many of the state's rivers; and herring and sardines canned at factories Down East. Not all the commerce was one-sided. Mainers were world-class shoppers, and during the 18th and 19th centuries world travelers — ship captains and merchants filled their homes with riches from Europe, the Far East, and ports to the south.

Shoes, paper, lumber, and seafood still comprise much of the industrial and commercial base for the state. Yet since the days the "rusticators" discovered

Bar Harbor and summer resorts began to sprout up along the coast and inland, much of the state's economy has focused on catering to seasonal residents and tourists. Shops and roadside stands sell everything from paintings, artwork, and nautical gear to T-shirts, balsam sachets, blueberry pottery, and lobster magnets — everything to remind the visitor that they have been here.

Antiques, pottery, and other handcrafts are especially big here. Until the past decade, many of the stores along the coast would close after the tourists went home on Labor Day. Now, in towns like Camden and Bar Harbor, they are open all year long.

In this chapter we mention some — but by no means all — of the shopping stops on the coast. Rte. 1, from where it first enters Maine at Kittery to far Down East, is a virtual shopper's paradise with outlets, galleries, junk stores, flea markets, and the occasional yard sale all along the way.

ANTIQUES

Shopping for antiques on the coast is almost as popular as outlet hopping, but slower paced. Most Maine coast antique shopping is done in two places: the region in the South Coast between York and Kennebunkport, and between Belfast and Searsport in the Midcoast. There is plenty of good stuff in between and beyond, only antique shopping in those places isn't as concentrated an experience.

To really know who has what and what it's selling for, pick up a copy of the *Maine Antique Digest,* the bible for coastal and inland antique shoppers. It's published in Waldoboro and can be found at most newsstands in the state.

South Coast

Antiques on Nine (207-967-0626; 75 Western Ave., Rte. 9, Kennebunk). A mishmash of American and continental furniture, architectural elements, books, art, and textiles — even old garden accessories.

The Barn at Cape Neddick (207-363-7315; Rte. 1, Cape Neddick). Recognized for its selection of American country furniture, accessories, and folk art.

The Farm (207-985-2656; Mildram Rd. off Rte. 1, Wells). Fine English antiques from the 18th and 19th centuries and oriental porcelain. Yankee magazine calls this one of the best in New England.

R. Jorgensen Antiques (207-646-9444; Rte. 1, Wells). Eleven rooms of period furniture and antiques from North America, the British Isles, France, and Scandinavia. This is the place for serious antique shoppers.

MacDougall-Gionet Antiques Associates (207-646-3531; Rte. 1, Wells). For more than a quarter of a century dealers — now there are 60 — have gathered in an old barn to show and sell formal and country period antiques.

Kenneth & Ida Manko (207-646-2595; on Seabreeze, one half mile off Eldridge Rd., Moody). An intriguing selection of Americana and folk art, including old weathervanes.

Riverbank Antiques (207-646-6314; Wells Union Antiques Center, Rte. 1, Wells). If we had a fortune, we'd consider spending a considerable portion of it here on old statuary, antique pots, and other stuff for our garden.

Casco Bay

F.O. Bailey (207-774-1479; 141 Middle St., Portland). Great showroom and a terrific mix of stuff from rustic pottery to highly polished highboys.

Portland Architectural Salvage (207-780-0634; 253 Congress St., Portland) Alice, the proprietor, usually has an ear glued to a cordless phone as she calls all over the state chasing down a good bargain. We've found many fine things to take home from here, from Tuscan garden ornaments to eight foot doors for our old Victorian parlor.

Red Wheel Antiques (207-865-6492; 275 Rte. 1, Freeport). We think some of this mix of old dishes, tools, furniture, and paraphernalia is overpriced. Still, we keep going back to find that occasional bargain. On summer weekends, it becomes an open air flea market.

Midcoast

Apex Antiques and Design Service (207-338-1194; 208 High St., Belfast). Eclectic mix of American and formal furniture, painted furniture, and custom-designed quilts.

Captain Pinkham's Emporium (207-548-6465; 34 Main St., Searsport) Old tools, furniture, old books, old paintings. This is just the kind of place you can make a "find."

The Ditty Box (207-882-6618; Rte. 1 at the No. Edgecomb/Newcastle town line). Antiques and collectibles including old samplers, china, Currier & Ives prints, and American country furniture.

F. Barrie Freeman (207-442-8452; Quaker Point Farm, West Bath). Old American maps. They also specialize in printed Americana and ephemera.

Avis Howell's Antiques (207-338-3302; corner of Pearl and Court, Belfast). Avis has collected and sold Shaker furniture for more than a quarter of a century.

The Palabra Shop (207-633-4225; 85 Commercial Street, Boothbay Harbor). Moses bottles, antique dolls, books, primitives, and nautical paintings.

Searsport Antique Mall (207-548-2640; Rte. 1, Searsport). About 20 dealers gather here in the heart of Maine's antique mecca.

Wee Barn Antiques (207-354-6163; 4$\frac{1}{2}$ Georges St., Thomaston). Gwen Robinson and Lee-Ann Upham have gathered a fun collection of antique "smalls," glass, furniture, jewelry, and silver.

A flea market in Searsport. Flea markets, yard sales, and garage sales yield some of the coast's best selections of antiques and other treasures.

Tom Hindman

Acadia/Down East

The Big Chicken Barn (207-667-7308; Rte. 1, Ellsworth). With hundreds of tiny windows rising several stories, this really is an old chicken barn. The feathers are gone, and it now is packed with a giant collection of old books, antiques, and fun junk.

E.L. Higgins (207-244-3983; Rte. 102, 4 miles past Southwest Harbor in Bernard) You've been looking for antique wicker furniture? Here's the place.

Hulls Cove Tool Barn (207-288-5126; Breakneck Rd. off Rte. 3, Hulls Cove). Antiques and old tools, books, paintings, and prints.

Liros Gallery (207-374-5370; Main St., Blue Hill). Interesting stuff, including old paintings, maps, and Russian icons.

South Coast

Bacon's Auction Co. (207-985-1401; Rte. 1, Arundel).
J. J. Keating (207-985-2097; Rte. 1, Kennebunk).
Richard Oliver (207-985-3600; Rte. 1, Kennebunk).

Auctions on the Coast

If you're looking for antiques or just a Victorian knick-knack to take back to your Aunt Pearl, auctions provide the chance to cut out the middleman and get a feel for the worth of something by competing against professional buyers. Estate auctions are even more fun, because they give you a truer sense of time and place than many historic homes or museums. Most of the auction houses listed below will be glad to put you on their mailing lists. The *Maine Sunday Telegram* and *The Maine Times* often run notices of upcoming auctions in their classified sections. Another source of auction notices, the *Maine Antique Digest* has auction news and an entertaining column of auction gossip complete with photographs.

Hap Moore Antiques Auctioneer (207-363-6373; York).

Casco Bay

F.O. Bailey Antiquarians (207-774-1479; 141 Middle St., Portland).
Southerland Auctions (207-829-3063; Yarmouth).

Midcoast

Andrews and Andrews (207-338-1386; 71 Cross St., Northport).

Downeast/Acadia

Mayo & Mayo Auctioneers (207-667-2586; Rte. 3, Trenton).

BOOKS

Friends who visit Maine love our bookstores. While many are small mom-and-pop affairs, they cater to a literate clientele. Several are known for their specialties — like women's studies or new age essays or fine old volumes only a bibliophile could love. Others you can count on for having a good translation of Homer as well as the top ten from *The New York Times Book Review* section. Maybe it's the long winter, and the fact that people here really do curl up by the fireplace with a good book. A couple of years ago Maine's preeminent weekly, *The Maine Times*, surveyed its readers and found they read, on average, fifty books a year. Herewith is a list of bookstores we have frequented and like. If you're into old books, you may request a directory of dealers by contacting the Maine *Antiquarian Booksellers Association* (207-443-1510).

This statue honoring the fisherman and his wife is on the town green in Kennebunkport.

Herb Swanson

South Coast

Kennebunk Book Port (207-967-3815; 10 Dock Square, Kennebunkport). Books sold in an old rum warehouse.

Harding's Book Shop (207-646-8785; Rte. 1, Wells). A book collector's paradise with old and rare books, maps, and prints. Bring your favorite first edition and they will do an appraisal.

Casco Bay

Allen Scott Books (207-774-2190; 89 Exchange St., Portland). Old, used, and rare books bought and sold. Good browsing for a rainy day.

Bookland (207-772-4045;1 Monument Sq., Portland). The biggest volume bookseller in Maine, and for periodical junkies, the place to go to get Italian *Vogue*. (They also have stores in Brunswick, Freeport and other locations on the coast.)

Books Etc. (207-774-0626; 38 Exchange St., Portland) This is one of our favorite Maine bookstores. Travelers take note, they have an excellent Maine and travel book selection.

Carlson & Turner Antiquarian Books (207-773-4200; 241 Congress St., Portland). We love to survey these dimly lit shelves. Ask to be put on their mailing list to receive their annual collectors' calendar.

DeLorme Mapping Company (207-865-4171; 2 DeLorme Drive, Yarmouth). This is the shiny new home of a favorite place of ours, just off Rte. 1 on the way to Freeport. A dozen or so years ago, DeLorme began charting the state's wilderness — urban and otherwise — from every possible point of view. Now they chart the world, and they do it with satellites, computers, and automobile navigation systems. Cool. If you love maps, globes, or computers, you'll love this place. Check out the giant globe in the lobby.

Harbour Books (207-846-6306; 106 Lafayette St., Yarmouth). Books for children and mariners in this small shop near the harbor.

Harding's Book Shop (207-761-2150; 594 Congress St., Portland). This is the younger sister of a well-known collectors' store in Wells (see above).

The Maine Writers Center (207-729-6333; 12 Pleasant St., Brunswick). More than 1,400 works by Maine writers, publishers, and small presses are represented, as well as Maine-related books. This is the home of the Maine Writers Alliance, a non-profit organization that sponsors seminars and workshops.

The Store at Maine Audubon Society (207-781-2330; 118 U.S. Rte 1, Falmouth). A good collection of books for those interested in natural history.

Midcoast

ABCDef (207-236-3903; 23 Bayview St., Camden). Fine, old, hard to find, and rare books.

Canterbury Tales Books (207-338-1171; 52 Main St., Belfast). Books for all ages, in addition to topographical maps and nautical charts.

The Fertile Mind Bookshop (207-338-2498; 13 Main St., Belfast). New and "recycled" books and a book and cassette rental collection.

Maine Coast Book Shop (207-563-3207; Main St., Damariscotta). Penguin novels and coffee table books, as well as a full selection of paperback and hardcover books.

Owl & Turtle Bookshop (207-236-4769 or 800-876-4769; 8 Bay View St., Camden). Not only do they encourage browsing, but if you get really absorbed in something, they have a few rooms available upstairs at the guest house. They specialize in children's and nautical books.

Thomaston Books & Prints (207-354-0001; 105 Main St., Thomaston). Books for kids, adults, and everyone in between, plus limited edition prints and art posters.

Down East/Acadia

Blue Hill Books (207-374-5632; 2 Pleasant St., Blue Hill). A healthy selection of books about Maine and New England. Books for children. Fiction for adults.

The Compass Rose (207-326-9366 or 800-698-9366; Main St., Castine). Books and antique prints.

Oz Books (207-244-9077; Main St., Southwest Harbor). Books for kids. Books for grownups. Books on Maine.

Pages of Time (207-288-3232; 227 Main St., Bar Harbor). New and used.

Port in a Storm Bookstore (207-244-4114; Main St., Somesville). This is a wonderful local bookstore, and a great place to spend an afternoon getting your bearings in a vacation town. Check their schedule — they often have local authors in for talks and signings. They also have a very entertaining biennial newsletter, a good music selection, and two amiable bookstore cats.

Sherman's Book Store (207-288-3161; 56 Main St., Bar Harbor). Books, gifts and souvenirs. Also hiking and road maps of Acadia National Park.

Maine Outlets

Maine's outlet trail runs from Kittery to Freeport and on to Ellsworth near Bar Harbor, and you can pick up the trail almost immediately after you cross the state line. There are few things an experienced shopper will not already know about shopping, but here are a few tips anyway.

1. <u>Try to avoid shopping on rainy days.</u> Visitors to the coast like to be outside whenever they can, and whenever they can't — that usually means when it's raining — they like to shop.
2. <u>Outlets have sales.</u> Even outlets have sales, and many times those coincide with sale seasons in regular retail stores (July 4, late summer, and early fall are particularly popular sale times here because of the summer tourist traffic).

(continued)

Outlets in Freeport.

Herb Swanson

3. <u>Not all outlet bargains are real bargains.</u> Many times, there's a reason, good or otherwise, these items did not sell elsewhere.

In Kittery, most of the outlets are for products you can purchase at many other outlet havens throughout the country. Anne Klein, Brooks Brothers, Corning/Revere, Timberland, Puma, Capezio, Villeroy & Boch, Crate & Barrel, Dansk, Black & Decker, and more.

It's much more of the same in Freeport in the Casco Bay region, except there you have L. L. Bean. You'll also find an outlet for high end Maine shoe manufacturer Cole-Haan (The Company Store), Calvin Klein, Reebok, The Gap (upstairs there are some great bargains), Banana Republic, J. Crew, Patagonia, and G. H. Bass (based just south of here in Falmouth). My quality-minded father-in-law especially likes to shop the Ralph Lauren store during their late summer sale. There he finds great bargains on his favorite polo shirts.

Ellsworth, the youngest outlet community on the coast, has the smallest selection of stores, but if you're an outdoors person, you'll want to check out the L. L. Bean Factory Store. Unlike their off-price store in Freeport, you occasionally can find significant markdowns on store samples of their sporting equipment — mountain bikes, steppers, tents, stoves, and the like. If you find something you like, grab it. It's usually the only one in stock.

Elsewhere on the coast, travelers will find hundreds of true factory stores and outlets, where the goods are made right there — or not far away. Here are some of our favorites:

Big Al's Odd Lot Outlet (207-882-6423; Rte. 1 Wiscasset) Big Al's is a Maine coast tradition that gets bigger every year. From funky gadgets, ugly sunglasses to some just plain weird and tacky stuff, you can find everything and nothing here. Still it's fun to wander the aisles.

The Company Store (207-865-6321; 66 Main Street, Freeport). An upscale "outlet" for Cole-Haan, the high-end shoe manufacturer that has its offices in nearby Yarmouth. Downstairs they stock beautiful shoes. Upstairs it's clothing from around the world.

(continued)

Cuddledown Factory Store (207-865-1713 or 888-235-3696; 231 Rte. 1 So. Freeport). Lush down comforters, comforter covers, sheets, and other linens sewn at a factory in nearby Portland. Buy them here and save 30 to 80 percent. Or ask to receive their catalog.

Maine State Prison Showroom Outlet (207-354-2535; Rte. 1, Thomaston). Everyone needs an outlet. Handcrafted furniture and gift items usually with a nautical theme. Here you can find patio furniture, lamps, ship's wheel mirrors, hutches, hand carved novelties, desks, and cedar chests. All are at reasonable prices.

The Moss Tent Outlet (at Maine Sport, 207-236-7120 or 888-236-8797; Rte. 1, Rockport). Moss Tents are considered by many experts to be the finest. Firsts, seconds, and discontinued models are sold at up to 30 percent off retail.

Portmanteau (207-774-7276; 191 Middle St., Portland). Elegant tapestry and leather clothing, bags, luggage, and accessories made on the premises.

Tom's of Maine Natural Living Store (207-985-3874; 106 Lafayette Center, Kennebunk). Since we've moved here, we've gotten hooked on their natural toothpaste (no saccharine), so we venture south every once in a while to stock up on toothpaste in slightly battered tubes, shaving cream, shampoo, and other natural personal care items and bathroom staples. Tom Chapell, the founder, graduated from Harvard Divinity School and is looking for new ways to fill the spiritual void in corporate America, as well as prevent tooth decay naturally.

CLOTHING

South Coast

Dock Square Clothiers (207-967-5362; Dock Square, Kennebunkport; and 207-646-8548; Perkins Cove). Classic, natural-fiber clothing for men and women sold at two locations.

Casco Bay

Amaryllis (207-772-4439; 41 Exchange St., Portland). Unusual women's clothing, shoes, and hats.

Joseph's (207-773-1274; 410 Fore St., Portland). The men's and women's clothing stores are as haut as Maine gets.

Levinsky's (207-774-0972; 516 Congress St., Portland). This is a bargain hunter's institution among tight-fisted Mainers, so much so the store had been immortalized in the pages of *Down East* magazine. This is a good place to outfit the kids for school.

L.L. Bean Factory Store (207-772-5100; 542 Congress Street, Portland). While all the tourists shop the mother store in Freeport, all the locals quietly buy their L.L. Bean products at this new store in downtown Portland. Don't tell anyone we told you.

Olympia Sports (207-772-7828; 544 Congress St., Portland). If you can't find what you're looking for in the L.L. Bean Factory Outlet, why not hop in here, it's right next door. Olympia carries sportswear and gear for all shapes and sizes.

Midcoast

Coyote Moon (207-338-5659; 54 Main St., Belfast) Natural fiber clothing and funky, New Age-like gifts.

Theo B. Camisole and Company (207-763-4297; 39¹/₂ Main St., Camden). There's nothing like great lingerie, and here is some of the best we've seen. Pretty, lacy things and soft cotton terry robes.

Down East/Acadia

Darthia Farm (207-963-7771 or 800-285-6234); Rte. 186, West Bay Rd., 1.7 miles off Rte. 1, Gouldsboro). Ikat dyed and handwoven clothing and accessories by Cindy Thayer, as well as hand spun yarns and hand knit items by other local craftspersons. In season you can purchase organic produce raised by Ms. Thayer and her husband on the saltwater farm.

The Grasshopper Shop (207-667-5816; 124 Main St., Ellsworth). Unusual, interesting, and comfortable women's clothing. They also have a shop in Camden.

Water Witch (207-326-4884; Main St., Castine). Jean de Raat sells amazing selection of hats, dresses, sundresses, and other summer weekend clothes made by local tailors and seamstresses from textiles she's gathered on travels around the world. Her sundresses may seem a bit pricey, but they are the kind you'll wear again and again. Want to buy a house in this pretty little town? Ms. de Raat is also the local realtor.

COLLECTIBLES

Midcoast

Duck Trap Decoys (207-789-5363; Duck Trap Rd. off Rte. 1, Lincolnville Beach). Hand-carved decoys by Walt Simmons and 32 other carvers. Furry animals, too. Prices range from under $10 to several thousand.

Ducktrap Bay Trading Co. (207-236-9568 or 800-560-9568; 28 Bayview St., Camden). Decoys, ships' models, carvings, prints, and original art.

Ye Olde Coin Shop Fine Jewelry (207-338-2663; 64 Main St., Belfast). A collector's mix including old comic books and collectors' supplies. If there has to be an Ye Olde anything, then, okay, this place.

Down East/Acadia

Belcher's Country Store (207-348-9938; Reach Rd., Deer Isle). They are big on Christmas here, all year round. Antique and collectible tinware, hooked rugs, hand blown glass, ceramics. Recently the owners opened a baby Belcher's on Water St. in Blue Hill.

Dakin's Quality Crafted Miniatures (207-548-6500; 21 Prospect St., Searsport). Wooden Breyer horses, horse show stalls, and accessories.

Downeast Decoys (207-469-2158; Rte. 1, Orland). Antique and old decoys, as well as new ones carved by Bill Conroy. He will appraise yours, if you ask.

Nancy Neale Typecraft (207-244-5192; Steamboat Wharf Rd. off Rte 102, Bernard). Irving Silverman and Nancy Neale began collecting antique wood type in 1969. Today they have the largest selection in the country in a shop near Bass Harbor on Mount Desert Island. In addition, Ms. Neal creates what she calls "framed assemblages" — type collages — for anniversaries, birthdays and other events. Open by chance or appointment.

East of Schoodic

The Sow's Ear (207-255-4066; 7 Water St., Machias). An engaging collection of clothing, books, toys, and gifts.

Yard Sales

There's nothing more Maine than a good yard sale. A yard sale begins when a homeowner piles the contents of his attic and garage on the lawn, hangs signs around town, and then sits and waits for the people to come.

The people do come, and they'll buy anything. Mainers hate to see anything go to waste. In fact it's noble to take something your neighbor outgrew or grew tired of and transform it into a family heirloom. We bought a dining room set for pennies that would have cost a thousand in a tony antique store. Why buy new, when used is as good as this?

Mid-August through mid-September is good yard sale season. Spring, after the ritual spring cleaning, can mean good yard sales in an economic boom time. Pick a road lined with large, prosperous-looking single-family homes. Then watch for the signs. Rte. 115 through Yarmouth and Rte. 88 through Falmouth are good yard sale routes. Read the Sunday classifieds; they often list good upcoming sales.

CRAFT SUPPLIES

South Coast

York River Trading Store (207-363-7734 or 888-227-7357; 90 U.S. Rte. 1, York). Craft supplies including stencil patterns, basket supplies, tole painting supplies, as well as local crafts.

Casco Bay

Halcyon Yarn (207-442-7909 or 800-341-0282; 12 School St., Bath). You can tell how long and cold the winter is by the quality of the local yarn shop. If you knit, spin, or weave or you know someone who does, check this place out.

Quilting Life (207-772-6568; 99 Exchange St., Portland). Marcia Whitney worked in the theater in New York before she moved to Maine and opened this quilters' haven in Portland. She has stocked it with great fabric and everything else for the quilter. If you like quilts but can't make them yourself, you can arrange to have one made for you here.

Midcoast

The Cat's Meow (207-548-2546; Rte. 1, Searsport). Patchwork quilts. Calicoes and solids. Also quilting supplies.

GIFTS

South Coast

Animal Instinct (207-646-7728; Main St., Ogunquit). Bear collectors alert! Great stuffed animals, puppets, dolls, and toys for the young and young at heart.

Brass Carousel & Kite Galleries (207-646-8225; 3 Oarweed Lane, Perkins Cove). Kites, brass, travel stuff, and gifts.

Brick Store Museum Shop (207-985-3639; 105 Main St.; Kennebunkport). Antique reproduction toys including a jacks set, rag doll kit, and old-time picture book. The shop also has grown-up gifts.

Compliments (207-967-2269 or 800-249-2269; Dock Square, Kennebunkport). An unusual gallery of outré pottery, mirrors, jewelry, lamps, and objets d'art. The "Time Bomb" clock with sticks of "dynamite" is worth a look alone.

Nestling Duck Gift Shop (207-883-6705; 350 Pine Point Rd., Scarborough). A collection of New England gifts, including candles, stoneware, jewelry, and Maine-made crafts.

Port Canvas (207-967-2717 or 800-333-6788; 9 Ocean Ave., Kennebunkport). Canvas suit bags, carpetbags, satchels, duffles, totes, raincoats in a variety of sizes and colors. Custom orders taken too.

Casco Bay

Indrani's (207-775-1901; 7 Moulton St., Portland and 149 Maine St., Brunswick). Indrani Dennen grew up in Africa, and she has brought some of the most beautiful traditions from that continent to Maine, including handsome wedding baskets which tell a story about the women who wove them.

Live music serenades shoppers in Portland's Old Port.

Herb Swanson

Midcoast

The Clipper Trade (207-442-8671; 110 Front St., Bath). Souvenirs, Maine crafts, and goods from the world over in a small shop created to resemble emporiums from the days of the clippers.

Enchantments (207-633-4992; 16 McKown St., Boothbay Harbor). Crystals, herbs, incense, and books. Gifts and stuff for the metaphysical crowd.

Granite Hall Store (207-529-5864; Round Pond). An old-fashioned country store in an historic building. Penny candy, antiques, and woolens. Closes after Christmas.

The Leather Bench (207-236-4688; 34 Main St., Camden). Great leather bags, belts, wallets, and clothing. Whenever a movie is filmed anywhere nearby, this is where the crew comes to get those cool leather jackets with their movie's name on it.

Maine Gathering (207-236-9004; 13 Elm St., Camden). Contemporary and traditional crafts by Maine residents with an extensive selection of Maine Native American baskets.

Narragansett Leathers (207-563-5080; Main St., Damariscotta). Leather goods — bags, belts, briefcases — handmade right here.

The Right Stuff (207-236-9595; 38 Main St., Camden). A gift and home store crammed with attractive reproductions, period lighting, and country-style accessories.

The Sheepskin Shop (207-273-3061; Rte. 90, Warren). If it can be made from sheepskin, these folks have it: seatcovers, gloves, footwear, hats, purses, blankets, rugs, and chamois cloth. A good shopping stop on the shortcut past Rockport to Camden.

Membership is not required to shop at H.O.M.E. (Homeworkers Organized for More Employment), a rambling complex of booths and stores, with everything from crafts to home-canned foods.

Herb Swanson

Down East/Acadia

Dollhouse Treasures (207-469-7832 or 800-743-7832; Acadia Hwy., East Orland). This store sells miniatures, dollhouses, and toy replicas. Everything's here for the doll lover, including building materials to make your own dollhouse. Know the building code in your own state.

Glass Workbench (800-564-2788; Rte. 1, Lincolnville Beach). Original stained glass designs for windows and gifts.

H.O.M.E. Craft Shop (207-469-7961; Rte. 1, Bucksport). A craft lover's dream, this sprawling store is a cooperative for more than 400 Maine craftspersons — H.O.M.E. stands for "Homeworkers Organized for More Employment." For sale are quilts, toys, jewelry, weaving, pottery, and other handcrafted items, as well as homemade, home-canned goods.

Island Artisans (207-288-4214; 99 Main St., Bar Harbor). Beautiful things, both practical and decorative, made by Mt. Desert Island craftspeople.

U. S. Bells (207-963-7184; Rte. 186, Prospect Harbor). Sculptor Richard Fisher began crafting bells more than 20 years ago. Now his bronze and brass bells are sold around the world. They're in all shapes, all sizes and for all purposes — including wind chimes for letting you know it's windy and doorbells for letting you know someone is at the door. He also sells beautiful handmade quilts in a "factory outlet" that sits next to the bell foundry.

HOME FURNISHINGS

Casco Bay

Robert Clements Gallery (207-775-2202; 81 West Commercial St., Portland). On a quiet side street just up the way from the Novia Scotia Ferry Terminal, Bob Clements frame shop offers more than your usual mouldings. He's crazy about fish, and among the mirrors, shadow boxes, and other stuff hanging on the walls, he sells his original fish paintings.

Decorum (207-775-3346; 231 Commercial St., Portland). Old house fanatics travel for hundreds of miles to find nifty, well made stuff for the house, including reproduction hardware.

Foreside Company (207-773-6282; 235 Commercial St., Portland). The first in a chain of stores where you can find nifty trinkets and furniture from around the world.

Maine Cabinetmakers

What is it about Maine and cabinetmakers? Ever since Thomas Moser quit his teaching job at Bates College to make his signature Shaker-style tables and chairs, dozens of other fine cabinetmakers have sprung up nearby. Some have worked in Moser's workshops. Here are a few of the cabinetmakers we know about in residence on the coast.

Casco Bay

Green Design Furniture Co. (207-775-4234 or 800-853-4234; 267 Commercial St., Portland) Doug Green has designed a line of furniture that is handsome and innovative, so much so *Time* magazine named him designer of the year.

Thos. Moser (207-774-3791 or 800-862-1973; 415 Cumberland Ave., Portland). The most famous of Maine's cabinetmakers, Moser was instrumental in making Shaker furniture fashionable again.

Midcoast

David and Susan Margonelli (207-633-3326; 780 River Rd., Edgecomb). Fine hand-made furniture.

Studio Mnemosyne (207-389-2027; HC 31 Box 323, Popham Beach). Jerry Moser designs and builds modern hardwood furniture with plenty of right angles.

Thomas C. Hinchcliffe — Cabinetmaker (207-326-9411; Rte. 176, Blue Hill). Hinchcliffe uses old woods and 18th-century joinery to make handmade copies of antique chairs, tables, cupboards, and armoires.

William Evans, Cabinetmaker (207-832-4175; 804 Main St., Waldoboro). Reproductions, restorations, and contemporary furniture.

Windsor Chairs (207-789-5188 or 800-789-5188; Rte. 1, Lincolnville). They make chairs. Windsor chairs. Watch them work. They also make other furniture, providing it complements their Windsors.

East of Schoodic

Jim's Smoked Salmon & Fine Woodworking (207-853-4831; 37 Washington St., Eastport) Jim's fly fishing boxes, humidors, and jewelry boxes are almost as good as his smoked seafood. This may sound like an odd combination to you, but here in Maine, it's thoroughly logical.

Master cabinetmaker Thomas Moser.

Courtesy of Thomas Moser

Heritage Lanterns (207-846-3911 or 800-544-6070; 25 Yarmouth Crossing Dr., Yarmouth). Handcrafted reproductions of 18th-, 19th-, and early 20th-century lanterns, sconces, chandeliers, and lamps.

Maine Cottage Furniture (207-846-1430; Lower Falls Landing, Rte. 88, Yarmouth). Summer furniture in colors that will appeal to modern day rusticators. Also, hooked rugs, quilts, lighting, vintage-cloth pillows, and sisal flooring.

The Whip & Spoon (207-774-4020 or 800-937-9447; 161 Commercial St., Portland). From Cuisinarts to lobster potholders, what to stock for the well-kept kitchen.

Midcoast

The Store (207-594-9246; 435 Main St., Rockland). Set in the heart of Rockland's old fashioned Main Street, this is an upscale kitchen store where you can find the perfect corkscrew or whatever other essential you need to make your vacation complete.

Village Store & Children's Shop (207-633-2293; 20 Townsend Ave., Boothbay Harbor). Gifts for the home, made here in Maine and elsewhere.

Well-Tempered Kitchen (207-563-5762; 122 Atlantic Highway; Waldoboro). Okay, we admit it. We have a soft spot for a good kitchen store, because you never know when you're going to find those perfect custard dishes or that sweet little sauce pot.

Down East/Acadia

Harbor Farm (207-348-7737 or 800-342-8003; Rte. 15 just over the causeway, Little Deer Isle). We can't believe this place has been around for more than 10 years, and we hadn't found it until recently. They have almost all the things we like to accumulate from wrought iron lamps, European and Maine made pottery, to very cool paving stones for our garden imported from England.

North Country Textiles (207-374-2715; Main St., Blue Hill). Home textiles and clothing. The cloth is the thing here.

Rooster Brother (207-667-8675 or 800-866-0054; 18 W. Main St., next to Union River Bridge, Ellsworth). Cooking equipment and tableware, plus gourmet foods and wine.

Scottish Lion Blacksmith (207-529-5523; Rte. 32, Round Pond). Blacksmith Andrew Leck's hand-forged iron home accessories include pot racks and fireplace tools.

Sleepy Hollow Rag Rugs (207-789-5987; Rte. 173, Lincolnville Beach). Hand-loomed rag rugs woven on antique looms and sold right in the studio.

Weatherend Estate Furniture (207-596-6483 or 800-456-6483; 6 Gordon Drive, Rockland). Reproductions of lawn furniture first crafted using yacht joinery techniques and considered by many to surpass the originals in style, construction techniques, and durability.

JEWELRY

South Coast

Swamp John's (207-646-9414; Oar Weed Rd., Perkins Cove, Ogunquit). They've been making and selling jewelry, including rings, earrings, and pins of Maine tourmaline, for more than two decades.

Casco Bay

Fibula (207-761-4432; 50 Exchange St., Portland). The showcases here are like the who's who of Maine jewelry making: Werner Reed, P.B. Las, Elizabeth Pryor, Sally Webb, Daniel Gibbings, and the shop's owner, Edie Armstrong, who makes beautiful custom wedding bands, earrings, bracelets, and necklaces at her workbench right in the store.

Geraldine Wolf Antique Jewelry (207-774-8994; 26 Milk St., Portland). Pretty baubles from the past, as well as antique china and decorative art.

Midcoast

A Silver Lining (207-633-4103; 21 Townsend Ave., Boothbay Harbor). Blueberry pendants and other originally designed memories of the Maine coast in metals past cast in sterling, gold, copper, brass, titanium, or gold electroplated.

NAUTICAL EQUIPMENT

Casco Bay

Chase Leavitt & Company (207-772-3751 or 800-638-8906; 10 Dana St., Portland). Half a block away from Portland's "working" waterfront, this old-fashioned marine store caters to pleasure boaters, with a good selection of charts, marine hardware, navigation equipment, and foul-weather gear.

Midcoast

Bohndell Sails (207-236-3549; Commercial St., Rockport). They've been making sails since 1870, which is nothing sailors around here don't know.

Hamilton Marine (207-548-6302 or 800-639-2715; East Main St., Searsport). Everything you need for your sailboat or motor boat. Should your radar — or any other nautical doodad — break down in some exotic far off port, call these guys. They ship replacement parts and hardware daily via UPS.

POTTERY

Casco Bay

Delilah Pottery (207-871-1594; 134 Spring St., Portland). Tucked into a tiny bubble gum pink antique saltbox, this lively potter's studio and store is just packed full of whimsical pottery and sculpture. We especially love their offbeat holiday ornaments.

Maine Potters Market (207-774-1633; 376 Fore St., Portland). Local potter's cooperative featuring stoneware, porcelain, and earthenware. An interesting mix of traditional to funky one-of-a-kind pieces.

Pottery by Peg & Dick Miller (207-846-4981; 19 Smith St. off Rte. 88, Yarmouth). The Millers fashion their wheel-thrown, slab, shingle, and coil pottery from local materials including native clay, beach sand, wood ashes, seaweed, clam, and mussel shells. Then they fire it in their own kiln. Their glazes are lead-free and all of their works are oven proof and dishwasher safe.

Midcoast

Andersen Studio (207-633-4397 or 800-640-4397; Rte. 96 and Andersen Rd., East Boothbay). Clay rendered and glazed to resemble seals, gulls, and ducks. Also stone-ware vases and bowls.

Edgecomb Potters (207-882-6802; Rte. 27, Edgecomb). Chris and Richard Hilton founded their potter's studio in 1976. Today their staff produce striking and functional pottery for the home, and the Hiltons manage three stores, including one on School St. in Freeport and another on Exchange St. in Portland's Old Port.

Down East/Acadia

Gull Rock Pottery (207-422-3990; 325 Eastside Rd., Hancock). Tori and Kurt Wray create wheel-thrown pottery decorated with birds, fish, and scenes from nature.

A Potter's Choice (Main St., just past Cottage St., Bar Harbor) A potter opened this shop more than a decade ago to show and sell work she liked by potters she knew. Over the years the collection has grown to include an impressive selection of ceramics, clothing, and jewelry by artists in Maine and throughout New England.

Rackliffe Pottery (207-374-2297 or 888-631-3321; Rte. 172, Ellsworth Road, Blue Hill). Younger than Rowantrees, but just as famous.

Rowantrees Pottery (207-374-5535; Union St., Blue Hill). They've been in business a long time — 50 years. Their glazes, made from locally found minerals, are famous.

East of Schoodic

Columbia Falls Pottery (207-483-4075; Main St., Columbia Falls). Potters April Adams and Alan Burnham have set up shop in a Victorian country store halfway between Cherryfield and Machias and next to the Ruggles House Museum. You can get a tour of their studio or just browse through their collection of majolica and terra cotta pottery. They also sell baskets, candles, and paintings by Maine artists and crafts people.

Dog Island Pottery (207-853-4775; 224 Water St., Eastport). Functional and decorative stoneware handcrafted by the shop's owner, Barbara Smith.

You can take the kayaks for a test ride at L.L. Bean.

Herb Swanson

L. L. Bean

The lore that surrounds L. L. Bean is almost as numerous as the items sold in the Maine company's mail order catalog, but here are some salient Bean facts.

- L.L. Bean was born Leon Linwood Bean in 1872, a name he changed soon after the turn of the century to Leon Leonwood.
- He was orphaned in 1884.
- He invented the Maine Hunting Shoe in 1911.
- He sent potential customers his first mailing in 1912, a small circular with an illustration and description of the Maine Hunting Shoe.
- In 1951, he threw out the keys to his famous store, making it one of the first stores in America to stay open 24 hours a day, 365 days a year.
- Since then the store has closed only four times: two Sundays in 1962 before the town fathers granted L. L. Bean dispensation from the state's new blue laws; the day in 1963 when President John F. Kennedy was assassinated; and the day L. L. Bean died in 1967.

OUTDOOR & SPORTING GOODS

South Coast

Kittery Trading Post (207-439-2700 or 888-587-6246; Rte. 1, Kittery). Just as Freeport's outlets grew up around Bean's, the shopping mecca here seemed to spring from the roots established by this rambling outdoor store full of canoes, sleeping bags, parkas, and pocketknives.

Stickman Surf & Sport (207-646-0565; 24 Shore Rd., Ogunquit). Get the latest wave report and check out this surfer's paradise on a summer's day. You'll find the local surfing crowd hanging out on the lawn behind a white picket fence and an island of cool in this busy New England summer colony.

Casco Bay

Bill's Surf & Skate (207-761-0174; 61 India St., Portland). Okay. We like the tenacity of this place. Maybe Maine doesn't have the best waves in the world, but hey, it's got the attitude.

Eastern Mountain Sports (207-772-3776; Maine Mall., So. Portland). Clothing, footwear, and gear for campers and hikers.

L. L. Bean (207-865-4761 or 800-221-4221; Main St., Freeport). The big daddy of all outdoor stores in Maine. The store stays open 24 hours every day of the year. The best time to shop — if you can stay awake — is in the wee hours. Then you have more time to chew the fat with the staff, who often have great stories to tell about fellow customers and their own outdoor exploits. (See sidebar.)

Surplus Store (207-775-0201; 28 Monument Sq. on Congress St., Portland). Before there were Marshalls, Loehman's, and shopping warehouses, surplus stores were the place to buy discounted jeans and old army fatigues. This store has all that, plus a good selection of respectably inexpensive camping and fishing gear.

Midcoast

Maine Sport (207-236-7120 or 888-236-8797; 34 High St., Rockport). They sell and rent mountain bikes, sea kayaks, canoes, camping gear, backpacks, and fishing equipment. They also serve as a true factory outlet for Moss tents.

Down East/Acadia

Cadillac Mountain Sports (207-667-7819; 34 High St., Ellsworth and 207-288-4532; 26 Cottage St., Bar Harbor). If you can do it outdoors on the island, you can find the gear and clothing to do it here. They have one of the best selections of sports footwear in the area, including more than 100 types of hiking boots. They have the stuff you need for rock and ice climbing and cross-country and telemark skiing. Open seven days a week throughout the year, and until 11 p.m. during the summer.

L. L. Bean Factory Store (207-667-7753; Rte. 1, Ellsworth). Brighter and more airy than their Freeport bargain basement, this store often has one-of-a-kind bargains on tents, bicycles, canoes, and sleeping bags, as well as outdoor clothing.

Only in Maine

During the Civil War one Maine paper manufacturer ran out of cotton rags from which to make his paper. As legend goes, he began importing the cotton wrapping from Egyptian mummies to use in his factory. Today, Maine entrepreneurs are equally as resourceful when making their livings, if not as ghoulish. Here are a few of the coast's most unusual producers of one-of-a-kind products.

Bar Harbor Weathervanes (207-667-3868 or 800-255-5025; Rte. 3, Trenton). For centuries weathervanes in the shape of boats and animals have been used by sailors and farmers to tell which way the wind blew. This store serves that tradition with hand wrought copper, brass, or cast aluminum weathervanes by Phil Alley. You can buy a whole cupola.

Joseph Gray Flagpoles (207-359-4448, Reach Rd., Sargentville). Handhewn flagpoles measuring 20' to 40'. Mr. Gray prefers to make his poles from Maine cedar because the wood is naturally water repellent. He'll deliver free of charge within 30 miles.

Product testing outside a typical Maine coast country store.

Tom Hindman

CHAPTER EIGHT
Practical Matters
INFORMATION

A traditional Lithuanian service at the Franciscan Monastery in Kennebunk.

Herb Swanson

Thy his chapter is meant to be a modest encyclopedia of useful information about the coast of Maine. Visitors can refer to it when planning trips to the coast and when on vacation here. It covers the following topics:

AMBULANCE/FIRE/POLICE

Emergency numbers differ throughout the coast. Here is an abbreviated listing for the major destinations. For other locations, check the local phone listings or dial "0" for operator.

Town	Fire	Police	Ambulance
Bar Harbor	911	911	911
Bath	911	911	911
Belfast	911	911	911
Blue Hill	207-374-2435	207-667-7575	207-374-9900
Boothbay Harbor	911	911	911
Brunswick	911 or	911 or	911 or
	207-725-5521	207-725-5521	207-725-5511
Camden	207-236-2000	911	207-236-2000
Castine	207-326-4322	207-667-7575	207-374-9900
Damariscotta	207-563-3131	207-563-3444	207-563-3200
Eastport	207-853-4221	207-853-2544	207-853-4828
			or 207-853-2771
Ellsworth	207-667-2525	207-667-2133	207-667-3200
Freeport	207-865-4211	207-865-4212	207-865-4211
Jonesport	207-483-2993	800-432-7303	207-497-2385
Kennebunkport	207-967-3323	207-967-3323	207-967-3323
Kittery	911	911	911
Lubec	207-733-4321	207-733-4321	207-733-4321
Machias	207-255-3535	207-255-4033	207-255-3535
Mt. Desert	207-276-5111	207-276-5111	207-276-5111
Ogunquit	207-646-5111	207-646-9361	207-646-5111
Old Orchard Beach	911	911	911
Portland	911	911	911
Rockland	911	911	911
Stonington	207-367-2655	207-667-7575	207-348-2300
Thomaston	911	911	911
Waldoboro	911	911	911
			or 207-832-5211
Winter Harbor	207-963-2222	207-667-7575	207-667-3200
Wiscasset	911	911	911
York	911	911	911

AREA CODE/TOWN GOVERNMENT & ZIP CODES

AREA CODE

Maine's area code is 207.

Therein Lies a Tale

[from the *Bar Harbor Times*]

CORRECTION

In a news brief in last week's edition of the *Times*, it was mistakenly reported that Janice Jones-Maxwell was fired from her position as executive director of the Mount Desert Chamber of Commerce after she was charged with embezzling chamber money. In fact, the position of executive director was eliminated due to lack of funds. The *Times* apologizes for the error.

—*The New Yorker*

TOWN GOVERNMENT

There are more than 250 cities, towns, villages and "plantations" (see definition below) along the coast of Maine from Kittery to Eastport. There are 16 counties in Maine and eight that line the coast. From west to east, they are: York, Cumberland, Sagadahoc, Lincoln, Knox, Waldo, Hancock and Washington.

Cities have their own charters and city councils. In Maine you don't have to be big to be a city; if you're big, there's nothing to prevent you from being a town. There are 2,000 city people in Eastport and 10 times that number of townspeople in Brunswick.

During the 19th century the annual town meeting was the social event of the year for most of Maine. Over the course of the day, men managed the town business; women set the noon table. Although more towns are electing officials and hiring professionals to govern and manage their communities, and women are regular fixtures in town hall, the annual town meeting still predominates. At a town meeting, usually held in March, every resident who shows up has as much pull as the person sitting or standing next to him. The government of the towns through the medium of the town meeting has been called the only existing type of "pure" democracy.

In addition to towns and cities, Maine has 33 plantations — a holdover from the time when the region was part of the Massachusetts Bay Colony. Originally intended to be temporary forms of government, many of Maine's plantations, such as Monhegan and Matinicus islands, have annual meetings, do not have home rule powers and are incorporated by county commissioners.

The state government, according to New England tradition, exercises relatively little power over the towns and cities — home rule predominates, in other words.

Don't forget that Maine had a thriving democracy long before European settlers arrived. Today, two Native American reservations, at Old Town near Bangor and Perry outside of Eastport, are self-governed nations and exist outside of U. S. federal jurisdiction.

For more information regarding the governing bodies of Maine's coastal plantations, towns and cities, contact the following town hall offices.

ZIP CODES

Town	*Telephone*	*Zip Code*
Bar Harbor	207-288-4098	04609
Bath	207-443-8330	04530
Belfast	207-338-3370	04915
Blue Hill	207-374-2281	04614
Boothbay Harbor	207-633-2144	04538
Brunswick	207-725-6659	04011
Camden	207-236-3353	04843
Castine	207-326-4502	04421
Damariscotta	207-563-5168	04543
Eastport	207-853-2300	04631
Ellsworth	207-667-2563	04605
Freeport	207-865-4743	04032
Jonesport	207-497-5926	04649
Kennebunkport	207-967-4243	04046
Kittery	207-439-0452	03904
Lubec	207-733-2341	04652
Machias	207-255-6621	04654
Newcastle	207-563-3441	04553
Ogunquit	207-646-5139	03907
Old Orchard Beach	207-934-5714	04064
Portland	207-874-8300	04101, 04102, 04103, 04104
Rockland	207-594-8431	04841
Stonington	207-367-2351	04681
Thomaston	207-354-6107	04861
Waldoboro	207-832-5369	04572
Winter Harbor	207-963-2235	04693
Wiscasset	207-882-8205	04578

BANKS

The major banks in Maine and several of the smaller local banks are linked to national and international instant teller machine networks. Following is a list of many of the banks with offices along the coast.

Bank	Phone	Cash Machine Networks
Atlantic Bank	800-745-8338	NYCE, Cirrus
Bangor Savings Bank	800-432-1591	NYCE, Plus, Cirrus, MasterCard/Visa, American Express, Novus Discover
Bar Harbor Banking & Trust	800-924-7787	Cirrus, Plus, Yankee24 NYCE, Visa
Camden National Bank	800-860-8821	Plus, Honor, NYCE, Cirrus,
First National Bank of Damariscotta	800-564-3195	Plus, Scott 24-Hour, Yankee24, NYCE, MasterCard/Visa
Fleet Bank	800-922-2882	Cirrus, NYCE, Yankee24, MasterCard/Visa
Key Bank	800-635-2265	NYCE, Cirrus, MAC, Maestro
Peoples Heritage Bank	800-295-7400	NYCE, Plus, Yankee24, The Exchange, TX

BIBLIOGRAPHY

BOOKS YOU CAN BUY

AUTOBIOGRAPHY, BIOGRAPHY & REMINISCENCE

Ames, Polly Scribner. *Marsden Hartley in Maine.* Orono, ME: University of Maine Press, 1972. 36 pp., illust., $8.95. Polly Scribner Ames writes about fellow painter Marsden Hartley's final three years living with lobsterman Forrest Young and his wife Katie in Corea, Maine (near Winter Harbor).

Coomer, Joe. *Sailing in a Spoonful of Water.* New York: Picador USA. 256 pp., $22. Coomer, a resident of Eliot, Maine, writes of the revival of his vintage craft *Yonder,* while reflecting on how his life journeys have drawn him again and again to the water.

Small, Constance. *The Lighthouse Keeper's Wife.* Orono, ME: University of Maine Press, 1986. 226 pp., photos, $13.95. Constance Small and her husband Elson tended a Maine island lighthouse for 28 years. This is her wry and moving account of that life.

Tatelbaum, Linda. *Carrying Water as a Way of Life.* Appleton, ME: About Time Press. 117 pp., $9.95. Series of feisty essays chronicling the author and her husband's quest to head back-to-the-land.

FICTION

Landesman, Peter. *The Raven.* New York: Penguin Books. 356 pp., $11.95. Based on the true story of a mysterious disappearance of a pleasure boat, *The Raven,* and its 36 passengers off the coast of Maine.

Maine Speaks. Maine: Maine Writers and Publishers Alliance. 464 pp., $19.95. An anthology of works by writers whose lives have been touched by Maine. E.B. White, Tim Sample, Ruth Moore, Steven King, and more.

McCloskey, Robert. *Blueberries for Sal.* New York: The Viking Press, 1948. 55 pp., illust. $4.99.

McCloskey, Robert. *One Morning in Maine.* New York: The Viking Press, 1952. 64 pp., illust. $4.99. Two of the best books about Maine to read, for adults as well as children.

Monroe, Judith W.. *Widdershins.* Durham, NC: Crone's Own Press, 1989. 240 pp., $9.95. Quirky, comic feminist novel about a group of women on a Maine island who discover their own power and independence.

Phippen, Sanford, Charles G. Waugh and Martin Greenberg, eds. *The Best Maine Stories.* Camden, ME: Yankee Books, 1994. 320 pp., $12.95. Short stories set in Maine written by some of America's most famous authors from Henry James to Caroline Chute.

HISTORY

Judd, Richard W. *Common Lands, Common People.* Cambridge: Harvard University Press. 335 pp., $35. The history of conservation ethics in northern New England.

Kurlandsky, Mark. *Cod.* New York: Walker and Company. 276 pp., $21. Spanning thousands of years and four continents, this book is a biography of the fish that changed the world and was a staple of the Maine fishery for centuries.

Rich, Louise Dickinson. *The Coast of Maine.* Camden, Maine: Down East Books, 1993. 400 pp., index, illust., photos. $14.95. A wonderfully rambling history of the coast from the Ice Age to the mid-1970s that is punctuated with the author's idiosyncratic interpretations of historical facts.

PHOTOGRAPHIC AND PAINTING STUDIES

Joseph, Stanley and Lynn Karlin. *Maine Farm: A Year of Country Life.* New York: Random House, 1991. Photos, $32.50. Beautifully photographed, warmly told account of life on a saltwater farm.

Skolnick, Arnold ed. *Paintings of Maine*. New York: Clarkson/Potter Publishers, 1991. 123 pp., illust., $27.50. Luscious reproductions of paintings of Maine by artists including Georgia O'Keeffe, Winslow Homer, Andrew Wyeth and Edward Hopper.

Tragard, Louise, Patricia E. Hart and W.L. Copithorne. *A Century of Color*: Ogunquit, Maine's Art Colony 1886-1986. Ogunquit, ME: Barn Gallery Associates, 1988. $24.95 Interviews and commentary from 100 years in the southern Maine art community.

RECREATION

Getchell, Dave and Kate Cronin. *The Maine Island Trail Book*. Rockland, ME: Maine Island Trail Association, 1991. The Maine Island Trail Association publishes this guidebook packed with charts and information for its members. It's worth joining just to get tips about touring the coast from the water. For information, or a copy of this great book, write to: Maine Island Trail Association, 60 Ocean St., Rockland, ME 04841.

Gibbs, David and Sarah Hale. *Mountain Bike! Maine*. Birmingham, AL: Menasaha Ridge Press, 1998. $12.95. This book is the only comprehensive reference for mountain bikers looking to get off the beaten trail in Maine. Hale and Gibbs detail 78 great rides, many of them within 10 miles of the coast.

Isaac, Jeff and Peter Goth. *The Outward Bound Wilderness First-Aid Handbook*. Lyons & Burford, 1991. 252 pp., index, illust., $14.95. A must-have for anyone discovering the coast by kayak, canoe, sailboat, foot or bike.

Taft, Hank. *A Cruising Guide to the Maine Coast*. New York: McGraw-Hill Publishing, 1994. 400 pp, illust., $39.95. The definitive guide for ocean-going travelers.

Venn, Tamsin. *Sea Kayaking Along The New England Coast*. Boston: Appalachian Mountain Club, 1990. 240 pp., maps, photos, $14.95.

BOOKS YOU CAN BORROW

Brault, Gerard. *The French-Canadian Heritage in New England*. Hanover and London: University Press of New England, and Kingston and Montreal: McGill-Queen's University Press, 1986. 264 pp., index, illust.

Caldwell, Bill. *Maine Coast*. Portland: Guy Gannet Publishing Co., 1988. 398 pp. Two collections of a journalist's rambling monologues about the people he has met and places he has visited.

Caldwell, Erskine. *Midsummer Passion and Other Tales of Maine Cussedness*. Camden, ME: Yankee Books. 192 pp. Fifteen short stories Erskine Caldwell wrote while living in Maine.

Carson, Rachel. *The Edge of the Sea*. New York: Houghton Mifflin Company, 1955. The famous naturalist and ecologist's essays on the coast. If you like this, you'll enjoy her other books, *The Sea Around Us* and *Silent Spring*.

Coffin, Robert Tristam. *Saltwater Farm.* New York: Macmillan, 1939. 114 pp., illust. Poetry by the premier poet and prose writer of Maine's middle coast.

Conkling, Philip. *Islands in Time.* Camden, ME: Down East Books, 1981. 222 pp., illust. Former Outward Bound naturalist, now head of the Island Institute, provides a lyrical history of Maine's coastal islands from an ecologist's point of view.

Doty, C. Stewart, ed. *The First Franco-Americans. New England Life Histories from the Federal Writers Project,* 1938–1939. Orono, ME: University of Maine Press, 1985. 163 pp., photos. Collected interviews of first-generation immigrants from Acadia and Quebec.

Eckstorm, Fannie Hardy. *Indian Place Names of the Penobscot Valley and the Maine Coast.* Orono, ME: University of Maine Press, 1978. An interesting journey through Maine by way of Penobscot Indian language and legend.

Federal Writers' Project of the Works Progress Administration, State of Maine. *Maine: A Guide 'Downeast.'* Boston: Houghton Mifflin Co., 1937. 458 pp., index, illust, photos. Try to get hold of this thick volume or the revised version, which was published in 1970 by Dorris Isaacson and the Maine Historical Society. It is a thorough account of all Maine: its history, natural wonders, and recreation.

Jewett, Sarah Orne. *The Country of the Pointed Firs.* Boston and New York: Houghton Mifflin Company, 1929. 306 pp.

Leeker, Robert and Kathleen R. Brown, eds. *An Anthology of Maine Literature.* Orono, Me: University of Maine Press, 1982. 260 pp. A collection of works by native and out-of-state writers, including Nathaniel Hawthorne, Henry David Thoreau, Harriet Beecher Stowe, Sarah Orne Jewett, and Kenneth Roberts.

Monegain, Bernie. *Natural Sites: A Guide to Maine's Natural Phenomena.* Freeport, ME: Delorme Mapping Company, 1988. 48 pp., index, maps, photos.

Monegain, Bernie. *Coastal Islands: A Guide to Exploring Main's Offshore Isles.* Freeport, ME: DeLorme Mapping Company, 1988. 48 pp., index, maps, photos, $4.95.

Pierson, Elizabeth Cary and Jan Erik Pierson. *The Birders Guide to the Coast of Maine.* Camden, ME: Down East Books. Birds that nest and visit, summer and winter, on the coast and its islands.

Shain, Charles and Samuella Shain. *The Maine Reader.* New York: Houghton Mifflin Company, 1991. Illus. Four hundred years of Maine through the eyes of explorers, writers, painters, and photographers.

Williamson, William D. *History of the State of Maine* (2 vols.) 1602-1820, 1832. An overview of Maine's history and geography before it became a state.

Willis, William, ed. *Journals of Rev. Thomas Smith and Rev. Samuel Deane, 1849.* The author of this book was a Portland minister whose record of daily life during the Revolutionary War is interesting in its thoroughness.

CLIMATE, WEATHER, AND WHAT TO WEAR

Digging out after a snowstorm in Cape Porpoise.

Herb Swanson

Whoever once said "character takes four seasons to make" must have been familiar with the seasons of coastal Maine. The seasons only serve to add drama to the already variable landscape from Kittery to Eastport.

Maine seasons go by their own timetable. Spring bulbs will often bloom as late as mid-June. Summer generally remains temperate throughout July and August. The cool days of autumn frequently extend well past the foliage's fall, and although it has been known to snow up to 70 inches in one winter (it snowed that much in Portland during the winter of 1970-71), harsh northern winter winds are usually softened by warmer ocean temperatures.

The state's climate is governed by the "prevailing westerlies," the belt of eastward-moving air that encircles the globe at the middle latitudes. The westerlies and warm currents of the Atlantic ensure that prolonged hot and cold spells are rare, although coastal weather — with the added moisture from the ocean — can be extremely changeable. Fogs frequently descend upon the coast, and are a reason why Maine mariners are famed the world over for their navigation skills. There are an average of 59 foggy days every year at Quoddy Head Light near Lubec.

Summer temperatures on Maine's coast range from 60 to 90 degrees, with the steadily warmest temperatures around 80, in mid- to late July. Even when the temperature climbs during the day, coastal nights are almost always cool and comfortable. Autumn generally brings sunny days, cool nights and a brilliant display of fall foliage colors ranging from vivid golds (birches, poplars, and ginkgos) and oranges (mountain maples, hickories, and ashes) to dazzling scarlets (red maple, red oak, and sassafras).

Frosts and freezing temperatures can occur from October to May, although Portland experiences only 132 freezing days every year and is usually only 4

What to Wear in Maine

Rainy days are tough on pedestrians, but I grew up in Maine, so I have no qualms about wearing really dorky clothes when it rains.

— Al Daimon, Maine's "walking" newsman,
quoted in *Casco Bay Weekly*

As I write this, I am wearing heavy long underwear, wind pants, three layers of insulation under a water-resistant jacket, wool socks, a wool hat and fingerless gloves. I look ridiculous, especially since it is now early June. But I'm on a small boat, and it is wicked cold out here .

— Jeff Isaac, Maine sailor

One could say fashion is a stranger to Maine. Dressing for a visit to the coast of Maine has everything to do with form and function. Versatility and comfort are respected. Strict formality is highly unusual, and probably transplanted from somewhere else. Any color is okay as long as it is brown, green or gray.

Knowing how to dress for coastal weather requires understanding the relationship between wind, water, and land. The overall climate of Maine is Northern Temperate with cold winters and warm summers. The effects of the ocean can significantly moderate the weather on the islands and for a few miles inland, depending on the direction of the wind. The water off the coast is part of an upwelling of the Labrador Current that has its origin under the polar ice cap. Although the water has traveled hundreds of miles to get here, it still feels like icebergs. The air — or wind — passing over coastal waters is cooled and humidified before it arrives ashore.

On a typical sunny summer day, warm air rises over the mainland and the cool and dense air over the ocean is drawn in to replace it. This produces the summer southwesterly sea breeze. Temperatures along the immediate coast and islands will reflect that of the ocean, which only reaches 60 degrees by late summer. Approaching the coast on a hot day you can feel the air temperature drop 10 or 15 degrees, and often a thick fog will roll in.

If you're headed for the shore, carry a jacket and a pair of long pants, no matter what the TV weather personality says. This is especially true if you're boarding a boat. Rain is almost always associated with larger and more predictable weather systems. Unless a frontal passage or storm system is expected, you can leave your foul-weather gear in the trunk.

Clothes should be loose and comfortable for scrambling over rocks and through spruce and raspberry bushes. Garments should be versatile enough to handle rapid changes in temperature. Shorts are fine for strolling or trail hiking during the day when it's warm. If you're going any distance, bring wind pants for protection against the sea breeze and bugs. Summer nights are almost always cool. A medium-weight sweater will get plenty of use. If you cannot bring all of them, choose wool or bunting over cotton. Those fabrics will keep moisture away from your skin, and therefore keep you warmer.

Hiking shoes are also a good idea. Maine is really just a very thin layer of topsoil over a very thick layer of coarse-grained granite. Since you don't want to damage the soil layer, most of your walking will be on the rocks. The soft soles of sandals

(continued)

and sneakers are quickly worn smooth by avid hikers. One of the most useful items is a pair of knee-high rubber boots. The tide range in Maine runs from eight to 20 feet, exposing thousands of tide pools and clam flats for exploring. Bare feet would be shredded by shells and barnacles, and sneakers can get lost in the mud. A good pair of "worm boots" can make your whole trip.

Never mind what the calendar says, fall can begin on the coast during the third week of August. By this time, summer has lost its grip. Increasingly frequent cold fronts bring the prevailing winds to the west and northwest. With the wind off the land, temperatures reflect the cooling mass of the North American continent.

This is a great time to visit Monhegan or Vinalhaven, because summer-like conditions often extend well into the fall on the islands. While the mainland cools, the islands' temperature is moderated by the still-warm ocean water.

For fall and winter travel in coastal Maine, bring everything from shorts to winter gear, and expect to change often. Good foul-weather gear is essential unless you plan to spend a lot of time indoors. When an approaching winter storm swings the wind to the south or east, the breeze brings relative warmth. Wind off the water can melt the snow out from under your skis as fast as it fell. The day can seem downright balmy, until the next front sends the temperature plummeting. Precipitation can alternate quickly between rain and snow as the conflicting land and ocean air masses meet.

Spring on the coast can be a real tease. The ocean is very reluctant to warm up. This creates a drastic difference between inland and coastal temperatures and an even more drastic difference between your expectations and reality. You pull out your bathing suit, head for the beach and find that the water is still 43 degrees. The key is to expect it. Remember your fall and winter wardrobe? Bring it. If the wind is off the water, you'll need it. Away from the shore, or with a shore breeze, you can lie around with as little on as at a summer picnic. It all depends on the wind.

Fogs in Maine

E. B. White gave us one of the best descriptions of a Maine fog in his 1948 *Atlantic Monthly* essay titled "Death of Pig."

We had been having an unseasonable spell of weather — hot, close days, with the fog shutting in every night, scaling for a few hours in midday, then creeping back again at dark, drifting in first over the trees on the point, then suddenly blowing across the fields, blotting out the world and taking possession of houses, men, and animals.

degrees cooler than Boston. The coast receives about 46 inches of precipitation annually. Of that precipitation, it snows only 15 or 20 days, and there are only 10 to 20 thunderstorms every year.

Meteorological extremes do occur. There was "the year without summer" in 1816 when it snowed in July. Hurricanes strike the coast about once every decade. The coast also experiences what have become known as "100-Year Storms," when severe wind and weather peak with high tide, creating tides 10 to 20 feet higher than normal. The most recent 100-year storm was on January 12, 1978. More common are "Nor'easters," coastal storms that come up the coast and pummel it with high tides, heavy rain — or snow — and gale force winds.

People who enjoy reading about the weather will want to look for The Weather Report column in the weekly newspaper *Maine Times*. The rambling weather-and-natural life accounts are gathered from residents who regularly observe the great outdoors from their windows onto the harbor or field. People from all places along the coast and inland give colorful reports of "flaming swamp maples" or a jack-in-the-pulpit discovered while out looking for mushrooms or pulling up the boat.

For frequently updated coastal and marine weather information, call the *National Weather Service*, 207-688-3210.

GUIDED TOURS

G uided and sightseeing tours on the coast of Maine can be divided into three categories. You can travel by bus or trolley in many of the more popular destinations such as Ogunquit, Kennebunkport, Portland and Bar Harbor. You can travel by water on regular guided boat cruises, including whale, seal, and puffin tours. You can also travel by air in a small plane because there are many small private airstrips and flying services along the coast. In this section we will discuss guided land and air tours. For lists of ocean-going guided tours, including windjammer cruises, whale, puffin watch tours, and harbor tours, see *Recreation*, Chapter Six.

South Coast

During the summer months, the *Ogunquit Chamber of Commerce* operates a free, unnarrated trolley that covers the town's high spots from Perkins Cove to the west and Footbridge Beach to the east. The four trolleys — all named after garden flowers — operate daily from Memorial Day weekend through Columbus Day.

The *Intown Trolley Company* in Kennebunkport (207-967-3686) has provided old-fashioned narrated tours of the seaport for more than 10 years, including historical notes, a drive-by of the Bush family summer home at Walker Point and stops at the Franciscan monastery, major inns, hotels, and shopping. There is a nominal fee for the service, and the fare is good for the entire day. The Intown Trolley leaves from the bottom of Ocean Ave. near Dock Sq. During July and August, and it is good to line up 15 minutes before scheduled departure.

Casco Bay

On-land tours are harder to come by in the Casco Bay region. The best opportunities are for chartered bus, taxi, and van tours operated by various companies. One of those is **Custom Coach of Portland** (800-585-3589) which provides personalized tours for groups ranging from one to fifty people. They are based in Portland, but will go anywhere in the state of Maine, 24 hours a day. Custom Coach also will lease a van, limousine, or bus to larger groups. **Mainely Tours** offers 90 minute guided tours of downtown Portland. Guides will point out historical sites while traveling from the city streets to the rocky coast at Portland Head Light. $11 adults, $10 seniors, $6 kids. Also call Mainely Tours for more information on their land & sea and Kennebunkport tours.

Town Taxi (207-772-0111) and **ABC Taxi** (207-772-8685) in Portland offer similar, custom tour service. You can book one of their Chrysler taxis for $20 an hour.

Greater Portland Landmarks (207-774-5561) provides downtown walking tours every Fri. and Sat. at 10 a.m. from July–late Sept. Tours meet at the Victory Monument in Monument Square, Portland and highlight the city's architectural history. $7 (includes $1.50 donation to Save The Monument).

Midcoast

Guided tours in the Midcoast are just as difficult to come by. Bill Sweet, a retired schoolteacher and history buff, was born and raised on Mount Desert Island. He operates the **Sweet William Tour Guide Service** (207-288-5443) in Bar Harbor. Cost for each two-and-one-half hour step-on guide service is $75 per coach. Bill will take you through Bar Harbor and Acadia. Park admission is not included with the fee. It's important to book at least 24 hours in advance during July and August.

If you want to view the region by air, **Downeast Charter Flights** (800-752-6378 out-of-state; 207-882-9401 in state) offers regular half-hour scenic flights over the coast near Wiscasset for $50. Their Cessna 172 seats three passengers. Regular routes include Boothbay, Pemaquid Point, and the small fishing villages nearby including Damariscove, one of the first fishing villages established in the New World; they also regularly offer an aerial view of Popham and Reid state parks on the Kennebec River where it empties into Sheepscot Bay. The flying service is open year round, although it's important to book at least a day in advance for summer weekend flights. For $50 they also offer seats aboard their 1-1/2 to 2 hour fire patrol flights conducted for the state of Maine. These two daily flights promise a good chance to actually see a fire as well as up to a third of the state.

Down East/Acadia

One of the best ways to see Bar Harbor and Acadia without having to deal with the summer traffic is on **Oli's Trolley** (207-288-9899), a one-hour or two-and-one-half hour ride. The old-fashioned brown bus seats 40 and travels the park loop with stops at Cadillac Mountain and Thunder Hole. The guided tour also includes Sieur de Mont Spring, Otter Cliffs and a running historical narrative of Mount Desert Island from prehistoric times through present day. Six daily tours run from May through mid-October. The summer months are busy, and reservations are encouraged. The bus leaves from downtown Bar Harbor in front of the Italian Fisherman restaurant.

To view Acadia by air, ***Acadia Air*** (207-667-5534), which operates out of Bar Harbor Airport in Trenton, offers several scenic flight tours for under $50 per person with two person minimum. The shorter, less-expensive flights fly over Acadia, Deer Isle, and Stonington in a Cessna 172. Longer flights go down the coast for views of Castine and Camden harbors. Acadia Air operates scenic flights on demand from June 1 through mid-October. The rest of the year tours can be arranged by appointment.

Jeff Miller and his drivers will take you on a tour of Bar Harbor in his ***Lobster Bike*** (207-288-3028), a pedicab disguised as a seven-foot-long Maine lobster. The comfortable cushioned seat sits at the front of this oversized tricycle and holds two adults or four kids. Go ahead, its fun. $5 for 10 minutes. Evenings. Reservations taken but not required.

HANDICAPPED SERVICES

A lmost all state and national parks in Maine provide access and facilities for the physically impaired. Most motels and hotels also have rooms easily accessible to the handicapped, although many historic buildings and inns have either not yet complied with or are exempt from the Americans with Disabilities Act. We have tried to provide information on individual restaurants in Chapter Five, and on inns and bed-and-breakfast establishments in Chapter Three that are accessible. To confirm, please call ahead.

To find out more about tourist facilities for the handicapped, contact the ***Maine Publicity Bureau***, P.O. Box 2300, Hallowell, ME 04347; 207-623-0363 in state and 800-533-9595 out-of-state.

HOSPITALS

South Coast
BIDDEFORD

Southern Maine Medical Center 1 Medical Center Dr., Biddeford 04005; 207-283-7000; Emergency Room open 24 hours.

YORK

York Hospital 15 Hospital Dr., York 03909; 207-363-4321; Emergency Room open 24 hours.

Casco Bay
BATH

Midcoast Hospital 1356 Washington St., Bath 04530; 207-443-5524; Non-life-threatening care. 7 a.m.–10 p.m.

BRUNSWICK

Parkview Memorial Hospital 329 Maine St., Brunswick 04011; 207-729-1641; Emergency Room open 24 hours.

PORTLAND

Brighton Medical Center Brighton Ave., Portland 04102; 207-879-8000; Emergency Room open 24 hours.

Maine Medical Center 22 Bramhall St., Portland 04102; 207-871-0111; Emergency Room open 24 hours.

Mercy Hospital 144 State St., Portland 04101; 207-879-3000; Emergency Room open 24 hours.

Jackson Brook Institute 175 Running Hill Rd., South Portland 04106; 207-761-2200.

Midcoast
BOOTHBAY HARBOR

St. Andrews Hospital 3 St. Andrews Ln., Boothbay Harbor 04538; 207-633-2121; Emergency Room open 24 hours.

BELFAST

Waldo County General Hospital 118 Northport Ave., Belfast 04915; 207-338-2500.

DAMARISCOTTA

Miles Memorial Hospital Bristol Rd., Damariscotta 04543; 207-563-1234; Emergency Room open 24 hours.

ROCKPORT

Penobscot Bay Medical Center 6 Glen Cove, Rockport 04856 ; 207-596-8000; Emergency Room open 24 hours.

Down East/Acadia

BAR HARBOR

Mount Desert Island Hospital 10 Wayman Ln., Bar Harbor 04609; 207-288-5081

BLUE HILL

Blue Hill Memorial Hospital Water St., Blue Hill 04614; 207-374-2836.

ELLSWORTH

Maine Coast Memorial Hospital 50 Union St., Ellsworth 04605; 207-667-5311.

East of Schoodic

MACHIAS

Down East Community Hospital Upper Court St., Machias 04654; 207-255-3356; Emergency Room open 24 hours.

LATE NIGHT FOOD AND FUEL

The coffee pot is always on all night at the service desk at L. L. Bean, the famous store that remains open 24 hours every day, including Christmas and Thanksgiving. If you need more than coffee — say fuel for your car or your body — here is a short list of notable late-night or all-night stores, restaurants, and gas stations.

South Coast

Howell's Auto Truck Stop (food and fuel), 207-439-2466, Rte. 1 bypass, Kittery. Open 24 hours.

Fishermen's floats and lines. The fishing village of Jonesport is in the background.

Herb Swanson

Rapid Ray's (food), 207-282-1847, Main St., Saco. Weekdays, 11 a.m.–1:30 a.m.; Fri. and Sat., 11 a.m.–3:00 a.m. High quality burgers.

Casco Bay

Cumberland Farms (food market and fuel), 207-772-9165, 801 Washington Ave., Portland. Open 24 hours.

Denny's Restaurants (food), 207-774-1886, 1101 Congress Ave., Portland (Congress St. exit off Rte. 295). Open 24 hours.

Midcoast

Christys Market, 207-338-3779, Rte. 1, Belfast. Open 24 hours.

Red's Eats (food), 207-882-6128, Rte. 1, Wiscasset. Open Mon.–Thur., 11 a.m.–11 p.m.; Fri.–Sat., 11a.m.–2 a.m.; Sun., noon–6 p.m.

Cappy's Chowder House (food), 207-236-2254, 1 Main St., Camden. Daily 8 a.m.–1 a.m.

MEDIA

Tr. [Trooper] Joseph Tibbets investigated a burglary at a private camp in Twp. 24. The only item stolen was a hand-operated well pump, however, a chain saw was used to gain entrance through the door.
— *The Downeast Coastal Press*, Sept. 16, 1991

The news business on the coast of Maine is dominated by two major newspaper companies, which publish the *Bangor Daily News* to the north and the *Portland Press Herald* and *Maine Sunday Telegram* to the south. To really learn about the area is to read about it through the eyes of the people who live and work here. For that reason, we recommend reading one of the several flourishing weeklies published on the coast.

Down East, based in Camden, is the granddaddy of Maine magazines, but during the past decade dozens of younger magazines have sprung up, from *Ocean Navigator*, rumored to have been Walter Cronkite's favorite magazine, to *WoodenBoat*, *National Fisherman* and *Coastal Fisheries News*. Many of these reflect the mariners' lifestyle. Then there are specialty magazines and newspapers like *Maine Antique Digest*, a thick tabloid packed with articles on art, antiques, and Americana, where to get it, and if you missed it, what it went for. The *Maine Times* (800-439-8866, 9 Union St., Hallowell 04347) is a great place to look for coastal summer rentals despite moving inland from its prior location in Portland. It's also a good source for those interested in Maine's liberal agenda. Following is a roundup of the media you will find on the coast.

South Coast

NEWSPAPERS

Journal Tribune, 800-244-7601, P.O. Box 627, Biddeford 04005; daily. Known as a photographer's paper, and a pleasant place to do serious journalism.

York County Coast Star, 207-485-2961, P.O. Box 979, Kennebunk 04043; weekly. Founded in 1877; several reporters for this aggressive tabloid have gone on to work for the *Boston Globe* and other big papers.

The York Weekly, 207-363-4343, 17 Woodbridge Rd., P.O. Box 7, York 03909.

RADIO

WPKM-FM, 207-883-9596, 106.3; Scarborough; Classical.

Casco Bay

NEWSPAPERS

Brunswick Times Record, 800-734-6397, Industry Rd., Brunswick 04011.

Coastal Journal, 800-649-6241, 361 High St., P.O. Box 575, Bath 04530.

Portland Press Herald/Maine Sunday Telegram, 800-894-0031, 390 Congress St., Portland 04101. The state's biggest daily.

Casco Bay Weekly, 800-286-6601, 561A Congress St., Portland 04102; free weekly. Great for entertainment news and the skinny on the state's largest city. A worthy alternative to the big daily.

MAGAZINES

Golf Course News, 207-846-0600, 106 Lafayette St., Yarmouth 04096. Trade tabloid for the greens crowd.

Gourmet News, 207-846-0600, 106 Lafayette St., Yarmouth 04096. Trade magazine for the fancy food industry.

National Fisherman, 207-842-5608, 121 Free St., Portland 04101. A color glossy founded in 1903, they cover commercial fishing and boat building, as well as other marine-related stories.

Ocean Navigator, 207-772-2466, 18 Danforth St., Portland 04101.

Salt Magazine, 207-761-0660, 19 Pine St., P.O. Box 4077, Portland 04102. Journalistic interviews and studies of the "real people of Maine"; great photos.

RADIO

WBLM-FM 102.9; 207-774-6364; Portland; Album-oriented rock, classic rock.
WCYY-FM 92.9; 207-774-6364; Portland; New rock.

WGAN-AM 560; 207-774-4561; Portland; Talk, Imus, news, sports.

WHOM-FM 94.9; 207-773-0200; Portland; Easy listening.

WJBQ-FM 97.9; 207-775-6321; Portland.

WJTO-AM 730; 207-443-6671; Bath, ABC; Oldies.

WMEA-FM 90.1; 800-884-1717; Portland; Public radio.

WMGX-FM 93.1, 207-774-4561; Contemporary and classic hits.

WMPG-FM 90.9; 207-780-4424; Portland; Full service, eclectic.

WPOR-AM 1490; 207-773-8111; Portland; Country.

WPOR-FM 101.9; 207-773-8111; Portland; Country.

WYNZ-FM 100.9; 207-774-4561; South Portland; Oldies.

WZAN-AM 970; 207-774-4561; Portland; News and talk.

TELEVISION

Maine Public Television Channel 10; 207-783-9101, Lewiston, PBS.

WCSH-TV Channel 6; 207-828-6666, Portland, NBC.

WGME-TV Channel 13; 207-797-9330, Portland, CBS.

WMTW-TV Channel 8; 207-775-1800, Portland and Auburn, ABC.

WPXT-TV Channel 51; 207-774-0051, Portland, Fox.

Midcoast

NEWSPAPERS

The Boothbay Register, 207-633-4620, 95 Townsend Ave., P.O. Box 357, Boothbay Harbor 04538; weekly.

The Camden Herald, 207-236-8511, Box 248, Camden 04843; weekly.

The Courier-Gazette, 207-338-5411, 1 Park Dr., P.O. Box 249, Rockland 04841; published Tuesday, Thursday and Saturday.

Lincoln County News, 207-563-3171, Box 36, Damariscotta 04543; weekly.

The Lincoln County Weekly, 207-563-5006, P.O. Box 1287, Damariscotta 04543.

The Republican Journal, 207-338-3333, Box 327, High St., Belfast 04915; weekly.

Waldo Independent, 207-338-5100, 107 Church St., Belfast 04915; weekly.

MAGAZINES

Down East Magazine, 800-766-1670, Box 679, Camden 04843. Bills itself as the magazine of Maine; two-thirds of their 85,000 readership live out of state.

Maine Antique Digest, 207-832-4888, 71 Main St., P.O. Box 645, Waldoboro 04752.

Rod & Reel, 800-766-1670, P.O. Box 370, Camden 04843.

WoodenBoat, 207-359-4651, P.O. Box 78, Brooklin 04616. Beautiful to look at. Covers the design, building, care, preservation and use of wooden boats, whether commercial or pleasure, old or new, sail or power.

RADIO

WMEH FM 90.9; 207-941-1010; Bangor; Classical.

WRKD-AM 1450; 207-594-1450; Rockland; Talk, news, sports, big band/nostalgia.

Down East/Acadia
NEWSPAPERS

The Bar Harbor Times, 800-479-3312, P.O. Box 68, 76 Cottage St., Bar Harbor 04609; weekly.

Castine Patriot, 207-326-9300, P.O. Box 205, Castine 04736; weekly.

The Ellsworth American, 800-499-2576, 63 Main St., P.O. Box 509, Ellsworth 04605; weekly. One of America's truly great small-town papers.

The Ellsworth Weekly, 207-667-5514, P.O. Box 1122, Ellsworth 04605.

Island Ad-Vantages, 207-367-2200, P.O. Box 36, Stonington 04681; weekly.

The Weekly Packet, 207-374-2341, Main St., Blue Hill 04614; weekly.

RADIO

WDEA-AM 1370; 800-640-4941; Ellsworth; Big band.

WERU-FM 89.9; 207-469-6600; East Orland; From cool to kewl, good stuff.

WEZQ-FM 92.9; 800-640-4941; Ellsworth; Adult soft and easy hits.

WKSQ-FM 94.5; 207-667-7573; Ellsworth; Adult contemporary, light/soft rock.

WWMJ-FM 95.7; 800-640-4941; Ellsworth; Oldies.

East of Schoodic
NEWSPAPERS

Machias Valley News Observer, 207-255-6561, P.O. Box 357, Machias 04654; weekly.

The Quoddy Tides, 207-853-4806, 123 Water St., Eastport 04631; weekly.

RADIO

WALZ-FM 95.3; 207-454-7545; Machias; Adult contemporary.

WQDY-FM 92.7; 207-454-7545; Calais.

Looking out onto Jordan Pond in Acadia National Park.

Herb Swanson

REAL ESTATE

If, after visiting the coast, you decide you want to own a piece of it, you can write to the *Maine Board of Realtors*, 35 State House Station, Augusta 04333 (207-625-8603) for a list of real estate agents in the areas you like. That office also can provide names of agents who handle seasonal rentals in coastal areas.

Also, good references for those looking to rent or own along the coast are the *Maine Times* and *Down East* magazine. During late spring, the *Maine Times* publishes a special summer vacation guide with classifieds for rental properties. The supplement is usually available all summer at newsstands throughout the state. *Down East* runs a monthly real estate classified section as well. See "Media," above, for further information about these publications.

ROAD SERVICE

Portland
AAA Maine 425 Marginal Way, 04104; Mon.–Fri. 8:30–6, Sat. 9–1. 207-780-6800 or 800-482-7497.

South Portland
AAA Maine 443 Western Ave., 04106; Mon.–Fri. 9–6, Sat. 9–1. 207-775-6211 or 800-336-6211.

TOURIST INFORMATION

Which way to Acadia?

There are several publicly funded information centers and state agencies that provide visitor information. In addition, most chambers of commerce will gladly send packets of information to people planning a stay in their area. Here is an abbreviated list of agencies and chambers for coastal Maine.

FISHING AND HUNTING REGULATIONS

Dept. of Inland Fisheries and Wildlife 284 State St., Augusta 04333; 207-287-8000.

VISITOR INFORMATION

Maine Publicity Bureau P.O. Box 2300 Hallowell 04347; 207-623-0363 in state, 800-533-9595 out-of-state.

South Coast

Kennebunk–Kennebunkport Chamber of Commerce P.O. Box 740, Kennebunk 04043; 207-967-0857.

Kittery Information Center I-95 and Rte. 1, P.O. Box 396, Kittery 03904; 207-439-1319.

Kittery Outlet Association 888-KITTERY.

Ogunquit Chamber of Commerce P.O. Box 2289, Ogunquit 03907; 207-646-2939.

Old Orchard Beach Chamber of Commerce, P.O. Box 600, Old Orchard Beach 04064; 207-934-2500.

Wells P.O. Box 356, Route 1, Wells, ME 04090; 207-646-2451.

Yorks P.O. Box 417, York, ME 03909; 207-363-4422.

Casco Bay

Bath-Brunswick Area Chamber of Commerce 59 Pleasant St., Brunswick 04011; 207-725-8797.

Chamber of Commerce of the Greater Portland Visitor Information Center 305 Commercial St., Portland 04101; 207-772-5800.

Freeport Merchants Association P.O. Box 452, Freeport 04032; 207-865-1212.

Portland's Downtown District 400 Congress St. Portland 04101; 207-772-6828.

Yarmouth Information Center U.S. Rte. 1/Exit 17, I-95, P.O. Box 1057, Yarmouth 04096; 207-846-0833.

Midcoast

Belfast Area Chamber of Commerce P.O. Box 58, Belfast 04915; 207-338-5900.

Boothbay Harbor Region Chamber of Commerce P.O. Box 356, Boothbay Harbor, 04539; 207-633-2353.

Camden-Rockport-Lincolnville Chamber of Commerce, P.O. Box 919, Camden 04843; 207-236-4404.

Damariscotta Region Chamber of Commerce P.O. Box 13, Damariscotta 04543; 207-563-8340.

Rockland/Thomaston Area Chamber of Commerce, P.O. Box 508, Rockland 04841; 207-596-0376.

Down East/Acadia

Acadia National Park Headquarters, P.O. Box 177, Bar Harbor 04609; 207-288-3338.

Bar Harbor Chamber of Commerce, P.O. Box 158, Bar Harbor 04609; 207-288-5103.

Blue Hill Chamber of Commerce, P.O. Box 520, Blue Hill 04614.

Deer Isle-Stonington Chamber of Commerce, Stonington 04681; 207-348-6124.

Ellsworth Area Chamber of Commerce, P.O. Box 267, Ellsworth 04605; 207-667-2617.

Mt. Desert Region, P.O. Box 675, Northeast Harbor, 04662; 207-276-5040.

East of Schoodic

Eastport Area Chamber of Commerce, P.O. Box 254, Eastport 04631; 207-853-4644 .

Machias Bay Area Chamber of Commerce, P.O. Box 606, Machias 04654; 207-255-4402.

IF TIME IS SHORT

With its ins and outs, the coast of Maine extends more than 3,000 miles. Even in a direct line, it is a five- or six-hour drive end to end. If your time is limited, you're traveling from the south, and you want to capture the flavors of the rocky coast, we recommend you use Portland as a home base and explore north and southward from there. Portland itself is a comfortable and interesting small city, and in addition to its attractions it is an easy drive north to Freeport and south to Kennebunkport, Ogunquit, and Maine's best sand beaches. If you're traveling from points north, we suggest your home base be Bar Harbor. It's the getting off point for Acadia National Park and its northeasternmost reaches on the Schoodic Peninsula. From either point, there's plenty of lobster, hiking, biking, shopping, cross country skiing, and rocky coast to be found.

What we really hope? That you will use our book to customize your own itinerary.

INNS

The Pomegranate Inn (207-772-1006; 49 Neal St., Portland). This is the city at its best and most eclectic. Great breakfast, amazing style, and smack in the middle of the city's historic West End.

Mira Monte Inn (207-288-4263; 69 Mount Desert St., Bar Harbor). If you think of the Rockefellers, the rocky coast, and Acadia National Park in one breathe, you've got a good picture of the Mira Monte. This is everything Bar Harbor is and was about.

CULTURAL ATTRACTIONS

Portland Museum of Art (207-773-2787; 619 Congress Ave., Portland). Designed by I. M. Pei, this is the oldest and most impressive art collection in Maine, with works by Van Gogh, Picasso, Degas, the Wyeths, and Winslow Homer.

Thuya Gardens at Asticou Terraces (Rte. 3, Northeast Harbor on Mount Desert Island). A formal English garden filled with country flowers — zinnias, dahlias, plume poppies, goatsbeards, and monkshood designed by landscape architect Joseph Henry Curtis. *The New York Times* describes Thuya Gardens as an "accidentally available private retreat left over from another time."

(continued)

SHOPPING

Exchange St. in Portland is the upscale downtown district near the city's working waterfront, with brick sidewalks, boutiques and art galleries, ethnic specialties, and funky stuff in general. Only 20 miles north on Rte. 295, you'll find **Freeport,** home of the great L.L. Bean and where the world shops when it's in Maine.

The shopping hub of this town is at the intersections of **Main and Cottage Streets,** just up from the harbor. There you'll find a proliferation of small stores from T-shirt joints to upscale galleries filled with art and handicrafts. Just over the bridge in Ellsworth, we suggest you stop in at the **L.L. Bean Factory Store,** where you can take home bargains from the famous outdoors store and catalog merchant.

RESTAURANTS

Zephyr Grill (207-828-4033; 653 Congress St., Portland). This is a very good restaurant that does everything well.

Le Domaine (207-422-3395 or 800-554-8498; Rte 1., Hancock). If you're going to be in the area two nights, you should have at least one dinner at the impeccably French country inn.

RECREATION

Portland Sea Dogs (207-879-9500; Hadlock Field, Park St., Portland) The Double A affiliate of the Florida Marlins. This is family entertainment at its best, and the intimate, friendly stadium is usually filled to capacity. Call well in advance for your tickets. Don't worry, there's not a bad seat in the house.

Acadia National Park (207-288-3338; Mount Desert Island). This is a year's worth of recreation in a weekend: 100 miles of trails through forests and past lakes; eight climbing peaks; great biking on old carriage roads; wonderful water view; good rock climbing, canoeing and cross-country skiing; a small sand beach; the tallest mountain; and only fjord on the eastern seaboard.

Index

LODGING BY PRICE CODE

Price Codes:
Inexpensive: Up to $65
Moderate: $65 to $125
Expensive: $125 to $180
Very Expensive: $180 and up

SOUTH COAST

Inexpensive
Econo Lodge, 48

Inexpensive–Moderate
Atlantic Birches Inn, 46
Green Heron Inn, 48

Inexpensive–Very Expensive
Edwards' Harborside Inn, 48

Moderate
Gundalow Inn, 49
The Trellis House, 49

Moderate–Expensive
Cape Arundel Inn, 47
Dockside Guest Quarters, 47

Hartwell House, 49
The Wooden Goose Inn, 50

Moderate–Very Expensive
White Barn Inn, 50

Expensive
Captain Lord Mansion, 47

CASCO BAY

Inexpensive–Moderate
Isaac Randall House, 56

Moderate
Captain's Watch B&B & Sail
    Charter, 52
Chebeague Inn, 52
Harpswell Inn, 54
Inn at ParkSpring, 54

Moderate–Expensive
Atlantic Seal B&B, 51
Captain Daniel Stone Inn, 52
The Danforth., 53

Inn on Carleton, 55
The Pomegranate Inn, 56
West End Inn, 57

Expensive
Portland Regency, 57

Expensive–Very Expensive
Harraseeket Inn, 53
Inn by the Sea, 55

MIDCOAST

Inexpensive
The Fox Island Inn, 61
Roaring Lion, 66
Trailing Yew Guest House,
    68

Inexpensive–Moderate
The Hichborn Inn, 61
Hotel Pemaquid, 62
The Owl & the Turtle Harbor
    View Guest Rooms, 65
The William & Mary Inn, 69

RESTAURANTS BY PRICE CODE

RESTAURANTS BY CUISINE

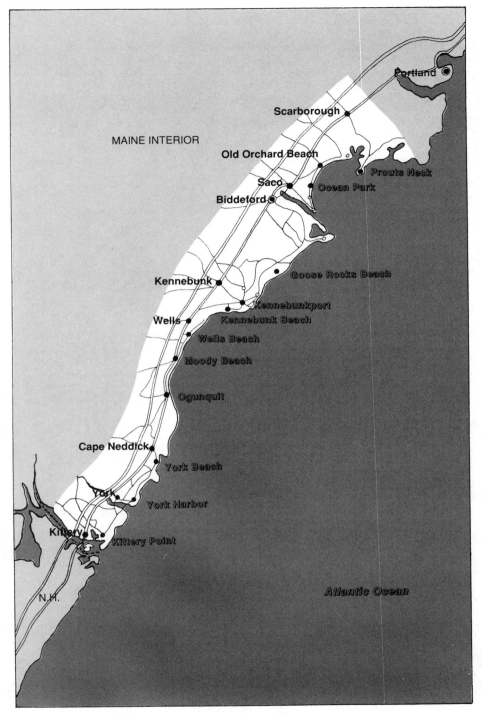

SOUTH COAST

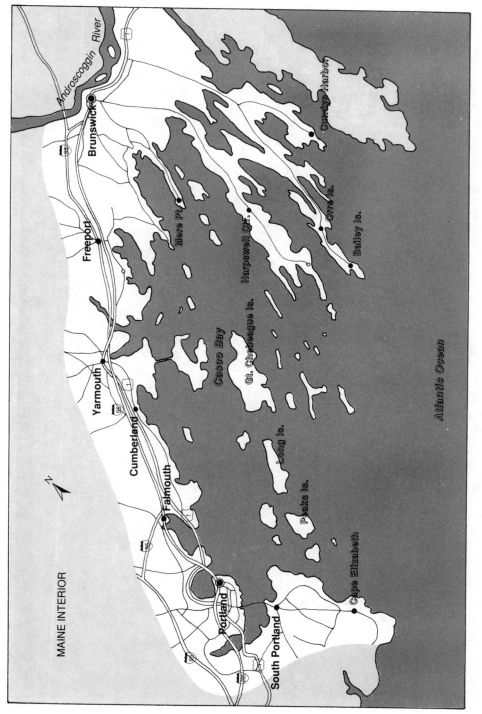

CASCO BAY

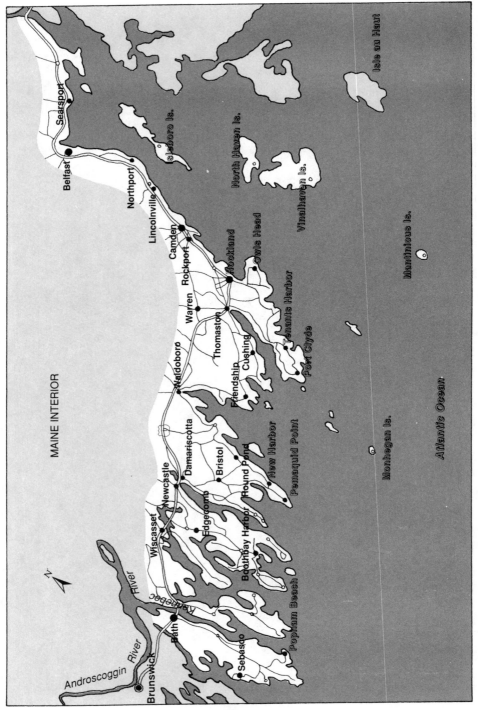

MIDCOAST

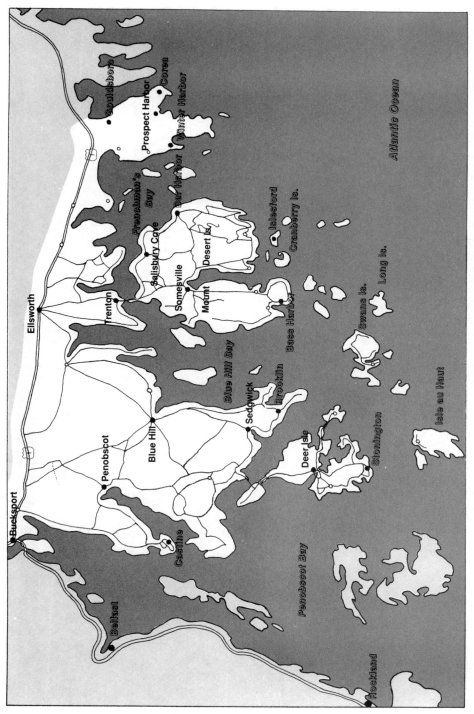

DOWN EAST/ACADIA

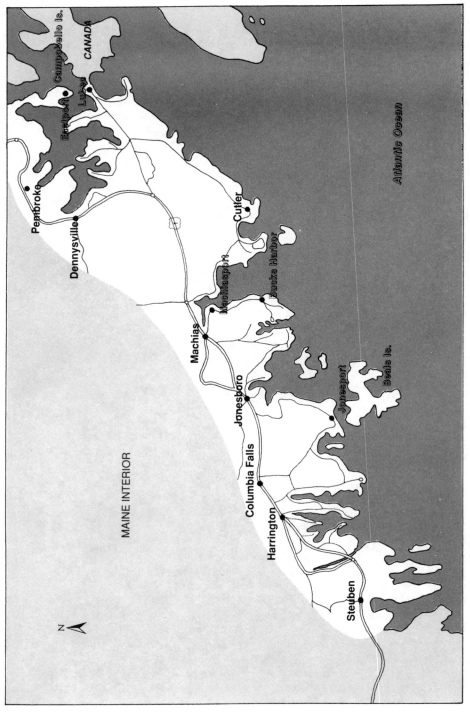

EAST OF SCHOODIC

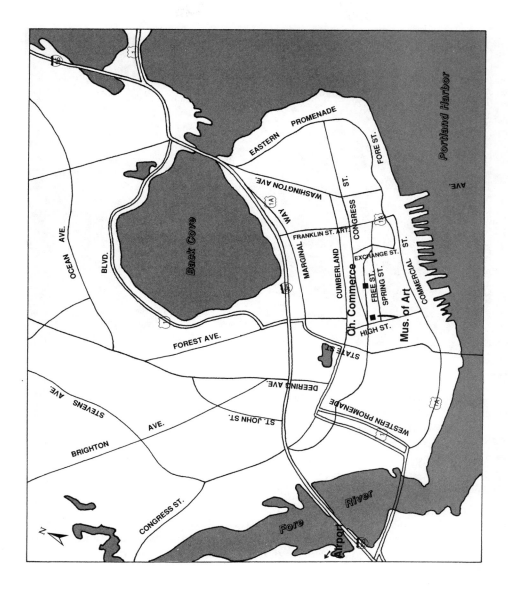

CITY OF PORTLAND

About the Authors

Herb Swanson

Rick Ackermann is a former journalist and Kathryn Buxton is a former film critic. They met while working for the *Palm Beach Post* in West Palm Beach, Florida. Their first cooperative writing efforts were as restaurant critics for *New England Monthly*.

Separately, they have written for several publications including *Town & Country*, *The Washington Post*, *The Palm Beach Daily News*, Reuters, *Yankee* and *Variety* magazines, *The Columbia Journalish Review*, *The Washington Journalism Review*, the *Maine Times* and the *Maine Sunday Telegram*. The authors live in Portland, Maine, where Ackermann is completing his first novel and Buxton writes advertising and promotions for companies and business clients including L.L. Bean, Bass, and the Norwegian Salmon Marketing Council.